Research and Policy:

The Uses of Qualitative Methods in Social and Educational Research

Social Research and Educational Studies Series

Series Editor
Robert G. Burgess,
Senior Lecturer in Sociology,
University of Warwick

1. Strategies of Educational Research: Qualitative Methods
    Edited by Robert G. Burgess
2. Research and Policy: The Uses of Qualitative Methods in Social
    and Educational Research
    Janet Finch

Social Research and Educational Studies Series: 2

Research and Policy:
The Uses of Qualitative Methods in Social and Educational Research

Janet Finch

 The Falmer Press

(A member of the Taylor & Francis Group)
London and Philadelphia

UK   The Falmer Press, Falmer House, Barcombe, Lewes, East Sussex,
            BN8 5DL

USA   The Falmer Press, Taylor & Francis Inc., 242 Cherry Street,
            Philadelphia, PA 19106-1906

First published 1986

Library of Congress Cataloging in Publication Data

Finch, Janet.
  Research and policy.

  (Social research and educational studies series; 2)
  Bibliography: p.
  Includes index.
  1. Social sciences—Research—Great Britain.
2. Policy sciences—Research. 3. Education—Research—
Great Britain. I. Title. II. Series.
  H62.5.G7F56 1986 300'.72041 86-2162
  ISBN 1-85000-098-0
  ISBN 1-85000-099-9 (pbk.)

Typeset in 11/13 Garamond by
Imago Publishing Ltd, Thame, Oxon

Printed in Great Britain by Taylor & Francis (Printers) Ltd, Basingstoke

Contents

Series Editor's Preface

The purpose of the *Social Research and Educational Studies* series is to provide authoritative guides to key issues in educational research. The series includes overviews of fields, guidance on good practice and discussions of the practical implications of social and educational research. In particular, the series deals with a variety of approaches to conducting social and educational research. Contributors to this series review recent work, raise critical concerns that are particular to the field of education, and reflect on the implications of research for educational policy and practice.

Each volume in the series draws on material that will be relevant for an international audience. The contributors to this series all have wide experience of teaching, conducting and using educational research. The volumes are written so that they will appeal to a wide audience of students, teachers and researchers. Altogether, the volumes in the *Social Research and Educational Studies* series provide a comprehensive guide for anyone concerned with contemporary educational research.

The series will include individually authored books and edited volumes on a range of themes in education including: qualitative research, survey research, the interpretation of data, self-evaluation, research and social policy, analyzing data, action research, the politics and ethics of research.

In recent years there has been much scepticism about the value of social and educational research. This book, therefore, tackles many of the critical issues that have been raised about research and policy in educational research by focussing on the use of qualitative studies. *Research and Policy* makes a distinct contribution to our understanding of social policy research in general and research on educational policy in particular. Janet Finch takes us beyond the narrow confines of education by focussing on the context in which policy related research is conducted in this field of study. Her book contains original case study material as well as critical discussion which will be of central importance to researchers, policy-makers and others who conduct and use social and educational studies.

Robert Burgess
University of Warwick

Author's Preface

This book is about the relationship between social research and social policy, using the field of education as the principal substantive area through which that relationship is explored. It is therefore addressed to two separate but overlapping audiences: to researchers, policy-makers, teachers and others whose interests lie mainly in education; and to researchers, students and policy-makers who are interested more generally in the relationship between research and policy. The main message to both audiences concerns the value and the potential importance of qualitative research in a policy context. In this book a 'policy' focus is seen as relevant not only to central government, but also to the various levels at which policy is made and implemented, including individual institutions such as schools, colleges and universities.

I see this particular overlap as useful and important from the perspective of both audiences. For the specifically educational audience, it is vital to contextualize the relationship between educational policy and research within broader debates. Historically, policy-related research in the educational field has not been generated in a vacuum, but frequently has grown out of broader social policy concerns such as the relationship between poverty in childhood and life opportunities. Equally, when considering the future development of policy-oriented research in education, this cannot be insulated from wider debates about what kind of research is appropriate and desirable. For the more general readership, I believe that focussing on one substantive area helps to make the debate about social research and social policy more concrete. Further, education provides a good illustrative case both for understanding why qualitative research has been relatively little used in the past, and for exploring its potential use in policy-oriented studies.

The overlap between education and broader social policy issues means that certain facets of what is broadly known as 'educational research' are highlighted in this book. No attempt is made to cover comprehensively the full range of questions which educational researchers collectively address. Rather, the focus is upon those situations where action in the educational sphere is part of a more general social policy strategy (see Finch (1984a) for discussion of education as social policy). This selective approach means, in terms of social science disciplines, that the discussion is rooted in sociology and social administration rather than, say, in psychology or economics. Further, in terms of substantive topics, the emphasis is upon the use of education as part of social policy — for example, to reduce social inequality, or to prepare the future workforce — rather than, say, on pedagogical issues.

The book therefore can be read in several different ways, with certain parts likely to be of particular interest to different audiences. It is organized into two main parts: Part I is about the past and Part II about the present and future. The main purpose of Part I is to document the relative importance of quantitative and qualitative research in policy-oriented studies, and to discuss why the former achieved and maintained its substantial dominance. Chapters 1 and 2 are about this dominant tradition which has relied heavily on quantitative research and devalued qualitative alternatives whilst nevertheless making some use of them. Chapters 3 and 4 are about what I call the 'alternative' tradition in which qualitative approaches have been much more prominent. Chapter 5 rounds off the first part of the book by discussing a range of possible explanations for the dominance of quantitative research. In Part II, the focus shifts to understanding the potential for policy-oriented qualitative research, and this is tackled in a variety of ways. Chapter 6 argues that an understanding of the ways in which research can influence policy is essential to the development of policy-oriented qualitative studies, and explores various models of the research-policy relationship. Chapters 7 and 8 examine ways in which such studies can be developed in the field of education specifically, and chapter 9 discusses ethical and political implications of this type of work.

Readers who are interested in policy and research generally rather than education specifically might want to pay less attention to those chapters which are principally about education: these are chapters 2, 7 and 8, although arguments presented in chapters 7 and 8 are central to the general case for policy-oriented qualitative research. Readers who are educationalists may be particularly interested in these chapters, although they do need to be set in the context of the argument of the book as a whole. Other chapters do use educational examples to illustrate the general points being made, with the exception of chapter 4, which is a case-study not centrally concerned with education, but which does offer a direct comparison of quantitative and qualitative research being used by government.

Finally, the conclusion sets out the case which has been developed about the importance of qualitative policy-oriented research, and for those who wish to read the book selectively this might be the best place to begin.

I should like to thank a number of people who have given me encouragement and assistance in preparing this book. Several people read and commented on the draft of one or more chapters: Martin Bulmer, Susan Clayton, Rosemary Deem, Dulcie Groves, David Morgan, Geoff Payne, Andrew Pollard, Penny Summerfield. I am indebted to all of these for their valuable comments, although they bear no responsibility for defects in this book. Bob Burgess was, as ever, a supportive but intelligently critical editor: I owe him thanks both for encouraging me initially to develop the ideas upon which this book is based, and for helping me in various ways to see the project through. I also would like to thank David Morgan for his continuing interest and support throughout the period of writing. Finally, Veronica Holmes typed drafts and the final manuscript with characteristic care and efficiency. I would like to thank her for this, and for the less quantifiable but splendid back-up services which she provides for myself and my colleagues.

Janet Finch
University of Lancaster

Introduction

Social Policy and Social Research

The history of social research in Britain over the past 150 years has both run parallel to and been closely intertwined with the development of social policies by central government, including educational policies. Yet predominantly the kind of research which has been both stimulated by and has been fed into social policy has been of a very specific type: positivist in conception, quantitative in orientation, and often relying on the social survey. In the late twentieth century, when the field of social research encompasses a much wider range of techniques and orientations, 'policy research' still essentially means research of that type. In particular, approaches which can be put under the label of 'qualitative research' at best play a minor part in policy-oriented studies.

The purpose of this book is first, to understand the reasons why a particular approach to research became dominant, and still substantially maintains its dominance, in the policy context; and second, to examine the opportunities which are presented in contemporary Britain for developing more policy-oriented work of a qualitative kind, and for claiming a place for this kind of work which accords it at least equal status and legitimacy. The book is, therefore, openly supportive of qualitative research, but not thereby necessarily hostile to the dominant tradition of quantitative research: in certain contexts the two are seen as complementary, in others one approach is clearly superior to the other.

Since much of the book is concerned with setting out the case for the utility of qualitative work from a policy perspective, it does therefore rather depend upon the assumption that social researchers with qualitative expertise would be interested in pursuing such

1

developments. At first sight, this may not seem too much of a problem. It is certainly the case that in the relatively recent past, some well-known educational studies based on qualitative techniques have been carried out by researchers for whom the prospect of engaging with social policy and stimulating social change provided a major inspiration for their work. These are the terms in which for example Colin Lacey has written about his study of Hightown Grammar (Lacey, 1970):

> My concern was to promote those sorts of intervention which would lead to an egalitarian society.... This concern remained a central underlying purpose.... I feel sure that my interest in sociology depends on my seeing it as a tool, as a means for progression towards a realization of that purpose. If I felt sociology was not 'useful' in this way I would probably turn to politics or journalism or something. (Lacey, 1976, p. 64).

The interest in policy issues displayed by Lacey, however, has not generally been characteristic of qualitative researchers in the field of education during the past two decades, for reasons which I discuss in chapter 5. Therefore the assumption that contemporary researchers with qualitative expertise would be interested in developing policy-oriented research may well not be justified. Many qualitative researchers may need to be convinced that it is worth engaging in policy-related research when their own approach may be regarded as illegitimate by policy-makers, or will fear that the intellectual status and independence of their work will become contaminated by this kind of use. It seems important therefore to tackle this 'why bother?' question at this stage, at least in a preliminary way.

It seems to me that there are at least four different kinds of reasons why any social scientist should adopt a policy-orientation, of which the last is the most powerful. The first is the somewhat cynical reason that — at the present time in both Britain and the United States — this is where the money is. Certainly, it has become increasingly the case in Britain in the 1980s that social scientists negotiating research grants have come under increasing pressure to demonstrate the policy-relevance of their work. As a policy for research funding, we may regard this as deplorable in that it excludes other important kinds of research, for example, research which contributes to the knowledge base of the social sciences. Many have nonetheless found themselves able to accept research money on these terms, and I find it difficult to see that the research produced as a result need necessarily be of poor quality, just because it has a social policy focus.

Second, it can be argued that a policy orientation brings positive benefits in the development of the knowledge created through research and the disciplines within which it is rooted. The most obvious example of this is that a policy-orientation focuses research upon those who make policy as well as those who receive it, therefore upon the relatively powerful — a group whom, as many others have recognized, have been conspicuously absent from social research studies (Bell and Newby, 1977; Scott, 1984). Other positive benefits may also ensue. Shils, writing in 1949, put forward an interesting argument about this which still has contemporary relevance, suggesting that in the past involvement government has stimulated the development of research techniques (mainly of course in the quantitative field), that it encourages interdisciplinary work, and that a concentration by more researchers on key issues of the day could in principle help to overcome the fragmented nature of social science research and theoretical developments within it (pp. 227–30).

The third argument for engaging in policy-oriented research is essentially a moral one, namely that a social scientist has an obligation to use her or his skills, usually acquired at public expense, to contribute to public debate about major issues of the day. I would endorse Barnes' (1979) view on this point, when he argues that the social scientist can be seen as 'a citizen with special skills', and that this can be regarded as imposing an obligation to intervene in public life to make the specialized knowledge acquired through the use of those skills more widely available (pp. 171–2).

The final reason — and I think the most compelling — for engaging in policy-oriented research is that it is actually impossible to avoid it. Social scientists are de facto part of the social world which we study, and the knowledge which we produce can always potentially be used to some effect; therefore the idea that one can pursue a detached social science which does not engage with public issues is at best very naive. That naive view is called 'critical-spectator sociology' by Payne and his colleagues (following Becker), who argue that:

> what this critical-spectator sociology, with its concern for disciplinary purity, fails to recognize is that however much it concentrates on non-involvement, sociology *is* involved in the policy field. Because of the very nature of the discipline, sociological knowledge will be used in the political arena. (Payne, Dingwall, Payne and Carter, 1981, p. 156)

The point about being inevitably involved in the political arena is seen most clearly in relation to the use of research findings, where researchers can on occasions be pushed into this whether they wish to be or not. Cohen and Weiss (1977), discussing the issue of schools and race in the American context, remind us that researchers have regularly found themselves testifying in courtrooms on the basis of their research findings — a situation which most found very uncomfortable but which was for them quite literally, unavoidable. Most examples are less dramatic than this, but there seems to be a growing awareness among British ethnographic researchers in the field of education that it is important for researchers themselves to spell out the political and policy consequences of their findings, lest other people should take different messages from those findings (Pollard, 1984, p. 175; Griffin, 1985, p. 102).

For all these reasons therefore, it seems to me that there are good reasons for all social researchers to see their work in relation to social policy, at least when it comes to presenting findings. But that leaves open questions about how far a specific research project is defined as a study *of* social policy, from whose perspective such a study would be undertaken, and how it would be funded. In its broadest sense, a 'policy-orientation' can be seen as a necessary part of all good empirical social research. In a narrower sense, 'policy-oriented research' encompasses a range of different types of research activity, some of which are closely tied into government, and others of which are definitely not. This theme of different types of policy-oriented research will be developed in later chapters, but to anticipate somewhat, there is a sense in which the rejection of policy research by many social scientists in Britain since the 1960s, including many qualitative researchers, has really been a rejection of one specific type of policy-oriented research: funded by government or other official bodies, commissioned by them and defining 'the problem' in policy-makers' terms, and reflecting the interests of dominant social groups.

What is Qualitative Research? Questions of Technique and Epistemology

The argument in this book concerns the practice of 'qualitative' research and the contrasting features and opportunities which it presents in relation to 'quantitative' research. It is important therefore to define these terms at the outset: a task which is not so straightforward as it perhaps first appears.

In focussing on qualitative research, I am discussing and promoting a tradition of social research which is essentially an oppositional tradition in relation to those social science disciplines which are pertinent to the study of social policy, namely (in the British context) sociology and social administration. The latter has seen only a very limited development of qualitative research, for reasons which I discuss in chapter 5. So far as sociology is concerned, there has been a debate about the relative merits of qualitative and quantitative approaches at least since the 1950s, although it has taken different forms. It is a debate which has been conducted principally by the advocates of qualitative research, arguing against a dominant tradition which has accorded quantitative approaches a much higher status (Bryman, 1984, p. 76). Typically, within that dominant tradition, a polarity is established between the two approaches in which qualitative methods are seen as soft, subjective and speculative, while quantitative methods are said to be hard, objective and rigorous (Halfpenny, 1979). The use of those particular metaphors has rather obvious gender-linked connotations, where the terms typically used to describe quantitative research also describe characteristically male attributes, whilst qualitative research is accorded rather more obviously 'female' terms. Recent feminist writers have indeed argued for the superiority of qualitative methods in relation to feminist research on women (Oakley, 1981; Graham, 1983) but in fact the history of the use of such methods is less gender-linked in terms of research personnel than one might expect. There have been many male, qualitative researchers and indeed Morgan (1981) has pointed out that one can identify a specifically 'macho' style of conducting such work.

The distinctive features of qualitative research concern matters of both research techniques and epistemology, that is the philosophical basis which underpins the research process, especially the question of how valid knowledge about the social world is generated. At the level of technique, 'qualitative' research is taken to encompass techniques which are not statistically based, but are especially suited to small-scale analysis, and in which the researcher attempts to get to know the social world being studied at first hand, especially participant observation and interviewing of an in-depth and unstructured or semi-structured variety, supplemented where appropriate by the use of documentary sources. Such techniques have their roots in social anthropology, and as in that discipline, the emphasis is upon studying social life in 'natural' settings (Popkewitz, 1981b, p. 156; Burgess, 1984b, pp. 2–3). These methods allow a much greater flexibility in research design than, for example, the large-scale social survey in which typically hypotheses are tested through quantitative measurement at a single point in time, and continued involvement with the research population enables the researcher to discover hypotheses (not just test them) and to change direction in the course of the research. The term 'qualitative research' in fact overlaps with others such as 'field research', 'case study methods' and 'ethnography'. Although these terms are not entirely synonymous, all denote, as Rist (1984) puts it 'a different way of knowing — one based on experience, empathy and involvement' (p. 160). I have chosen to use the term 'qualitative research' and the range of approaches which it encompasses because it is the qualitative/quantitative distinction which has been most apparent in relation to research on social policy issues. In my discussion of the potential of educational research, however, ethnography (which I take to be one important type of qualitative research) plays an especially significant part, because of the expansion of research in Britain over the past decade which has identified itself as ethnography in educational settings (Burgess, 1984b, p. 3).

Even at the level of technique, the qualitative/quantitative distinction is not as simple as it first appears. One can, for example, take the technique of 'observation', and demonstrate that this is used in quite different ways in different projects, and even within the context of the same project. A good illustration of this is provided by Galton and Delamont's (1985) discussion of the ORACLE project, which was a study of classroom learning principally concerned with children in the top primary age range over a five-year period. This project utilized classroom observation as a major research technique, but in two very different ways. First, observers were trained to record observations in a standardized way on observation schedules which had pre-specified categories, which were then available for quantitative analysis. Many well-known educational studies have used systematic observation in this way (see, for example, Bennett, 1976; Bennett and McNamara, 1979). Second, other observers used ethnographic observation of the classic type characteristic of qualitative or field research (see, for example, Burgess, 1984b, pp. 78–100). In this instance, although the researchers experienced some difficulties in putting the different types of data together, in general they felt that their approach was vindicated since the contrasting types of observation did produce different kinds of data therefore the project would have been more limited if only one type of 'observation' or the other had been used.

At the level of epistemology, qualitative research is usually seen as gaining its contemporary impetus from the strong reaction within social science against positivism and its limitations. In this context, 'positivism' is taken to mean an approach to the creation of know-ledge through research which emphasizes the model of the natural sciences: the scientist adopts the position of the objective researcher, who collects 'facts' about the social world and then builds up an explanation of social life by arranging such facts in a chain of causality, in the hope that this will uncover general laws about how the society works. The underlying logic is deductive, where an hypothesis is generated from a universal statement, then tested by empirical research, which then leads to a verification or a modifica-tion of such universal generalizations about the social world (Hughes, 1980, chapters 2 and 3).

By contrast, qualitative research characteristically draws on alternative philosophical traditions, of which symbolic interactionism has been especially important in studies of education. Woods (1983) offers a clear account of how the interactionist perspective has been used in studies of schools and classrooms in particular. This perspec-tive essentially sees human actions as constructed by the actors, rather than the product of external forces which mould the individual. Another important focus is upon the meanings which people attri-bute to their actions, and the processes by which such meanings are constructed, negotiated and shared in the course of human interac-tion. In relation to studies of schooling, this has meant that resear-chers have focussed on the detail of how pupils and teachers interact with each other, how they experience each other, how they interpret the processes going on in the school, and how they each organize their school activity. The characteristic methods associated with such studies are qualitative, with participant observation being used exten-sively (pp. 1–16).

Qualitative research therefore looks not so much for 'causes' as for 'meanings', rejecting the natural science model and seeing the task of social research as uncovering the meaning of social events and processes, based upon understanding the lived experience of human society from the actors' point of view (Bryman, 1984). I shall use the term 'interpretivist' to refer to the underlying epistemology of this kind of work. Characteristically, the logical procedures adopted are inductive rather than deductive, in that data from case studies are used to develop, not just to test, generalizations (see chapter 7 for further discussion). It is at this epistemological level that the opposi-tional nature of qualitative research within social science has been most obvious. For example, Cicourel's (1964) important and influential work sets out not merely to demonstrate that there are different ways of knowing, but to establish that conventional sociological research based upon positivist epistemology can never produce valid knowledge about the social world.

It is not my purpose here to discuss these contrasting positions in general terms, but it is important to note some difficulties with them which are significant for the ensuing discussion of policy-oriented research. One difficulty concerns the concept of 'positivism' used in this context. The approach to research which I take to be indicated by that term is characteristic of the dominant approach within social policy research in the last 150 years (see chapter 1). However, there are grounds for seeing the terms 'positivist' as an inaccurate and perhaps a misleading way of describing this. In recent social science in Britain, the term has been used very loosely (often defined very broadly) to cover almost all empirical research or else not defined at all, and has become effectively a term of abuse, along with the associated concept of 'empiricism'. In the 1970s, it became the orthodoxy to see positivism as having been both discredited and superceded (Husbands, 1981; Platt, 1981a). Platt, in her interesting discussion of positivism and British sociology in this decade, based on an analysis of journal articles and research methods textbooks, is able to demonstrate that there was in fact no obvious diminution of sociological research using features associated with positivism, and she goes on to suggest that 'positivism' has outlived its usefulness as a meaningful label. She argues persuasively the point that, although there certainly are important differences between styles of research and the 'ideology of research methods', the positivist/non-positivist distinction does not capture them accurately (Platt, 1981a, p. 82). The points which Platt makes about the term 'positivism' are clearly important, but do not of course mean that one can simply overlook the important epistemological differences which do underlie different approaches to social research. Where appropriate in the following chapters, I shall in fact use the term 'positivism' because it is a readily understood descriptive label, which denotes an approach to research emphasizing the natural science model, the objective researcher and the collection of facts. I accept, however, that this label is loose and inaccurate, if also convenient, and I certainly do not intend to use it as an automatic term of abuse.

Another very important issue in relation to the contrast between qualitative and quantitative research described above is the question of whether epistemological differences necessarily imply different research methods or techniques; and conversely, whether the use of a particular technique must inevitably mean that a particular epistemological position is adopted. Conventionally, epistemology and method are regarded as inevitably intertwined. Positivist epistemology is taken to imply a search for 'causes' requiring quantitative measurement and statistical analysis, using most characteristically the technique of the social survey; whilst interpretivist epistemology is taken to be concerned with uncovering 'meanings', which requires non-statistical in-depth approaches, based on techniques such as unstructured interviewing and participant observation. Although epistemology and methods may often be bracketed together in this way in practice there are good reasons for questioning whether this is a *necessary* alignment. These reasons have been set out cogently in Bryman's article (1984), where he argues that discussions of the quantitative/qualitative distinction often hopelessly confuse matters of epistemology and matters of technique. In his view, there is a clear distinction between the two. Positivist and phenomenological epistemologies are, he argues, very different and resist attempts to reconcile them. However, qualitative and quantitative techniques are not straightforwardly related to these. Confusion frequently arises because different techniques are used to symbolically represent different epistemological positions.

The point that there is no automatic and necessary alignment between techniques and epistemologies can be illustrated in a variety of ways. First, Catherine Marsh (1982), writing from within the survey research tradition, puts forward a strong case for defining the survey in broad terms, encompassing far more than conventional questionnaire studies. She argues that a survey can be conducted using a variety of methods including observation, content analysis of newspapers or post-coding tape-recorded interviews. In her view, the important feature which makes any piece of research a 'survey' is that the relationship between cases is considered systematically (pp. 6–7). Marsh's view, whilst not representing a conventional approach to surveys, does challenge the assumption that the underlying quantitative logic of the survey need necessarily be linked with a single technique for collecting data. Further, she rejects the view that surveys concentrate on causal explanations and that meaningful explanations are elicited through participant observation. She argues that this apparently neat separation cannot be sustained in practice, and that surveys can and should employ techniques which produce explanations that 'take cognisance of the meaningful aspects of social action' (p. 98) (see chapter 7 for further discussion).

A parallel argument can be pursued in relation to methods which are characteristically qualitative. Delamont and Atkinson (1980), writing about ethnographic studies in educational settings, also argue that there is no straightforward and invariable relationship between ethnographic work and a single theoretical school, but that ethnography can 'serve several masters'. Perhaps the most graphic illustration of that is the use which has been made of ethnographic techniques in recent years not only by those who adopt a symbolic interactionist or phenomenological position, but also by some Marxists, who argue that qualitative *techniques* do not have to imply 'merely descriptive' accounts, nor Weberian theory, but can be used to good effect in the context of a Marxist theoretical framework (Grimshaw, Hobson and Willis, 1980, p. 74). A parallel and important development has been the use of ethnographic techniques by feminists working in the field of education, where again empirical study is both informed by specific theoretical perspectives and also further contributes to the development and refinement of theory (see, for example, Davies, 1984 and 1985; Fuller, 1984; Porter, 1984; Scott, 1985). The use of ethnographic techniques can therefore range from a study informed by Marxist theory on the one hand, through symbolic interactionist studies, to work which does not acknowledge an explicit theoretical basis. They can also be used in ways which essentially are positivist. As Willis puts it, conventional participant observation incorporates a 'covert positivism', in its belief that theoretical issues can be postponed to a stage following the collection of data, and in its implied notion of the passive participant observer, which suggests that research subjects are actually objects (Willis, 1980, pp. 89–90). Bryman (1984) also takes the view that the epistemological basis of participant observation can in fact be positivist; and Delamont and Atkinson (1980), themselves actively sympathetic to this technique, argue that many researchers have turned to ethnography because they reject 'positivism' or 'mindless empiricism', only to run the risk of reproducing the same inadequacies in their own work (p. 139).

A definition of qualitative research therefore must encompass both techniques and epistemology, but the two cannot be easily and neatly linked. In the following chapters, I use the term 'qualitative research' to refer to an approach which both uses qualitative techniques and also draws upon an interpretivist epistemology which emphasizes understanding the meaning of the social world from the perspective of the actor. Frequently, however, I find it necessary to distinguish between techniques and epistemology, and indeed I take the view that certain facets of the status and the potential of qualitative research in the social policy field can only be fully appreciated if the two are distinguished.

Part I

1 The Dominant Tradition in Social and Educational Research in Britain: Quantitative and Qualitative Methods

It is commonly acknowledged that the distinctive character of the relationship between social research and social policy in Britain was shaped during the expansion of both activities in the nineteenth century and consolidated in the twentieth. Accounts of the research-policy relationship commonly emphasize the clear historical continuity of particular conceptions of how research can be used in policy-making (for discussion, see Abrams, 1968; Bulmer, 1982a).

No attempt is made here to go over this general ground covered very adequately by others, but the purpose of this chapter is to re-examine that relationship from the perspective of the *methods* of research which were thought to be useful for social policy purposes, and in particular, to examine the notable dominance achieved by quantitative methods, and the (at best) secondary place which qualitative methods were accorded.

For most of this chapter, educational concerns are interwoven with social policy more generally, as characteristically they were during the nineteenth and the early part of the twentieth centuries. Indeed it is only after the Second World War that one can identify a substantial and distinctive body of social research concerned with education specifically, and this is discussed in the final section of the chapter. This body of work, however, very clearly has its origins in the broader tradition of policy-oriented research which is discussed in the earlier sections of the chapter. A single — but key — illustration will perhaps serve to underline the importance of contextualizing education in this way. The issue of educational opportunities, which was so central to educational research and social policy in the two decades after the Second World War, did not arise from 'educational' concerns as narrowly defined, nor from the activities of educational researchers as such, but was an integral part of socialist politics in the social policy field as they developed in the 1920s and 1930s, the principal concern being to demonstrate the links between educational underprivilege and social underprivilege (Silver, 1973, p. xii). Further, the methods considered appropriate for studying those links in the 1950s and 1960s derived directly from the dominant tradition of the research-policy relationship developed during the previous century in relation to broader policy concerns — a point to which I return in the final section of this chapter.

This chapter discusses the dominant tradition of policy-oriented research sequentially, focussing on key periods. It is therefore a selective account, with the principles of selection being first, to sketch in an overview of the development of this tradition for the benefit of those who are not familiar with it; second, and more importantly, to explore what part was played by qualitative methods in a tradition whose bias is commonly acknowledged to be heavily quantitative.

Social Research and Social Policy in Early Nineteenth Century England

The origins of social research in England are usually dated in the 1830s. The Royal Commission on the Poor Law 1832–34 was, as Bulmer (1982a) puts it, the first 'dramatically obvious' instance of the use of social research in policy making (p. 2). It is also conventionally regarded as the beginning of modern British social policy. It is therefore of particular significance in understanding the research-policy relationship. What kind of research methods were used by the Royal Commission?

When one examines the Commission's methods, in many ways the techniques look more qualitative than quantitative. The Commission did initially attempt what we would now call a postal question-naire, sent to all districts which administered poor relief but the result — as is so frequently the case with this method — was a very poor response rate. They then turned to a quite different technique of investigation. They appointed twenty-six Assistant Commissioners who were sent out to make personal enquiries among the poor and amongst those who administered poor relief. The resulting reports — especially the report of one of the Assistant Commissioners, Edwin Chadwick — have become key documents in the history of social policy. Despite this, however, the techniques used in the production of these reports have been much criticized: the evidence was mostly extremely impressionistic and moralistic in tone, and insufficient attention was paid to geographical variations (Bulmer, 1982a; Marsh, 1985).

The Commission marked the beginning of the great expansion of social enquiry by government itself, the products of which were known collectively as 'blue books' because of the covers in which they were printed, and which have provided a fertile source for many subsequent social investigators, including Karl Marx. The blue books combined reports compiled by government inspectors, evidence given by witnesses to Parliamentary committees and to Royal Commissions and reports compiled by government departments, as well as official statistics from the General Register Office (Bulmer, 1982a, pp. 5–6). Apart from the latter, which are unambiguously quantitative, the material generated clearly derived from a variety of techniques including personal observation, often incorporated in these reports at second hand through the questioning of 'expert' witnesses whose occupations brought them into contact with the poor — a technique which was to remain standard in research designed to serve social policy until the end of the century when Rowntree (1902) introduced — for the first time in a social survey — the revolutionary technique of questioning the poor themselves about their condition. Marsh (1985) has argued that the convention of questioning 'informants' about the poor rather than the poor themselves was quite consistent with the prevailing view that the problem of poverty was essentially a moral problem. Those philanthropists and industrialists who undertook these early investigations therefore had a profound distrust of the people they were researching which was not conducive to direct interviewing.

Within these general developments of social research-social policy relationship in the mid-nineteenth century, education held an important place. First, participation of children in education was seen as one key indicator of the state of the poor. Second, the provision of education for the poor was seen as a central tool of social policy. Third, individuals who were involved in developing applied social research were also active in developing educational provisions; Kay-Shuttleworth being the major example.

The name of Kay-Shuttleworth occupies a prominent place in the history of education in England, because in 1839 he became the first Secretary of the newly-established Committee of the Privy Council on Education (the forerunner of the Board of Education and subsequently the Ministry) and for the following decade, as the first educational administrator at central government level, shaped the early involvement of the state in education. In the five years which preceded that, he had been an Assistant Poor Law Commissioner, and had pioneered the education of pauper children (Morris, 1973; Smith, 1974).

From the point of view of this discussion, the events which are important occurred before he achieved this national prominence when, as a doctor in Manchester, he wrote a pamphlet in 1832 on the moral and physical condition of the working classes, and subsequently became a founder member of the Manchester Statistical Society (Kay, 1832). In his autobiography, Kay (who added his wife's name to his own when he married) describes how he was led to investigate the condition of the poor as a result of having been a doctor practising in Manchester at the time of the cholera epidemic. The municipality conducted an enquiry into this epidemic, which formed the basis of Kay's pamphlet along with his own observations. This led him to the conclusion that the health and well-being of the population was intimately connected with the 'physical and moral' conditions in which the poorest lived (Bloomfield, 1964, pp. 8–12). The pamphlet itself not only documents these conditions in some detail but also spells out the causes as Kay saw them and suggests remedies. In Kay's view the remedy lay in a mixture of public health and sanitary measures, repeal of the corn laws (which had pushed up the cost of food), reform of the poor laws, and the moral and religious education of the poor themselves (Kay, 1832). His interweaving of 'moral' with 'physical' conditions gives education a prominent place in social policy as Kay formulated it: participation in education was a measure of the state of the poor, and the expansion of education was seen as a remedy for their moral condition. Education is needed he wrote, so that:

> all the children of the poor (may be) rescued from ignorance, and from the effects of that bad example to which they are now subjected in the crowded lanes of our cities. (p. 44)

Like many other subsequent commentators, he also saw the education of young women as crucial not so much for the benefits which they themselves would derive, but as a means to ensuring that the domestic economy of poor households was managed in a frugal manner (for discussion, see Lewis, 1980; Dyhouse, 1981). Institutions were needed:

in which the young females of the poor may be instructed in
domestic economy ... and may receive wholesome advice
concerning their duties as wives and mothers. (Kay, 1832,
p. 45)

This early concern with the education of the poor as one of the key
means of improving their condition remained an inspiration in his
later national work. As Morris writes, it followed quite naturally that
Kay should sponsor the development of elementary schools under
religious sanction, since the churches had always been the bodies
which had sought to exercise a normative influence over the population (Morris, 1973, p. ix).

This concern with education as a central tool of social policy was
not merely a personal obsession of Kay's, but was reflected in the
activities of the Statistical Society which he helped to found. He
describes in his autobiography how the Society was formed after the
publication of his pamphlet by a group of his friends 'of the highest
intelligence and warmest political sympathies' (Bloomfield, 1964,
p. 12). They quickly set about further investigations, expanding their
activities from Manchester to six other Lancashire towns, and in 1835
they produced a report on elementary education in these towns
(Ashton, 1934; Smith, 1974, pp. 24–6).

What methods were favoured by Kay and by the Society in these
early reports? Kay's 1832 pamphlet in fact opens with a discussion of
research methods, and in particular, he is critical of the methods used
by committees of the House of Commons when they needed
information on specific subjects. Because the interests of such
committees are various, argued Kay, they rely upon taking evidence
from people 'supposed to be most conversant with the subject'. But
the results of such investigations are unconvincing because they often
contain 'opposing testimonies' and 'partial evidence'. In his view
much more accurate — and therefore more satisfactory — results can
be obtained from statistical investigation (Kay, 1832, pp. 2–3). The
pamphlet is actually based upon a mixture of data derived from
different methods. It contains a good deal of statistical data based
upon returns collected by Board of Health inspectors on the state of
the houses and the streets; information gained from public offices in
the town; and finally the author's own personal observation. A good
deal of the pamphlet consists of vivid description based upon his
observations, but it is interesting to note that the justification which
he gives for his work rests upon the statistical data not upon this
observation, and essentially upon the criterion of accuracy: the

objective facts about the poor were what was needed, so the main question was, how can they be most accurately collected? The Society was also concerned with the thorough and accurate collection of facts, and decided that this could only be done through paying investigators, with the Society itself preparing the forms which the investigators would use, and supervising their enquiries. The resulting statistics, Kay proudly says, were more exact, searching and exhaustive than any previously obtained (Bloomfield, 1964, p. 13).

We find therefore in the early work of Kay-Shuttleworth and the Manchester Statistical Society the dominant orientations of social research in the 1830s: the accurate collection of facts about the poor, the primacy of statistical data, the immediate use of such facts in the formulation of measures of social reform, and in the administration of social policy. So far as education is concerned, this approach to social research was consolidated in the later part of the century in ways which were closely related to that major piece of policy-making: the introduction of universal elementary education in 1870. The Newcastle Commission, which reported in 1861 and which was the first national commission concerned entirely with education, undertook extensive statistical studies with a view to establishing the adequacy or deficiency of educational provision (for discussion, see West, 1975, pp. 95–110). Foster, in preparing his Bill which eventually became the Education Act 1870, undertook his own surveys which enabled him to argue that there was a greater deficiency of provision than the Newcastle Commission found, since he concentrated upon schools with a religious base. The accuracy of either set of figures is a matter of historical dispute (pp. 98–106). The important point in this context however is that — whatever the accuracy of the outcome — both the Newcastle and Foster studies were firmly grounded in the quantitative research tradition which has its roots in the 1830s and which was clearly maintaining its dominance in relation to social policy in the field of education, as elsewhere.

In summary, in this section I have argued that important characteristics of the research-policy relationship can be discerned at least in embryo form in the 1830s, and these were to set the parameters for the subsequent development of that relationship. First, there was a belief in the importance of collecting accurate facts about the social world, and especially about the working classes, as the basis for formulating government policies. Second, quantification and accurate statistics rapidly came to be seen as essential to the definition of such facts, although at the same time some use was made of methods which we would now call qualitative. Third, there was an adherence to a simple model of the relationship between social research and social reform which posited a direct and unproblematic relationship between knowledge and action.

Social Research in the Late Nineteenth Century: The Work of Charles Booth

This section will consider the developments which occurred in the late nineteenth century in policy-related social research, in particular the poverty studies of Charles Booth which set the pattern for the subsequent work of Rowntree and others in the twentieth century. These studies represent in some ways a continuity with earlier work and in other ways a decisive break from it, especially in the way in which they conceptualized poverty and its causes. From the perspective of education, as I shall show later, these studies are important because they subsequently formed the basis of the dominant approach to researching educational disadvantage, transferring to the educational arena their concern with carefully documenting the correlates of material poverty.

When Booth began his study, which eventually resulted in the seventeen volumes of *Life and Labour of the People of London* (1902), he set out to study poverty in a systematic and precise manner, so that competing claims about its extent and causes could be settled. The intellectual background against which developed his work, and from which these competing claims derived was first, the traditions of statistical study set down in the earlier part of the century; second, popular journalistic accounts of the life and conditions of the poor (see chapter 3 for further discussion); and third, the ameliorist tradition in social research, which had developed in the second half of the nineteenth century and whose concerns were with the immediate practical use of research to devise measures of social reform (McGregor, 1957; Abrams, 1968). The principal outcome of Booth's study in policy terms was an advance on all three approaches, in that Booth uncovered the underlying structural conditions associated with poverty (such as unemployment), as opposed to the dominant assumption that poverty is caused by the inadequacy and fecklessness of individuals.

Booth's study is a comprehensive survey of the social conditions of the population of London and in research methods literature it is regarded as the forerunner of detailed, extensive, statistical work which forms the basis of the twentieth century social survey (Bulmer,

1982a, pp. 10–14). However, Booth used a variety of techniques in his study, including some which we would now call qualitative. Indeed he saw that such techniques were essential to complement quantitative, statistical methods. As he put it:

> in intensity of feeling and not in statistics lies the power to move the world. But by statistics must this power be guided if it would move the world right. (Quoted in Bulmer, 1982a, p. 14)

The base of Booth's studies, which he financed himself, was the Census figures for London from the 1881 Census, updated later with the 1891 Census. He had access to the Registrar General's records, and used the Householders Schedules completed for the Census. Some of his data derived directly from these: for example, the 1891 schedules included questions about numbers of rooms in the house and the number of occupants, including servants. Booth used this to chart levels of overcrowding. For the most part, however, Booth regarded the Census data as of limited usefulness because necessarily only very basic data could be recorded, and furthermore there was no check as to its accuracy. He therefore embarked upon other research strategies, which aimed at gathering comprehensive and accurate information about every household in London. This was done through extensive interviewing, again not of the population directly, but of respectable intermediaries, people who were assumed to be able to present accurate information about the households of the poor. A particularly interesting feature from the point of view of education is that he used School Board Visitors as his principal informants, because of their presumed extensive knowledge of the homes of the poor, and he employed interviewers to question them (Booth, 1902, Vol. I, pp. 5–6). Finally, Booth himself engaged in covert participant observation, taking lodgings in places where he was not known on three separate occasions, for several weeks at a time. (See Webb, 1926, pp. 194–200 for a detailed discussion of these methods.)

Booth's presentation of his data reflects the mixture of quantitative and qualitative methods which he employed. The core of his work was detailed statistical quantification and classification of the population, reflecting a concern with classification which was characteristic of his times and was paralleled, for example, in the development of the mental testing of schoolchildren during the same period (Sutherland, 1984, pp. 5–24). Alongside this material, however, Booth gives illustrative examples which have come either from direct observation or from interviews. To illustrate this, I shall draw upon his discussion in Part 2 of Volume 3, which is entitled 'London children' and which covers elementary and secondary schools and the children who attended them. This volume offers a six-fold classification of elementary schools quite typical of Booth's approach. Schools are classified in relation to the 'types' of children who attend them, and they range from Class I schools which accommodate 'the "poor" and the "very poor" with a sprinkling of the lowest criminal class' to Class VI schools which accommodate 'those who are fairly well-to-do only' (Booth, 1902, Vol. 3, p. 196). On the basis of this classification, he builds a discussion of policy in relation to schools in the lowest group which he identifies as 'special difficulty schools', describing these in terms which were closely paralleled some seventy years later in the Plowden Report and the designation of Educational Priority Areas which was built upon it (Department of Education and Science, 1967; see also chapter 2). Booth's discussion of special difficulty schools elaborates on his classification by using more qualitative, descriptive material as, for example, in this extract where he is describing the children who attend such schools:

> Puny, pale-faced, scantily clad and badly shod, these small and feeble folk may be found sitting limp and chill on the school benches in all the poorer parts of London. They swell the bills of mortality as want and sickness thin them off, or survive to be the needy and enfeebled adults whose burden of helplessness the next generation will have to bear.
>
> Unhappily, in many cases, this semi-starved condition of the child is due not to poverty alone, but to drink, neglect, or vice at home. The practised eye can readily distinguish children of this class by their shrinking or furtive look, their unwholesomeness of aspect, their sickly squalor, or it may be by their indescribable pathos, the little shoulders bowed so helplessly beneath the burden of the parents' vice. 'How was it you came to school without any breakfast this morning?' I asked a forlorn little lad one day. 'Mother got drunk last night and couldn't get up to give me any,' was the reply, given as if it were an ordinary incident in the child's daily life. (Booth, 1902, Vol. 3, pp. 207–8)

One might well want to question the assumptions underlying this kind of work, or the viability of the techniques employed, but there is no doubt that his great poverty study — usually regarded as the base for the development of survey methods — did contain substantial qualitative elements which were not taken further within the survey research tradition. Indeed, Booth had difficulty in gaining recognition for this work from the Royal Statistical Society, whose members initially reacted badly to it (Norman-Butler, 1972, p. 91). In the view of Everett Hughes, a key figure in the development of qualitative sociology in the United States, these early social surveys such as Booth's entailed an element of observation and field research which was subsequently lost from the survey tradition: they 'discovered and described customs and institutions as well as opinions' (Hughes, 1960, p. vi). As Simey puts it, Booth's survey has a 'surprisingly modern ring', attempting a balance between personal observation and statistical measurement, and between inductive and deductive reasoning (Simey, 1957, p. 125).

However, despite this use of qualitative methods, Booth's work was in essence a quantitative social survey, presenting an extensive and detailed documentation of the extent and distribution of poverty. Like all such surveys, the picture it presents is essentially a static one. This was a criticism levelled at Booth's work at the time by Beatrice Webb, who had worked as one of Booth's interviewers. Webb (1926, pp. 193–211) argued that this kind of static picture had certain weaknesses as well as many strengths; in particular, it could not capture and understand the process of social change — as she put it 'the actual processes of birth, growth, decay and death' of social institutions (p. 211).

The fact that the fieldwork elements in Booth's study have often been de-emphasized, and were dropped in the subsequent development of social surveys except as a preparatory stage, can perhaps best be understood in relation to questions of epistemology rather than techniques (see Introduction for discussion of this distinction). Booth's work, although innovative in its methods and its policy implications, nonetheless represents a continuity with the dominant conception of fact-gathering which earlier policy-oriented researchers had predominantly accepted. This underlying positivist epistemology more readily incorporated quantitative rather than qualitative methods into its concept of appropriate research for policy purposes (although as I argued in the Introduction this alignment is not a logical necessity). Despite its qualitative elements, the way in which Booth's work was used and built upon served to consolidate that position.

The Webbs and the Fabian Tradition of Social Research and Social Policy

During the late nineteenth and early twentieth centuries, while the work of Booth and Rowntree was continuing, the establishment of the Fabian Society and the social investigations undertaken by some of its members, especially Sidney and Beatrice Webb, was developing a distinctive approach to the research-policy relationship which in some ways represented a continuity with the poverty surveys, and in others, a break from them. Sidney Webb was also active as a politician both at central and local government level, and played a key role in particular in reshaping educational provision in London (Brennan, 1975; see chapter 5 for discussion). The research work of the Webbs will be outlined here, and is considered further in chapter 5, which contains a detailed discussion of the research-policy model which they established, and the importance of that model subsequently.

Within a short time of the founding of the Fabian Society in 1883, the key figures whose names are predominantly associated with the early Fabian Society had become members: George Bernard Shaw, Sidney Webb and Beatrice Potter (later, Webb). Quickly, the Society's orientation crystallized around a version of socialism which rejected the 'very frothy revolutionary socialism of the eighteen eighties', as it is described by John Parker, who was a later General Secretary of the Society. Instead they 'insisted on the need for working out practical schemes for applying Socialist ideas to particular problems that had to be faced' (Parker, 1974, p. 241). As Shaw himself explained, he and Sidney Webb decided to join the Society because they saw it as a suitable group with which to align their own concerns. Sidney Webb, he said:

> had far too much knowledge of practical administration to believe in versions of socialism such as (William) Morris'....
> We were both strong on 'the inevitability of gradualness'.
> (Shaw, 1974, pp. 6–7).

Very soon, the Society turned to social investigation as a major means of pursuing its aims of social reform, and produced the first of its famous pamphlets, entitled *Why Are The Many Poor?* in 1884. Its most famous pamphlet was the fifth one, largely the work of Sidney Webb and entitled *Facts For Socialists*. The very title of this pamphlet indicated that from an epistemelogical standpoint, the Fabian approach to social research was firmly rooted in the same tradition as the other nineteenth century approaches represented in the statistical movement, the ameliorist tradition and the great poverty surveys, namely a belief in the collection of facts which would speak for themselves as the basis for social reform.

However there were distinctive features of the research-policy relationship as developed by the Webbs in particular, who devoted their lives and Beatrice's private income to a mixture of social research, fostering contacts with politicans and administrators as a way of influencing policy, and public service in central and local government. The distinctive features were, first, the crystallization of an approach which has its roots in the ameliorist tradition, namely the practical use of research in the services of both formulating social policies and administering them. Abrams regards the work of the Webbs as the key instance of this particular approach to social policy: research of a quantitative nature, emphasizing the collection of administrative intelligence followed by effective action taken by government (Abrams, 1968, p. 27). Their concern to 'humanize and liberalize social administration', as John Brown has put it, is important not only because of its significance at the time, but because it has provided the language and the conceptual framework within which social policy subsequently developed (Brown, 1978, p. 126). Second, and in contrast with other contemporary socialist traditions which were concerned with bringing about social change by pressure from mass movements, the Fabian approach to social reform operated entirely with closed intellectual and political circles: the vision was 'objective research and expert opinion as the arbiters of policy' (p. 127). This 'top down' model of social reform and the role of research within that model also have had profound consequences subsequently for the types of research that have become acceptable in a policy context, as I shall argue in chapter 5. The implications of this model were seen clearly by the Webbs and pursued vigorously by them, especially in the period 1900–1910, when the cultivation of administrators and politicians in the cause of social reform formed a major part of their activities. Beatrice Webb's diaries for this period are full of descriptions of social events which they set up for this purpose, described with phrases like 'a brilliant little luncheon' (Webb, 1948). They regarded any politician whatever their party affiliation as a suitable target, provided they were influential.

For the Webbs, extensive and systematic social research was a key element in developing effective strategies for social reform (see chapter 5). So far as the methods which they employed are concerned, in a very real sense, the tradition established by the Webbs combined both quantitative and qualitative methods. Beatrice Webb, as a young woman, admired Charles Booth's plan for his study precisely because it offered 'a subtle combination of quantitative and qualitative analysis' (Webb, 1926, p. 186). Subsequently, however, she came to emphasize the limitations of Booth's approach precisely because it represented a cross-sectional survey approach which — however accurate — could say little about social process and social change, as I have already indicated.

Their own approach had a strong historical dimension, based upon the analysis of documents plus observation and interviews with key informants. F W Galton, who was Sidney Webb's personal secretary (in effect, research assistant) in the 1890s has provided an interesting account of how he worked under their direction. He was sent to visit trade union officials and interview them to collect printed material which they issued and to attend meetings of local branches and Trades Councils when he could get permission. He then wrote full reports, which had to be done in particular format which facilitated systematic analysis: on paper of uniform size, 'with strict attention to the necessity of using separate sheets for separate subjects . . ., I was enjoined to see that matters relating to, say, the history of a Union should not be mixed up with matters relating to trade practices, regulations etc.' (Galton, 1974, p. 31).

This sounds very much like classic fieldwork methods, carried out and analyzed in a systematic way. That impression is confirmed by reading the Webbs' own writing on research methods, including their book published in 1932, much of which would stand comparison with any contemporary text. Beatrice Webb had been writing about research methods for some years, and her discussion of interviewing, for example, makes it clear that her concept of the interview was much closer to ethnographic than to survey research. She describes the interview as 'an instrument of research and discovery through the process of skilled interrogation' (Webb, 1926, p. 361), and includes extremely pertinent advice on how to make the interview a pleasurable occasion so as to encourage the free flow of information, how to ask questions perceptively but not intrusively, and the importance of being well prepared for each interview (pp. 361–3).

All this sounds very promising from the viewpoint of using qualitative methods in social policy research and certainly it challenges the supreme dominance of statistics. However, little work in the Fabian tradition has built upon a fieldwork base. The reason for this lies partly in the concept of combining methods: a concept which, when examined carefully, accords a secondary role to qualitative data. Beatrice Webb thought that all studies should use both quantitative and qualitative methods, and that either alone is inadequate. Of personal observation she writes that, however vivid, 'it must be put to the hard and fast test of statistical enquiry ... we may admire it as a work of art, but we cannot accept it as verified statement of fact' (Webb, 1926, p. 360). Therefore, despite the sensitive and appreciative understanding of what we would now call qualitative methods displayed in the Webbs' textbook, the concept of facts contained within the Fabian approach meant that the ultimate test would always be found in quantitative data. Qualitative methods then came to be seen as especially appropriate to the initial stages of study, 'a preliminary step to statistical enquiry' (p. 358). The epistemology contained within the model therefore placed limits upon the use of qualitative methods.

This was further reinforced by the administrative orientation of the Fabian model of the research-policy relationship, in which gathering administrative intelligence was seen as the basis of effective policy (Abrams, 1968, p. 27). To employ field research as the main strategy could prove profoundly uncomfortable if the researcher is taking the perspective of the administrator. In the case of research on the recipients of welfare benefits, almost by definition the work will reflect the perspective of what Becker (1967) calls the 'underdog', a perspective which may well challenge the status quo. This is unlikely to commend itself to the administrator concerned with the long-term management of welfare services.

The Webbs' approach to research methods therefore in a sense represents a potentially important shift within the dominant tradition of social policy research, in the direction of legitimizing and extending the use of qualitative methods. Ultimately however, that potential was not realized.

Surveys and Social Policy in the Twentieth Century

The discussion of the development of surveys in relation to social policy in the twentieth century will be much briefer than the discussion of the nineteenth-century material for two reasons. First, Part II of this book contains detailed discussion of a number of recent examples of both qualitative and quantitative work. Second, developments in the twentieth century for the most part were modifications of the basic parameters of the research-policy relationship laid down in the nineteenth century, rather than significant departures from them. Indeed, many commentators would place work on poverty done by Peter Townsend in the 1970s in the direct line of studies which began with Charles Booth, although it is recognized that the level of conceptual sophistication is substantially different (Golding, 1980).

Although the growth in the amount of social survey work being done slowed down somewhat at the beginning of the twentieth century (Dyos, 1967–68), the most significant changes were not so much in the quantity of work produced as in the context within which that work was undertaken. More substantial discussions of twentieth century developments are available elsewhere (Bulmer, 1982a; Marsh, 1982), and for the purposes of this chapter, I simply wish to highlight three features.

First, there were technical developments in survey technique, and especially the development of random sampling, which created quite different opportunities for the more extensive use of surveys, if anything further strengthening the position of survey work in relation to social policy. The development of random sampling was made initially by A L Bowley, who conducted his main work in the period before and after the First World War and was Professor of Statistics at the London School of Economics (Bulmer, 1982a, pp. 23–4).

The second change in the context in which applied social research took place was the increasing institutionalization of social research. On the one hand academic institutions began to provide a base for it — in the first instance the LSE. Bulmer considers that the academic institutionalization of research was slow in Britain, but that eventually it did make social research rather different in character (pp. 22–3). On the other hand, social survey work eventually became institutionalized within government itself, as the principal means whereby research was used to inform policy-making. The Haldane Report in 1918 reviewed government provision for research and argued that it should be substantially expanded (see chapter 2). However, it was not until the Second World War that central government set up its own survey organization. The Wartime Social Survey was founded in 1940 by the Ministry of Information's Home Intelligence Division, and is discussed in detail as part of the case study presented in chapter 4.

The institutionalization of survey work within government was consolidated after the end of the war, with the organization renamed the Government Social Survey and established as a permanent part of the machinery of government, despite threats by the Conservatives in

1950 to close it down (Whitehead, 1985). The form in which survey work became institutionalized within government was therefore one which saw research as a non-political, fact-finding activity. This is confirmed by an article written by Louis Moss in 1953, in which he describes the range of work undertaken by the Government Social Survey, and highlights the use of sample surveys to the government administrator. It is indeed the administrator rather than the politician he sees as the major client for this factual information about aspects of social life related to policy, and sees it as much as part of the process of putting into effect decisions made as informing the nature of those decisions:

> For the administrator, sample survey research can never be regarded as a substitute for the play of political forces. It becomes relevant as a tool of the administrator only after political decisions have been made and when the administrator has the clearly assigned duty of making political decisions effective. (Moss, 1953, p. 482)

This emphasis upon the perspective of the administrator is reminiscent of earlier work, especially in the Fabian tradition, and it will be argued in chapter 5 that the administrative perspective aligns well with quantitative research. Another factor which helped to strengthen the position of survey work at the end of the Second World War was the publication of the Clapham Report, which is discussed in chapter 2.

The third development in survey work in the twentieth century which I wish to highlight came in the inter-war period, namely the development of local social surveys with a clear focus on social reform. Writing in 1935, Wells notes the expansion of social surveys based in a locality, and sets out to analyze their character and potential. A typical example which he cites is Mess' study of Tyneside, published in 1928. This in fact originated in a church conference on citizenship, in which the participants decided that a survey was the most practical contribution which they could make to the welfare of the area, and they set up a committee to direct this survey which was composed of senior church figures, academics, union officials and employers (Mess, 1928, pp. 7–8). Although they saw their task as a 'survey', the Committee explicitly rejected direct questioning of people who lived in Tyneside. The report is in fact based upon a compilation and analysis of data in official and other reports which already existed, checked by obtaining information from 'persons with direct contact and experience' (p. 17). These local surveys were notable therefore not so much for their methods as for the fact that they were local initiatives, intended to highlight the social problems of a local area in order to directly stimulate policy change. In this they achieved some success (Bulmer, 1982, p. 26). It is apparent from the Tyneside survey that these initiatives in many ways were parallel to the work of the Statistical Societies in the 1830s: they were conducted by a committee of local worthies, their methods were not dissimilar, and they expected social research to lead directly to social reform. However, by contrast with work a century earlier, the Tyneside survey focusses upon inadequacies of public provision rather than the inadequacies of the poor. In its chapter on education for example, it is highly critical of elementary school provision, with classes too large, facilities poor, and staffing levels unsatisfactory. Its general impression of provision is that 'the Tyneside towns have much leeway to make up in the matter of public elementary education' (Mess, 1928, p. 123). The concern with education as an indication of the moral state of the poor and a remedy for their condition — central to the local surveys of the 1830s — is completely absent.

These local social surveys of the inter-war period are conventionally considered part of the survey tradition (Bulmer, 1982a; Marsh, 1982) and at the level of methods their emphasis certainly was upon statistical work, while their view of the research-policy relationship was a simple and straightforward one. At the same time, however, they had certain features which depart from those very simple models: the control of the work was in the hands of local individuals, not administrators or policy-makers, and an explicit part of their activities concerned the educative value of taking part in the exercise (Wells, 1935). This rather distinctive line on the purpose, control and use of data makes these local surveys something of a departure within the survey tradition, and these aspects will be considered more fully in relation to the 'alternative' approach to research and policy discussed in chapter 3.

With this exception, however, the dominant position of surveys and statistical work was maintained in the twentieth century, despite a challenge from the alternative tradition represented most clearly by Mass Observation (see chapter 3). Further, the dominant themes in the research-policy relationship remained substantially the same: accurate and impartial collection of facts, the primacy of statistical material and the immediate use of data for purposes of social reform.

Social Research and Social Policy in Education Since the Second World War

The final section of this chapter on the dominant tradition of social research and social policy concerns education specifically, in the period since the end of the Second World War in Britain. In this period, developments both of the welfare state and within social science make it possible to focus down upon an identifiable area around educational research and policy, and specifically an identifiable sub-discipline within sociology. The period is divided clearly into two halves, with a break around 1970. Before this date, the orthodoxy of social research on educational issues followed closely the dominant paradigm set out earlier in this chapter; and in terms of methodology, studies conducted were principally (although not exclusively) quantitative. From the begining of the 1970s a clear challenge was mounted to this dominant position which, inter alia, rejected the kind of studies which had previously been undertaken and promoted methodologies which were more recognizably qualitative; at the same time, however, the work which developed in this genre was not specifically targeted upon social policy issues.

The dominant tradition of social research on education in the two decades following the end of the Second World War was recognizably the inheritor of the model of social research set out in the early poverty studies and developed within the Fabian tradition. Its concerns were also shaped by the political context of the period following the 1944 Education Act, with its explicit emphasis upon extending equality of educational opportunity (Floud and Halsey, 1958, p. 179). The dominant concerns were the links between education and social stratification, and the extent to which education was either continuing to reinforce the structure of a hierarchically ordered society, or was providing a channel through which the children of the poor could be upwardly socially mobile (Williamson, 1974). Such questions were pursued principally through large-scale quantitative analysis, through many famous studies in the 1950s, a number of which are collected in the volume edited by Halsey, Floud and Anderson (1961) — a period during which sociologists 'invaded' educational research on a large scale (Karabel and Halsey, 1977, p. 2). Work in this tradition has come to be called 'political arithmetic' — a phrase which its critics used as a term of abuse, but which its advocates regard as an accurate description of a legitimate approach to research: essentially it means 'calculating the chances of reaching different stages in the educational process for children of different class origins' (p. 11). Work of this type has indeed survived into the 1980s with the publication of the results of the Oxford Mobility Study, which the authors place explicitly within this tradition (Halsey, Heath and Ridge, 1980, p. 1).

The historical roots of this tradition are important in the context of this book. M F D Young, who was a central critic of the political arithmetic tradition (see below), saw its roots in the methodology of Booth and Rowntree and the ideological perspective of the Fabians, pursuing studies in education which 'broadened the notion of poverty from lack of income to lack of education which was seen as a significant part of working-class life changes' (Young, 1973, p. 343). In fact the first conscious use of the term was by Lancelot Hogben who, as a professor at the London School of Economics in the 1930s, edited a book entitled *Political Arithmetic* (Hogben, 1938). Significantly, one of the research team who produced this book was David Glass, who subsequently held a chair at LSE himself and whose major work on social structure and social mobility made precisely the kind of links in relation to education which Young describes (Glass, 1954). In turn, A H Halsey, a key post-war exponent of 'political arithmetic' studies in relation to education, was a student of Glass. He has described his own work as directly building upon Glass and 'consciously carrying on the tradition of political arithmetic — marrying a value-laden choice of issue with objective methods of data collection and analysis' (Halsey, 1985, p. 161; see also, Szreter, 1984).

Therefore in a sense, those who have worked within the political arithmetic tradition would accept the classification of their work as part of the tradition which incorporates both the Webbs and Charles Booth, but would regard that as a strength not a weakness. Halsey, for example, has argued that both before and after the war there was a strong socialist influence on the choice of problems to be studied, and that the way data were used followed the classic Fabian model of research related to policy (Karabel and Halsey, 1977, p. 3). As scholars still working in the political arithmetic tradition, Halsey, Heath and Ridge (1980) have defended it as 'this indigenous style of social science':

> It has a long and distinguished history. Its origins can be traced back at least as far as Booth and the Webbs, and perhaps earlier to Mayhew in the nineteenth century and William Petty in the seventeenth. These writers were concerned to describe accurately and in detail the social conditions of their society.... Description of social conditions

was a preliminary to political reform. They exposed the
inequalities of society in order to change them . . . it has been
an attempt to marry a value-laden choice of issue with
objective methods of data collection. (p. 1)

Social research on education in the two decades following the
end of the Second World War can therefore be seen as the direct
inheritor of the dominant tradition of social research and social
policy, with all that entails: a belief in collecting objective facts about
the social world, principally through quantitative methods; a commitment to using those facts as the basis of social reform; and a belief
in the efficiency of government action to create a more just society
(see chapter 5 for further discussion of the Fabian model). This
particular blend of policy orientation and quantitative methodology
was indeed part of a continuing tradition in British social science, but
it can also be said to have been supported in the post-war period by
such factors as increased government sponsorship of research and,
within the discipline of sociology, the developing theoretical orthodoxy of structural-functionalism with which it fitted quite comfortably (Karabel and Halsey, 1977, p. 17). In a real sense the area of
education in the post-war period was not only an inheritor of the
dominant tradition of social research and social policy, but also its
high-point. As Reynolds puts it, the 1960s was the high point of
social engineering in Britain and many academic proponents of the
political arithmetic of educational research were instrumental in
shaping Labour Party policy on education during this period, first in
opposition and then in power (Reynolds, 1980–81, p. 79). Their
impact was considerable on such matters as the 11+ system, the
concept of a limited pool of ability, the comprehensive reform of
secondary education and strategies for positive discrimination (Bernbaum, 1977, pp. 28–29).

The period of Labour government in the 1960s may have been
the high point for this approach to research and policy but a period of
rapid disillusionment followed, in which it became increasingly
apparent that these 'social engineering' policies were failing to deliver
the kind of social change which their proponents envisaged. It is in
this period that commentators locate the breakdown of the social
democratic consensus in British politics generally, and in the sphere
of educational policies in particular (Williamson, 1974; Centre for
Contemporary Cultural Studies, 1981). So far as education is concerned, it led to a disillusionment both with the role of the academic

expert, and with the established methods of research (Reynolds, 1980–81, p. 79).

It was against this background that loudly-voiced criticism of the 'old' orthodoxy emerged within the sub-discipline of sociology of education, and the 'new' order was proclaimed. The critics focussed upon all those features which made the political arithmetic tradition so clearly part of the dominant tradition of policy-related research: its subject-matter, its methodology and its policy orientation. In relation to subject-matter, the central criticism was that there had been an almost total neglect of the content of education, and especially of 'how knowledge is selected, organized and assessed in educational institutions' (Young, 1973, p. 339). In Young's view, this limitation can be traced directly to the Fabian origins of the work, which directs attention towards life-chances within a stratified society, and therefore to a preoccupation with access to education rather than with its content (pp. 343–4). As to the methodology of the 'old' sociology of education, this was roundly dismissed as positivist epistemology mixed with normative orientations. Particular attention was paid to critiques of measurement techniques and to the idea that if knowledge is quantifiable it must be scientific — criticisms which even certain proponents of the political arithmetic approach find well placed (Karabel and Halsey, 1977, p. 17). Finally, so far as the policy orientation of the 'old' school is concerned, Young in particular was highly critical of the willingness of academics to 'take' the problems of administrators rather than to 'make' their own — a distinction which was important more generally during this period (see chapter 5). Young argues that sociologists failed to question the assumptions behind the problems which they were 'taking' — assumptions which were principally concerned with the maintenance of social order and the failure of socialization in working-class families — whereas in his view, educators' problems, and those aspects of the social world which they take for granted, ought always to be considered as phenomena to be explained. The consequence was that, although the work of sociologists did question procedures for grouping and selecting children, it failed to question more fundamental processes of categorization such as the concepts 'able' or 'dull' (Young, 1971, pp. 1–2).

From 1970 onwards therefore it must be said that the political arithmetic tradition no longer represented the dominant mode of social research on educational issues, although it did not disappear completely, as has already been indicated. The gap left by the demise of the 'old' approach has, in relation to empirical studies, largely been filled by work which draws upon naturalistic and ethnographic methods, making what constitutes social research in education much more varied in the 1980s than it was in the 1960s (Karabel and Halsey, 1977, pp. 51–8; Reynolds; 1980–81; Burgess, 1984a). Work in what most commentators refer to as this 'interpretivist' style utilizes principally qualitative methods, and draws upon epistemologies which emphasize the social construction of reality and the political nature of social knowledge, rather than empiricist concepts of objective facts. From this point onwards, therefore, the dominant paradigm within social research in the educational sphere was no longer heavily quantitative, and gave much more space to qualitative work. This does not mean, however, that there followed a significant shift in the kind of social research targeted upon social policy and used by policy-makers. Indeed, as Pollard puts it 'interpretive work as a whole has made very little impact on policy in the last decade' (Pollard, 1984, p. 177; see also Parkinson, 1982; Burgess, 1984a.)

Why did not this new development of qualitative work not concern itself with issues of social policy, except peripherally? A variety of answers can be given to this, some of which touch upon the character of that research itself, and others of which concern the academic and political context in which it was developing. One also needs to distinguish between different strands of work within an interpretivist framework and using qualitative methods (Woods and Hammersley, 1977; Delamont and Atkinson, 1980). Those who have aligned themselves specifically with the 'new' sociology of education and with phenomonology or ethnomethodology as its core seem to have rejected a policy orientation much more explicitly than other ethnographic researchers, whose work owes much more to anthropology — for example, the studies of schools undertaken by Ball (1981) and Burgess (1983), which stand quite explicitly in the line of school studies initiated by Hargreaves (1967) and Lacey (1970) in the 1960s, and which were concerned very explicitly with issues of social policy. This is made clear in Lacey's retrospective discussion of the development of these latter two studies in the context of a department in Manchester steered by the vision of the social anthropologist, Max Gluckman (Lacey, 1982). A detailed discussion of the range of qualitative research in education is beyond my scope here, but I shall suggest some answers to the important question of why the links between qualitative work and social policy have been so loose.

First, the political context within which this research has developed has not on the whole been conducive to a strong policy orientation. The collapse of the social democratic consensus and a recognition on the political left that previous attempts at social engineering through education (and elsewhere) had largely been ineffective have called into question the whole enterprise of creating social knowledge for direct use by governments. A rejection of the Fabian model of research and policy was a specific part of the critique developed by the 'new' sociologists of education, and the removal of that model of the research-policy relationship has left a void which there has been no particular incentive for other researchers within the interpretivist tradition to fill. The fact that the Labour party has had only a tenuous hold on power since 1970 provides a further lack of incentive to develop policy links, since it has been principally through the Labour party that academics have had an impact on social policy in Britain — a point which will be elaborated further in chapter 5.

Second, the academic scene has also been changing in ways which made it unlikely that research within sociology would embrace a strong policy orientation. In particular, the clear separation of the disciplines of sociology and social administration (discussed in detail in chapter 5) has meant that — during the 1970s at least — sociologists appeared to wish to leave policy studies to the discipline of social administration, concentrating rather on the kind of work which was regarded as high status, principally theory. Since qualitative research in education developed mainly within the discipline of sociology, there was no incentive for researchers to orient their work towards policy — quite the reverse, if the main problem was to establish the validity of empirical work in a discipline which was placing the highest value upon theory.

I am suggesting therefore that at least part of the explanation for the lack of interest in policy studies lies in the fact that researchers doing qualitative work after 1970 had no particular incentive to develop in this direction — if anything an incentive to keep their distance. This lack of incentive is important given that, from the perspective of policy-makers, the kind of work being produced in qualitative studies was unlikely to automatically commend itself because its methodology does not conform to the dominant paradigm of fact-gathering (see chapter 5). At the very least, this means that qualitative researchers needed to actively promote their work with policy-makers if it was to make any impact — something which there seems to have been little incentive to engage with as far as most were concerned. An important exception to this perhaps is represented by the research on the curriculum developed by Lawrence Stenhouse and his colleagues, which I discuss in chapter 8 (see, for example,

Stenhouse, 1975 and 1980). But in aspects of education related to broader social policy concerns, there seems to have been little incentive for qualitative researchers to become involved.

The reasons so far offered apply to all kinds of qualitative work. The final reason which I suggest for the lack of policy orientation concerns the 'new' sociologists of education specifically: that is, the highly relativistic concept of knowledge which the work of some (but not all) displays. The most vociferous proponents of 'new' sociology of education defined their task as a branch of the sociology of knowledge and questions of the organization and control of knowledge as their 'core concern' (Young, 1971, p. 3). The book called *Knowledge and Control* edited by Young *(1971)* contains papers which elaborate this from a variety of perspectives. Although there are some differences between contributors, there is a clear sense that most are easing towards the position in which all knowledge is seen as the creation of specific social groups with specific sets of interests which means — as Bernbaum puts it in his highly critical discussion — that knowledge cannot be judged with reference to any external criteria and reality, and that there is no indication of what 'being wrong' might constitute (Bernbaum, 1977, pp. 59–61). Without any clear sense of what constitutes valid knowledge or how items of knowledge relate to social reality, it is not difficult to see how proponents of this approach shied away from involvement with policy: their stance is almost the polar opposite of the committed, left-wing academics who used political arithmetic studies to push politicians and administrators in directions which they believed to be right.

I have suggested that there are grounds for understanding why the range of qualitative work in education which developed after 1970 did not have a significant policy focus, but none of those reasons suggest that it is in principle impossible for a different focus to develop. As Williamson (1974, p. 5) has noted, whilst the 'new' sociology of education was 'not in the least concerned' with policy, nor does it preclude totally the development of such studies, especially studies of the social construction of social policy. Indeed, at least one researcher in the ethnographic tradition has recently argued that the time is now ripe for ethnography to begin to make a broader contribution to policy, and to renew its concern with material and structural issues (Pollard, 1984, p. 178). Pollard, like Stenhouse and his collaborators (1975 and 1980), argues that there are particular possibilities for ethnography to feed into policy at the level of classroom practice. This view in a sense is shared by Karabel and Halsey, although they also clearly believe that its impact can extend to broader levels of policy-making. They argue that — ironically, since the 'new' sociology of education began by specifically rejecting the 'taking' of educators' problems — that there is considerable potential in interpretivist work from the perspective of educational policy-makers. The political arithmetic tradition pointed to structural reforms in the education system, but it is now well recognized that many of these left behaviour in schools substantially unchanged. The interpretive paradigm can now be of more use because it 'focusses precisely on those classroom processes that must be understood if there is to be any chance of reducing the class and racial differentials in academic achievement that concern the administrators of the Welfare State'. They point to factors such as the way in which self-fulfilling prophecies affect student performance as an illustration (Karabel and Halsey, 1977, pp. 60–1).

In principle, therefore, there are grounds for seeing space for the development of qualitative work oriented to social policy issues in the field of education. In practice, such developments have been very limited, and certainly there has been no sign of an 'alternative' policy-oriented, qualitative tradition of research to replace the dominant quantitative paradigm, represented so clearly by the political arithmetic tradition in the educational sphere.

Conclusion

This review of the dominant tradition of social research and social policy in Britain has traced the major distinctive features of that tradition, as they developed through key periods in the nineteenth and twentieth centuries. The recurring themes are: the impartial collection of facts; an unproblematic conception of 'facts', based on a positivist epistemology; a belief in the direct utility of such facts in shaping measures of social reform which can be implemented by governments; and a strong preference for statistical methods and the social survey as the most suitable technique for fact-collecting. The development of this tradition has been traced through the past 150 years, and it has been argued that although some use has been made of qualitative techniques they have always been accorded a secondary place, principally because of the unchallenged position of positivist epistemology. Ironically, when a clear body of qualitative research based on a different epistemology did develop in the field of education, little interest was shown in social policy. However, this rather gloomy picture does not necessarily hold for the future, as I shall suggest in chapter 5.

2 The Dominant Tradition and Government Reports

The previous chapter offered a selective history of the development of policy-oriented social research in England and documented the substantial dominance of research conducted through quantitative techniques and within an intellectual framework of positivism (see Introduction for discussion of these terms). At the same time I argued that there has been a greater use of qualitative methods — at least at the levels of techniques — than is sometimes acknowledged, albeit accorded a secondary role. This chapter attempts a parallel exercise: it considers the same issues, namely what kind of social research has been regarded as appropriate and useful in a policy context, but through the rather different focus of central government reports produced since the Second World War. An examination of these reports affords the opportunity to explore the 'official view' — from the centre of policy-making at national level — about the utility of social research and to examine concrete examples of its use.

The chapter is presented in two sections, each covering rather different kinds of documents. In the first part, I discuss a series of reports about social research itself and government support for it, considering specifically the balance between quantitative and qualitative approaches which they envisage. This section is about social research in general rather than about education specifically, although the kind of support for social research which these reports encouraged itself formed an important part of the context in which research on education (as much as other kinds of social research) has developed in the post-war period. Further, these reports have had a direct relevance for higher education since for the most part they envisaged that government support for research would mean an expansion of research opportunities (and to an extent teaching provision) in universities especially.

The second, rather longer, part of the chapter, concentrates on education, examining a series of key reports on educational provision in England produced since 1959. In this period, there has been a substantial input of social research into such documents, and hence more indirectly into policy-making, at central government level. This series of reports therefore provides an opportunity to examine the balance of quantitative and qualitative research inputs into educational policy specifically.

Government Reports on Social Research

In the twentieth century, and especially since the Second World War, it is possible to trace 'official' thinking about the usefulness of social research through a series of government reports. This section considers in particular: the Haldane Report (1917); the Clapham Report (1946); the Heyworth Report (1965); and the two reports produced by Lord Rothschild in 1971 and 1982. The concerns of these reports range widely and encompass the use of research *within* government, the usefulness of research *to* government (whoever produces it) and the sponsorship of research *by* government (the grounds for which may be different from the issue of usefulness). In this section, I shall not attempt a general evaluation of these reports, but concentrate upon two issues: What are the models of the research-policy relationship being promoted by these reports? What kind of research is envisaged, and especially, are the reports hospitable to qualitative work?

The Haldane Report (1917)

The Haldane Committee was asked to enquire into the 'machinery of government' in general, not specifically research, but its brief included the request to 'advise in what manner the exercise and distribution by the government of its functions should be improved' (Haldane Committee, 1917, paragraph 2). Part of the Committee's advice was to expand research and information services, and a whole section of the Report was devoted to this (Part II, Chapter IV). Beatrice Webb was a member of this Committee, and there is evidence that she placed great importance on her membership, seeing it as a prime opportunity to advance her own view of social reform, that is, that reform should be based upon administrative intelligence gathered through government sponsored research, followed by effective action through efficient government machinery. The Haldane Committee encompassed both concerns (Abrams, 1968, p. 27; and for further discussion of Beatrice Webb's position, see chapter 5). More generally, the context in which the Committee was set up was planning for change after the end of the First World War, and the concerns of the Report do indicate that the Committee wanted to mobilize social science in the task of reconstruction. Increased amounts of money for research were made available subsequently (Cherns, 1979, pp. 33–4). These developments of course have to be seen in relation to the social circumstances in which they occurred where, for example, state provision of social welfare, education and medical services was much more limited than it became after the end of the Second World War; and where social science was not yet established in academic institutions in England (Bulmer, 1982a and 1985).

The Committee was in general enthusiastic about the potential of research, and thought that the machinery of government, especially policy-making, would be improved by a greater input:

> in the sphere of civil government, the duty of investigation and thought, as preliminary to action, might with great advantage be more definitely recognised. It appears to us that adequate provision has not been made in the past for the organised acquisition of facts and information, and for the systematic application of thought, as preliminary to the settlement of policy and its subsequent administration. (Part I, paragraph 12)

There is a twin emphasis in the Committee's view of research apparent here: information-gathering on the one hand, and systematic thought on the other. However, in its specific discussion of the expansion of research, the former is given far more prominence than the latter. This, of course, is quite consistent with the view that social research for government equals administrative intelligence, and it is clearly reflected in the survey which the Committee conducted into the existing 'intelligence work' in government departments. In this survey, the Board of Education is praised for the work of its Office of Special Inquiries and Reports, whose work included gathering information from other countries, keeping the Department's library, making 'extensive enquiries into various educational problems' and maintaining a survey of the education service (paragraph 11). In the Committee's view, such work was exactly the kind of development it wished to encourage: work which, in its view, had greatly assisted the work of the Board, the Inspectors and the local education authorities, and had been instrumental in identifying fresh education needs and helping the Board to devise ways of meeting them (paragraph 13). So, although the Committee does not explicitly spell out the methods of research which it favoured, it is clear from the rest of its discussion that quantitative work was seen as the norm, being the form in which administrative intelligence can be most effectively collected.

A major proposal of the Committee's should be mentioned because — had it been accepted — it would have given research (of all kinds, not just social research) a position of prominence in government which it has never actually enjoyed. The Committee proposed that, whilst all departments should continue to expand research and intelligence for their own specific use, there should be an additional Department of Intelligence and Research which would 'take its place among the most important departments of government' (paragraph 74).

The Committee's main reason for advocating a separate Department of Research became known subsequently as the 'Haldane Principle'. This is the argument that only a minister freed from other administrative concerns can make proper and unbiased recommendations about the use of research:

> It places responsibility to Parliament in the hands of a Minister who is in normal times free from any serious pressure of administrative duties, and is immune from any suspicion of being biased by administrative considerations against the application of the results of research. (Part II, Chapter IV, paragraph 67a)

On one level, this seems to contradict the idea that research is useful to government only when it is oriented to administrative concerns, since it opens up the possibility that research which runs counter to such considerations should nonetheless be used. On another level, however, it is quite consistent with the Committee's concern to promote efficient government machinery, which might well mean that entrenched departmental interests would have to be bypassed if efficient and effective policies were to be promoted. In other words, it represents a strong faith in the efficacy of research and in its direct applicability, and a view of the research-policy relationship which was indeed characteristic of Beatrice Webb: that the application of research results by intelligent, progressive administrators is the route to enlightened social reform (see chapter 5).

The Clapham Report (1946)

The Clapham Report, like the Haldane Report, was produced in a period of social reconstruction following a major war. Its terms of reference asked the Committee to consider 'whether any additional provision is necessary into social and economic questions' (Report of the Committee on the Provision for Social and Economic Research, 1946, paragraph 1). It was focussed therefore upon social research specifically and therefore in that sense was much narrower in scope than Haldane. In another sense, however, its scope was broader. Whereas Haldane's concern for research had been confined to its use directly within the machinery of government, the Clapham Committee (operating in the very different political and intellectual climate of the late 1940s, in which central government was attempting to create a comprehensive welfare state) was concerned also with questions of how far, and in what ways, government should sponsor social and economic research both inside and outside government, some of which would not necessarily have direct policy relevance. The Committee in fact took the view that it is 'inherent in the nature of things' that governments should be involved in social and economic research both directly and indirectly, and produced proposals for the expansion of these activities (Payne, Dingwall, Payne and Carter, 1981, p. 143).

Cherns regards the report produced by the Committee as characteristic of the atmosphere of social reconstruction of the late 1940s, in that it saw social scientists as a potential resource in the task of building a welfare state (Cherns, 1979, pp. 35–6). The Committee certainly took a strong view of the efficacy of social research in developing sound policies and doubted whether 'even in the present day the great practical value of knowledge in these fields is appreciated' (paragraph 17). However, their view of what counts as useful research was once again heavily oriented towards the quantitative and the statistical. For example, they argued that, 'an adequate supply of statistical competence is quite fundamental to the advancement of knowledge of social and economic questions' (paragraph 18). So far as sociology specifically was concerned, the Committee felt that it should be expanded as a fundamental study and not just tied to the training of social workers (as it was predominantly at that time); but when they spelled out their reasons for this, the emphasis again was on statistics:

We feel that, in particular, there is scope for the development of the study of social organisation and the use of social and regional surveys. (Paragraph 17)

As to the relationship between research and policy envisaged by the Committee, this again was fairly direct, but with some acknowledgement of the complexities of translating social science research into policy. Within government itself, their view of research was essentially the same as the idea of administrative intelligence promoted by Haldane (paragraphs 7–8). But in discussing the need for strengthening contacts with researchers outside government, they suggest that 'outside experts' should be used to keep those who work in government abreast of developments in 'speculative branches of the field' and ought to be used to assist in 'assessing the value and possible uses of material which is already being collected' (paragraph 9). This seems to imply a faith in the potential usefulness of research, coupled with a degree of recognition that there has to be interpretation and assessment of research before it can be translated into policy. As Robin Williams puts it, the Committee's view of research was clearly interventionist, but they drew a distinction between information needed by government directly in its administration and planning and more purely academic research, which should not take place within government (Williams, 1980, pp. 135–6). It was this latter kind of research which would require interpretation.

The distinction between these two different types of social research was expressed in a major proposal of the Committee: that the expansion of social research should take place principally in the universities. They argued that the existing small number of teachers of social science in universities were grossly overstretched and that research was underresourced. They emphasized that support for social science research in universities should be *'on a permanent and routine basis'* (paragraph 24). Specifically, they proposed the establishment of more university chairs and other teaching posts in social science, more library provision, and more research support, including the provision of calculators and computing assistants (again, a strong clue about the kind of research which they envisaged) (paragraphs 24–6). Administratively, they proposed that this should be accomplished through the earmarking of specific grants for this purpose by the University Grants Committee (the body which distributes the grant given by central government to fund the universities), and at central government level, an interdepartmental committee should be set up to advise the UGC on social science matters. The Clapham

Committee also considered a proposal that social science research should be stimulated by setting up a Social and Economic Research Council financed by central government like research councils in scientific disciplines, but considered that such a move would be premature 'at this stage' (paragraphs 29–31).

The Clapham Committee therefore clearly accorded government a role in sponsoring and developing the social sciences per se, not merely those aspects of social science which are useful in the policy-making and administrative process. Government's sponsorship of the social sciences was located firmly as part of higher education policy in contrast, as Cherns argues, with what happened after 1965 when the sponsorship of social research was seen as part of science policy, not education policy (Cherns, 1979, p. 42). At the same time, as has already been noted, the Committee's view of social science emphasized its great practical value; and as far as methods are concerned, its concepts seem to have been entirely quantitative. So although in some ways it represents a radical departure in government sponsorship of social science, in terms of the concerns of this chapter, it represents a continuity with the dominant models of the past.

The recommendations of the report were substantially accepted by the government and the progress of these policies was subsequently reviewed by the Heyworth Committee (Report of the Committee on Social Studies, 1965, paragraphs 24–8). The UGC did apply the principle of earmarked grants between the years 1947 and 1952, although not totally with the results that Clapham had envisaged (Payne, Dingwall, Payne and Carter, 1981, pp. 255–6). Indeed the Heyworth Committee also was dubious about this policy of earmarking grants because, on the whole it had not succeeded in stimulating more research, but rather had financed the expansion of social science teaching in universities.

The Heyworth Committee (1965)

The work of the Heyworth Committee can in some senses be seen as a continuation of Clapham. The Committee's brief was:

> To review the research at present being done in the field of social studies in Government departments, the universities and other institutions and to advise whether changes are

needed in the arrangements for supporting and co-ordinating this research. (Report of the Committee on Social Studies, 1965, paragraph 1)

Like Clapham, therefore, the Committee's concern was with the sponsorship of social research by government as well as its direct use in policy and its major recommendation (accepted by the government) was that the time was now right to set up a Social Science Research Council (whose name was changed in 1983 to Economic and Social Research Council).

The purposes delineated for the SSRC in the Report make it clear that this is a case of sponsorship by government of a wide range of research, not only that which is of direct use — an issue which subsequently was to become important (see following section). Its purpose was to be: to provide support for research; to keep under review the state of research; to advise government on the needs of social science research; to keep under review the supply of trained research workers; to give advice on research in the social sciences and its application (paragraphs 145–70). So far as research in the field of education is concerned, the Committee 'carefully considered' the case for recommending a separate Educational Research Council. This was finally rejected, on the grounds that it would be better not to cut education off from the main stream of social sciences, since most research in education draws upon social sciences disciplines. There should, however, be a Board within SSRC to cater for the needs of educational research (paragraph 158). This was indeed established, although there are few signs that it stimulated work in anything other than the dominant tradition. Indeed, in the reorganization of the Council's committees which took place in 1982, the Education Committee was merged with Psychology, thus making its links with other social science displines and their concerns much more tenuous.

The Heyworth Committee also devoted a good deal of its report to the use of social science research by government. Robin Williams argues that the very setting up of the Committee was a characteristic move for the early 1960s, which period represents a high point of faith in the efficacy of the social sciences and in the possibility of planned interventions by government to secure social reform, citing a parliamentary debate on the social sciences in 1961 as evidence. During this period, he argues, there were remarkable expectations about the extent to which social science could provide the information upon which government could plan social interventions (Williams, 1980, pp. 138–9). Certainly these remarks would apply to the field of education (see following section).

In the view of the Heyworth Committee, the government was using social scientists in its own departments to a very limited extent, and then mainly economists and statisticians. It recommended a review of how social scientists from all disciplines could be useful (paragraphs 125–7). Thus the Heyworth Committee envisaged a much more extensive use of social scientists *within* government departments, and their view of what such people could do was fairly sophisticated. These people should not simply conduct research but also should translate research already done by others to administrative use, and should help policy-makers to identify how social problems emerge, and how they might be tackled. As Blume puts it, the Heyworth Committee was concerned to establish the importance of the research-policy relationship, but they had a clearer view than many that the findings of social science research cannot be 'applied' in a straightforward way (Blume, 1979, p. 321; see also, Thomas, 1983).

The relatively sophisticated view of the research-policy relationship taken by the Heyworth Committee is most apparent in the distinction which it drew between research and fact-finding:

> the difference between research and fact-finding (is) an extremely difficult distinction to make and research may require, or alternatively emerge from, fact-findings exercises or surveys. We would not, however, regard research as either routine fact-finding or fact-finding for specific administrative purposes. (Paragraph 9)

Building upon this distinction later in the Report, the Committee argued that fact-finding perhaps can be relatively easily assimilated and put to use by government whereas research in the social sciences cannot so readily be used:

> Problems in government or industry do not usually present themselves to administrators in a fashion which at once shows how they can be clarified by research in the social sciences. (Paragraph 123)

The conclusions which the Committee drew from this were first, that administrators and managers need to be familiar with the scope of the social sciences not only as 'direct aids to administration' but also as 'disciplines which are able to limit the uncertainties within which decisions are taken and to evaluate their outcome'; and second, that social scientists need to 'work at the points where problems first emerge' to help identify and deal with them (*ibid*).

The Heyworth Report therefore represents not only a high point of faith in the potential and efficacy of the social sciences, but also a much more sophisticated view of the research-policy relationship than had hitherto been expounded in official reports. It is one which, to anticipate the discussion in chapter 6, sounds rather like an 'enlightenment' model and which for the first time states that fact-finding is *not* research. Because of this, although methods of research are not explicitly discussed, the Report leaves potentially far greater scope than its predecessors for qualitative work to be developed, especially in its emphasis upon identifying the real nature and origins of social problems, and evaluating their outcomes. It is, therefore, a Report potentially far more hospitable to qualitative research than the others, whilst not directly making a case for such work. However, a marked development in policy-related qualitative research did not follow, certainly not in the field of education — something of a missed opportunity which was partly the consequence of developments with academic disciplines, as I shall argue in chapter 5.

The Rothschild Report (1971)

The first Rothschild Report called 'The Organisation and Management of Government R and D' was published by the Government in a Green Paper in 1971 (A Framework for Government Research and Development, 1971). Included in the same document is the Dainton Report, which is on the future of the research council system. Dainton's major recommendation was that the research councils should be kept in their existing form, but since the SSRC was explicitly excluded from this review, that Report will not be discussed here.

This first Rothschild review also excluded social science in general (on the grounds that it was not suitable for inclusion in the concept of research and development) and the SSRC in particular (on the grounds that it was in its infancy). However, the issues which Rothschild raised *have* subsequently been applied to the social sciences, including in his own second report, so it is important to consider them. Rothschild reviewed the use of all kinds of research by government departments and, drawing a sharp distinction between fundamental and applied research, he defined the latter in severely practical and instrumental terms. Applied research, he said, had as its end-product or objective a product, a process for making a product or an improved method of operation of some service (paragraph 7). The basic principle which Rothschild enunciated for government use of applied research is that it should be commissioned on the basis of the customer-contractor principle:

> This report is based upon the principle that applied R and D, that is, R and D with a practical application as its objective, must be done on a customer-contractor basis. The customer says what he wants, the contractor does it (if he can) and the customer pays. Basic, fundamental or pure research ... has no analagous customer-contractor basis. (Paragraph 9)

In a sense, this very clear distinction between fundamental and applied research — with the latter only being of direct use to government — was similar to the distinctions developed in the Haldane and especially the Clapham Report. It is a distinction, however, which is very difficult to apply to the social sciences (as Rothschild acknowledged in his later report), and represents a much cruder version of 'research' than was elaborated by the Heyworth Committee (Thomas, 1983). It was, however, an important distinction, especially since Rothschild stressed that government's prime interest must inevitably be in applied rather than fundamental research, whilst acknowledging that some funds should go to the latter. The issue here, as Rein has argued, is how immediately useful research can be to government, and Rothschild offers a strong view that it is the needs of government (as defined by those within it) which should shape the research agenda (Rein, 1976, pp. 113–4). This is a model of the research-policy relationship which relegates the researcher to the role of technician who produces the facts upon which policy-makers take decisions, a model which I shall argue in chapter 6 is not likely to be hospitable to qualitative work.

The government, in their introduction to the Green Paper, welcomed Rothschild's recommendation that government's commissioning of applied research should be in accordance with the customer-contractor principle, and they subsequently took action to implement Rothschild's recommendations although there was substantial hostility from the scientific community (Kogan, Korman and Henkel, 1980, p. 11). Most contentiously, they transferred part of the budgets of three of the research councils to the relevant government departments, so that they could implement the principle of commissioning research relevant to their own needs. Maurice Kogan and his colleagues have made a detailed study of how this worked out in the case of the Department of Health and Social Security, who had funds transferred from the Medical Research Council, to enable them to fund research in the field of health. On the basis of this study, the authors show that the DHSS tried to implement a system which was an elaborated version of the over-simple model which Rothschild had provided, building into the system various levels of negotiation about the feasibility and desirability of research which might be commissioned. Nonetheless there were substantial difficulties in developing mechanisms for this kind of close research-policy collaboration (Kogan, Korman and Henkel, 1980; Kogan and Henkel, 1983).

The Social Science Research Council was exempted from all of this, because the government accepted Rothschild's view that it was 'in its infancy'. However, the context in which the SSRC developed its own work was strongly coloured by the Rothschild Report and its application: the Council could 'see the writing on the wall and, on its own initiative attempted to ensure that its research programmes incorporated strong elements of policy relevance' (Kogan, Korman and Henkel, 1980, p. 20). Meanwhile, government departments quickly started to apply the consumer-contractor principle to social research which they funded, despite the exclusion of social science from Rothschild's brief (Thomas, 1983).

The Rothschild Report on the SSRC (1982)

The circumstances under which the Rothschild Report on the SSRC was undertaken contrast markedly with earlier reports, especially Heyworth. By this stage, the social sciences were politically under attack, rather than seen as the means to the creation of a better society; and the expansionist climate of the 1960s had turned into an era of public expenditure cuts in which the social sciences looked particularly at risk. This latter point is evidenced by the Report on Government Statistical Services produced the previous year (1981), whose main theme was the reduction of public expenditure upon statistical services of government departments, an area of work which must be regarded as relatively innocuous by comparison with some other social sciences. So far as the Department of Education and Science is concerned, the Report indicated that they planned to make a 12 per cent saving in their statistical services by ceasing to publish the annual volumes of Statistics of Education. The effect of this is to reduce the data available to social scientists who might wish to examine and comment upon government policy.

Against this background, Lord Rothschild was asked to carry out an exercise on the SSRC parallel to that which he had undertaken for the other research councils in 1971, and was invited explicitly to have regard to the customer-contractor principle which he had enunciated then (Rothschild, 1982, paragraph 3.1). The Report which Rothschild produced was in many ways far more supportive of the SSRC and of the social sciences than many had feared. His Report quotes the Heyworth Committee in some detail, and states that there are 'no serious arguments to rebut' what Heyworth had said about the social sciences (paragraph 5.1). As far as the Council was concerned, Rothschild recommended that it should continue (with some internal changes) and should be free both of further enquiries and further cuts in its budget for at least three years (paragraph 1.10).

In his discussion of the customer-contractor principle, Rothschild is clear that this principle could be applied to very little of the work sponsored by SSRC. This is true even of 'applied' social science research which — drawing on the criteria enunciated in the 1971 Report — he says is directed towards an end-product 'only in the metaphorical sense' (paragraph 3.9). The position which Rothschild spells out therefore is in stark contrast to the nineteenth century ameliorist tradition and to the Fabian model of the research-policy relationship, both of which stress the immediate practical utility of social research, and also differs from the line taken by the Haldane and Clapham reports. However, it is much closer to the Heyworth Report, especially in the role which Rothschild *does* envisage for social science research in relation to social policy; that is, that it essentially should inform debate rather than lead directly to policy outcomes:

> The main purpose of applied social science research is to provide the material upon which it may be possible to conduct more informed debate and make better decisions . . . the social science 'customer' includes all those who have a part to play in the decision-making process . . . . These decisions in a democratic society are not the sole concern of Ministers or officials. Members of Parliament on both sides of the House, journalists, academics, the public at large — all of these are beneficiaries of applied social science research. (Paragraph 3.10)

This passage also makes clear that Rothschild sees the essentially contested nature of social science research, which means that it cannot be 'applied' in any neutral sense, and also that he rejects the straightforward 'top-down' model of social reform which was characteristic especially of the Fabian model of the research-policy relationship (see chapter 5).

One obvious conclusion of this of course is that government departments are much less likely to fund social research, once it is recognized that it cannot be easily used to solve administrative problems, and that it may be interpreted and used in ways which are not necessarily supportive of the government's position. Rothschild sees this implication, and argues that there is a certain amount of social science research which government may fund directly, but they cannot be expected to fund the majority — an argument which he uses as a basis for the continuation of SSRC:

> The need for independence from government departments is particularly important because so much social science research is the stuff of political debate. All such research might prove subversive of government policies because it attempts to submit such policies to empirical trial, with the risk that the judgement may be adverse. It would be too much to expect Ministers to show enthusiasm for research designed to show that their policies were misconceived. But it seems obvious that in many cases the public interest will be served by such research being undertaken. (Paragraph 3.12)

The Rothschild view of the research-policy relationship therefore is one which sees research being fed into policy, and especially debates about policy, at many levels, and used on behalf of a variety of interests. This is far removed from the concept of research as administrative intelligence for use by government, and it not only opens up a quite different model of the research-policy relationship, but also creates the conditions under which a variety of *types* of research are more likely to be able to flourish, including policy-related qualitative work (see chapter 6 for further discussion). Those possibilities were opened up to an extent by the Heyworth Report in the 1960s, but that opportunity was not really taken in education and many other social policy fields. The 1980s could perhaps prove a more auspicious time, as I argue in chapter 5.

Government Reports on Education:
Their Use of Social Research

In this section, I shall discuss the use made of social research in a series of key reports on educational provision in England published since 1959: Crowther (1959), Newsom (1963), Robbins (1963), Plowden (1967), Warnock (1978), Rampton (1981) and Swann (1985). The reason for beginning at this point is that the late 1950s was the point at which social research began to feed into such reports to a significant extent, although psychological research had been extensively used as early as the Hadow Report of 1931 (Kogan and Packwood, 1974, p. 34). Alongside these, I shall discuss the major research projects undertaken under the Educational Priority Areas programme, which is the single most important example in Britain of major research projects being directly linked to a social policy initiative in the field of education. Finally, I shall consider some recent reports of Her Majesty's Inspectorate where there is an explicit 'research' element. In relation to all these reports, three questions will be considered: first, what kinds of data were used (having in mind especially the use made of qualitative as well as quantitative data); second, what use was made of different types of data in developing policy recommendations; third, were the kinds of data used appropriate to the policy issues which the committee was considering?

Before discussing these questions, it is important to indicate some key features of the context within such reports are produced, which in turn helps to explain some features of the products. The series of reports on educational provision mentioned above were produced by various kinds of advisory committee appointed by the Department of Education and Science. The background to the appointment and operation of such educational committees has been discussed by Kogan and Packwood (1974) and need not be repeated in general terms here. However, it is useful to highlight certain features which are important for understanding how these committees have made use of research, and what type of research has been considered relevant.

First, in terms of their operation and orientation these committees are the descendants of the nineteenth-century Commissions which I discussed in chapter 1. Classically such Commmissions operate by 'taking evidence' (both oral and written) from interested parties and expert witnesses. All the educational reports considered in this chapter include lists of individuals and organizations who have 'given evidence' in this way. However since the Second World War they have increasingly drawn on social research evidence, which Bulmer (1980) suggests reflects increasing dissatisfaction with relying upon these classic methods and a belief that research is a useful means through which commissions can properly pursue their task of impartial collection of the facts. However, the increasingly close links between research and government which I documented in the previous section make it unsurprising that committees and commissions in the last two or three decades have made extensive use of social research. Nor is it surprising to find that the type of research which they have used has leaned heavily towards the quantitative. Bulmer provides a helpful categorization of the different ways in which research has been used by commissions, and it is clear that much of it has been seen as basic intelligence-gathering of a statistical nature, with a view to the descriptive documentation of the area under study. Less frequently, it has been used to develop causal analysis or as general illumination of the issues at an analytical level; and hardly ever, to test theoretical models (pp. 5–6). Therefore the context in which these commissions and committees operate define impartiality and fact-gathering as central to their task — a definition which strongly favours quantitative research. Further, research evidence is only *one* kind of evidence which they properly should take into account and therefore it is unlikely that one will find a very direct relationship between research findings and policy recommendations made by the committees.

Second, the composition of such committees clearly reflects — and is intended to reflect — a range of established interests in the field of education: typically administrators, headteachers and principals of colleges, academic experts and one or two parents, with women being under-represented (Kogan and Packwood, 1974, pp. 28–33). Thus, although their task is seen overtly as the impartial collection of the facts and formulating policy recommendations based upon them, they are set up in such a way as to ensure that their recommendations will reflect conflicts and compromises between powerful educational and political interests, rather than simply the informed conclusions of dispassionate advisers.

Third, the reasons for setting up such committees and the use to which their reports are put are many and varied. Seldom are their recommendations totally original, but rather pick up on developments already under way in the education service, and serve to endorse, legitimize and strengthen these. Sometimes they play the role of providing a vision — 'deliberate attempts to evangelize by eulogy', as Kogan and Packwood put it — which presents new thinking or good practice in a way that seeks to inspire teachers, teacher-trainers and administrators (pp. 2–7). All of this suggests a much more fragmented and indirect role for research in these reports than is indicated by the simple, direct model in which investigation is carried out in an area about which little is known, the facts are established, and policies are formulated on the basis of those facts (see chapter 6 for further discussion of this model).

A separate comment needs to be made here about the reports on the EPA action research projects which are included in this analysis of official reports. Although this was not a committee of enquiry like the reports previously discussed, the EPA initiative was a direct consequence of the Plowden Report and represents an important attempt sponsored by central government to develop the policy recommendations contained there, especially to put into effect the principle of positive discrimination by designating Educational Priority Areas. The report of the research projects set up alongside them was published under the authorship of the Department of Education and Science, and the main volume is frequently referred to as 'The Halsey Report' and mentioned in the same sentence as Crowther, Newsom and Plowden (Department of Education and Science, 1972). Reference is made elsewhere is this book to the significance of the EPA projects as an instance of research input to policy, and to the importance of the research director, A H Halsey, not only as researcher but as adviser to Labour politicians and lobbyist with administrators (see especially chapter 6). In this chapter, I simply want to consider the research methods used in the research projects, in the light of the questions posed about other reports discussed in here.

The Research Input to Educational Reports: Quantitative and Qualitative Data

The first question which I shall explore in relation to these official reports on education is: what kind of research did they use; in particular, did they make use of qualitative as well as quantitative data? In this section, I shall consider the reports chronologically as they were produced.

The Crowther Report on education in the 15–18 age group was the first of this series of major reports on aspects of the educational system to make substantial use of social research. Like the others which followed, the Crowther Committee commissioned major pieces of research to assist its deliberations, emphasizing in this case the need to undertake their own research because they found gaps in existing knowledge about what goes on in schools and colleges, especially in relation to girls, and because they wanted information on those young people who had lost touch with the educational system as well as those who had stayed within it (Ministry of Education, 1959, Vol. I, paragraph 5).

All the research commissioned by Crowther was quantitative, and consisted of three surveys, carried out by the government Social Survey Division (see chapter 1). These were: 'the social survey', consisting of a random sample of young men and women who left school in 1954–55, based on interviews with them and their parents; the 'national service survey', based on a random sample of young men entering the army and the RAF as conscripts in 1956–58, based upon interviews and intelligence tests; and the 'technical courses survey' which was in two parts, first a 5 per cent random sample of men enrolled for any National Certificate course in the autumn of 1956, based on postal questionnaires, and second, information on the same percentage of men enrolled for City and Guilds courses in 1957, based on information from college records. This of course again gave them far more information about boys than girls, a problem which the Committee clearly recognized as partly consequent upon girls' very low participation in technical courses (Vol. I, paragraph 5).

The pattern which Crowther adopted was followed with variations by several subsequent committees: large-scale sample surveys, commissioned within government, using a mixture of methods consisting of postal questionnaires, interviews and information from the records of educational institutions. This methodology is entirely consistent with the emphasis upon collecting 'the facts' which Bulmer identifies as a feature of such committees' approach to their task, and which is repeated in the other reports considered here.

The Newsom Report on the education of 13 to 16 year olds of 'average or below average ability' (Ministry of Education, 1963) was unusual among the reports considered here insofar as its research data was not wholly based on statistical and survey methods, and did include data which in some senses can be classified as 'qualitative'.

Most of the research which the Committee commissioned was in fact quantitative, consisting of surveys conducted in a one in twenty-four sample of secondary modern and comprehensive schools stratified by size, sex and religion. An additional twenty schools were included on the basis of nomination by HMI, as being especially 'difficult', since one of the Committee's major concerns was education 'in the slums' (see chapter 3 and Appendix V of the Report). The first stage of the research requested written reports from headteachers, and this was followed by four questionnaires completed by headteachers (on the timetables of fourth year pupils; staffing; school premises; examination and non-examination candidates). Data were subsequently collected on individual pupils, by means of questionnaires (completed by teachers, not the pupils) for one-third of boys and girls in the fourth year, and tests of ability administered to all fourth year pupils in the survey schools (see chapter 21 of the Report for details). Some of the data were then linked to the findings of the national service survey which had been undertaken for the Crowther Committee.

Much of the data used by the Committee were therefore in the familiar quantitative form, but the Report contains two examples of data in a rather different form. The first of these is comments made by headteachers in their reports, which formed the first stage of the 'survey'. At this stage, heads were not sent a structured questionnaire but 'were asked to write freely about their problems, the backgrounds of their pupils, their school and their staff; about their methods, their difficulties and their successes' (paragraph 552). The data collected from headteachers were therefore qualitative documentary data. The Report makes use of verbatim quotations from these documents especially in the chapters on 'Education in the slums' and 'The school community', and in many cases these provide very vivid descriptions of both the schools and the localities which they served. They convey a sense of the social situation in which the schools operate and a sense of social interaction and social processes which cross-sectional survey data cannot provide. There are, however, problems about the way these data were used in the Report, as I shall indicate later.

The second use of 'qualitative' data in the Newsom Report is of a rather different order. These are the well-known case-studies of imaginary characters — the Browns, the Joneses and the Robinsons, constructed from the survey data (chapter 22). I have put quotation marks round 'qualitative' data in this instance, since the source is survey data and test material, but the *use* to which these data are put injects an additional element, presenting aggregate data on three 'types' of pupil (with the basic divisions based on the test scores) but portraying each category as rounded individuals. Thus aggregate data on children who fall into the 'most able' quarter of the secondary modern pupils who were studied are presented in the classic political arithmetic mode, calculating the likelihood that they will come from certain areas, that their fathers will have a given type of occupation, and so on; and then these data are expressed by describing the imaginary characters of John and Mary Brown; and so on. This classification of children into 'types' is of course wholly consistent with the tripartite system established at the end of the Second World War and the Hadow, Spens and Norwood Reports which foreshadowed it; and before that the studies of Charles Booth (see chapter 1). In the Newsom Report, each of the 'characters' constructed from survey data is compared with a description of the 'real' people who fall into these categories, but those descriptions seem very flat and sketchy by comparison with the imaginary characters. The Committee was clearly reaching after qualitative data to complement its quantitative studies but not quite finding it. As I shall argue later, 'real' qualitative data would actually have been more appropriate to the task they set themselves.

Next, the Robbins Report (Committee on Higher Education, 1963) is very different from the two previously considered both in its use of research, which was more extensive, and in its relationship to policy. Whereas both the Crowther and Newsom Reports made proposals which were accepted only in part and then sometimes half-heartedly, Robbins had been established on the assumption that higher education would need to expand substantially. Its proposals were accepted speedily, and implemented in substantial measure (Layard and King, 1973).

The Robbins Committee commissioned a substantial programme of research, but again it was of a wholly quantitative nature. They commissioned what they called 'six major surveys' (four of students in various sectors of higher and further education; one of university teachers, and one a survey of 21-year olds in the general population). They also initiated several smaller studies (see Committee on Higher Education, 1963, pp. 298–301 for an outline of the research studies). The distinguished social statistician Professor C A Moser acted as adviser to the Committee, and all the work which they commissioned used essentially quantitative methods, principally survey methods. The six major surveys were conducted by a mixture of interviews, postal questionnaires and questionnaires administered by the institution, the four student studies being conducted by the government's Social Survey Division. The other studies also used sample surveys, plus quantitative information taken from the records of institutions and the reanalysis of existing statistical data. In the Robbins data as published, there are no discernable qualitative elements of any kind.

Like most of the other reports considered here, the Plowden

Report on primary education (Department of Education and Science, 1967) commissioned substantial research projects, but of a wholly quantitative nature. The main part of this was conducted by the government's Social Survey Division, but research was also commissioned from academics (for example, a survey of schools in Manchester by Stephen Wiseman), and from the National Children's Bureau, who were asked for a report based upon their 1958 cohort study (details reported in Vol. II of the Plowden Report).

The Plowden research requirements built explicitly on the previous Reports which had provided 'powerful evidence linking home circumstances and pupils' educational progress'. Plowden wished to both build upon and move beyond these studies, by substituting the crude measure of father's occupation as a way of categorizing home background, and to distinguish between material circumstances and parental attitudes, treating 'attitudes' as a separate variable (Vol. II, p. 91). A central finding of the research, as presented in the Report, was that 'circumstances' and 'attitudes' appear to operate relatively independent of each other in terms of their effect on children's educational progress. This was the finding upon which the Committee apparently based its optimistic conclusion that there is some possibility of changing parental attitudes towards their children's education, and subsequently its major recommendation that a variety of measures should be adopted to ensure that parents become more actively involved with schools and with their children's education (Vol. I, p. 36).

Quite apart from the issue of using solely quantitative research, the Plowden findings can be questioned purely on their own terms. Acland (1980) on the basis of his own reanalysis of the Plowden data, has been able to show that the support in the research findings for both the policy of parental involvement and for the establishment of Educational Priority Areas (another major recommendation — see below) was at best tenuous. He shows, for example, that some of the items categorized as 'attitudes' could — on different assumptions — be classified as material circumstances; for example, responses to a question about whether parents take children on outings was used to generate an 'attitude' variable, but one equally could argue that this is mainly a matter of affluence (Acland, 1980, p. 45). Examples such as this fundamentally undermine the claim that the Plowden data show that 'attitudes' are more important than 'circumstances'. Further, Acland argues that there was a fundamental problem in interpreting causal connections in the way which Plowden did. The writers of the Report reasoned that, because there was a strong association between measured parental 'attitudes' and children's educational performance, the former caused the latter. But one might equally argue that it works the other way round, namely that parents' attitudes change when their children do better at school; or of course that both phenomena might be attributable to a third factor (p. 51). These are classic problems in the interpretation of survey data, but the Plowden Committee seemed to be unaware of them. In fact, Acland argues that Plowden's use of research was not ever a matter of a rationally based model where research findings lead to policy recommendations, but a case of 'stage management', that is, of research being used to both communicate and support certain recommendations which actually were reached on quite other grounds.

The research commissioned by the Warnock Committee on special education was again entirely quantitative, following the pattern of earlier committees of enquiry (Department of Education and Science, 1978a, see especially Appendices 5–8). They commissioned five surveys, two of which were undertaken by the DES: a survey of teachers' and headteachers' opinions about special education, based on a postal questionnaire, and also a survey of the cost per place in special education in nine local education authorities. The other three studies were commissioned outside government and were: a survey of parents with handicapped children under five; a study of provision for handicapped children in pre-school services; and a study of the employment experiences of handicapped school leavers, commissioned from the National Children's Bureau, and based on their cohort data. The Committee also commissioned a review of existing research on special education.

In accordance with what by now is the familiar pattern, the Warnock Report made specific use only of quantitative data, and opportunities within their commissioned research for using qualitative analysis apparently were not taken. For example, the postal questionnaire to teachers included both fixed-choice and open-ended questions, but the latter were treated quantitatively, with the answers being coded from the questionnaires before use (Appendix 8, p. 393). One might question whether a more qualitative analysis of these answers might not have been more illuminating, especially since claims to representativeness of this study were substantially reduced by a poor response rate of 56 per cent — a common problem of course with postal questionnaires. Further, the cohort study data on handicapped school leavers, whilst based on a large-scale random sample and structured questionnaires, clearly yielded more detailed and rich data than is apparent from the Warnock Report itself. Alan

Walker, who directed this study, has written it up separately (Walker, 1981), and it is clear from this publication that the interviews were both lengthy — up to three hours in some cases (p. 23) — and carefully recorded. In consequence, Walker is able to make extensive use of case study material to complement statistical analysis, which highlights the very limited use of the commissioned data in the Warnock Report itself.

The Rampton Committee was set up in 1979 to investigate the education of children from ethnic minority groups. Its final Report was produced in 1985 under the chairmanship of Lord Swann (see below), but an interim report on the West Indian community specifically was requested because of the high level of political concern about this group, and this Report was published in 1981 (Committee of Inquiry into the Education of Children from Ethnic Minority Groups, 1981).

The research input to this Committee again followed the familiar pattern. A review of existing research — not available for the interim report — was commissioned from the National Foundation for Educational Research, and some statistical work was also commissioned. Most importantly, the DES Statistics Branch was asked to include additional questions in its school leavers' survey for 1978/79. This statistical information was important, insofar as it enabled the Committee to document the extent to which children of West Indian origin do leave school with more limited achievements in terms of formal qualifications than do other school leavers, including Asians. This amounts to documenting the dimensions of the problem in the familiar style of political arithmetic (this time with an ethnic dimension), with all the strengths and weaknesses of that approach (see chapter 1).

The main report of the Swann Committee (Report of the Committee of Inquiry into the Education of Children from Ethnic Minority Groups, 1985), took a rather different approach to research, partly of necessity. The Report contains a very interesting 'Note on Research' written by James Carnford, the Director of the Nuffield Foundation, who was a member of the Committee (Annex G, pp. 171–82). Carnford describes the attempts made by the Committee to set up a research project which would respond to the criticisms made of its interim Rampton Report. This new project was to focus upon educational success rather than failure, and would try to isolate the factors which are associated with success for black pupils. In the event, this research had to be abandoned because of strong criticisms of its approach; most importantly, that the research design focussed too much on home and social background of pupils, and too little upon schools and the educational experiences which they offer to black pupils (pp. 171–2). Instead of commissioning major research of its own, therefore, the Committee relied upon commissioning reviews of published research, and upon using the findings of other research projects which were already underway. They also commissioned two retired local authority inspectors to make a series of visits to all-white schools, to assess the development of multi-ethnic curricula in these settings (Annex C and D, pp. 244–314) — and use inspectors as quasi-researchers which is interesting in the light of the discussion of HMI 'research' reports which follows later in this chapter. The many annexes and appendices included in the Report contain material from all these sources.

Carnford's Research Note for the Swann Committee is also interesting in relation to the relative merits of quantitative and qualitative research. Whilst the discussion is not couched in those terms specifically, Carnford acknowledges that their own abandoned research project could be legitimately criticized for using inappropriate methodology. He accepts that its proposed methodology (which was, of course, the orthodox approach to research adopted by previous committees and was essentially quantified documentation of the characteristics of a given school population) would have thrown very little light on the difficulties which black children encounter in school, or upon questions of how classroom practice and school organization contribute to their success of failure. He assents to the view that a more fruitful strategy would involve 'research of a more qualitative, interactive nature' (p. 177). This represents a clear acknowledgement of the limitations of the approach to research adopted by all the committees of enquiry since 1959, and offers some hope that in future any such committees might see qualitative research as a serious possibility. Any optimism of this kind, however, needs to be tempered by the fact that Carnford's view may not be widely shared in government. Indeed, Lord Swann's personal summary of the Report takes a much more limited view of research and refers to it in very orthodox terms (Swann, 1985, pp. 3–5).

Finally, in this section, I shall consider the research methods used in the EPA action-research projects (Department of Education and Science, 1972). The EPA research is the best known and the most ambitious example of 'action-research' in British social policy at national level. That is, the research was set up as the projects themselves were set up, and its role was conceived not simply as a passive monitoring exercise, but much more actively. Research was to feed into the planning of the projects at every stage, and social science knowledge was therefore to be used directly to plan social interventions. This of course is a very different role for research than that accorded to it in the reports so far discussed, where research is essentially seen as providing factual information, upon which committees can then formulate policy recommendations. In his discussion of how the action-research model was actually applied in the EPA projects, Halsey argues that, of the possible variations of that model, there was a strong element of what he calls the 'research approach'. That is, the agenda of the researchers significantly determined the shape of the action, in such a way as to enable the research not merely to describe 'what works' but also to contribute to the development of social science knowledge (p. 166). In fact, Halsey suggests that the researchers played an even more significant role in developing the agenda for action than had originally been envisaged, and this facilitated the development of studies which could be conducted with reference to rigorous research criteria (p. 172).

The relationship between research and policy intervention was therefore highly innovative in these projects. However, when one actually looks at the research which was done, in terms of its methods it bears remarkable similarity to the kind of work done for earlier committees of enquiry. In other words, it was heavily quantitative, concentrating upon mapping the dimensions of the problem under study, in the classic political arithmetic style — hardly surprising, since Halsey was already a leading and distinguished contributor to this style of social research (see chapter 1). As with earlier reports, material from school records was analyzed, and a series of national surveys based on questionnaires was conducted: a survey of EPA teachers; of parents of children in the project schools, and a survey of attainment among EPA pupils. Halsey in fact calls these 'descriptive surveys' (Department of Education and Science, 1974, p. xii).

Alongside these standard research tools, the other major research initiative was based upon an experimental design, and concerned the introduction of the Peabody Language Development Kit into nursery classes and playgroups, accompanied by tests of the children's language development both before and after the period of use (Department of Education and Science, 1972, chapter 7). The use of this research strategy of course reflected the 'action' element of the research, since it entailed both the introduction and monitoring of a specific social intervention. Nonetheless, the way in which this was done again was based upon quantitative methods, using standardized tests, control groups, and with the findings subjected to statistical analysis.

Within the overall framework of the coordinated national study, involving four localities in England and one in Scotland, there was clearly space for the staff of each project to develop separate initiatives. In the West Riding project in particular, there was a recognition of the limitations of surveys and 'the traditional form of educational research' with clear and bounded objectives, predicted changes, measured outcomes and control groups. Where action itself is exploratory, the team argued, 'a different form of evaluation is needed', and the form which they developed relied heavily upon what they called 'participant evaluation', that is, as full as possible a documentation of the action as it develops, principally by the participants, with some attempt to link this with social science knowledge (Department of Education and Science, 1975b, pp. 68–9; see also, Poulton and James, 1975). This shift in the direction of qualitative methods and away from positivist epistemology certainly made an impact upon the research produced by this team; for example, their official report makes substantial use of direct quotations as data. Appendix 3 of their Report consists of the full text of the diary kept by one of their home visitors, as she visited a particular household on a number of occasions, to administer tests to a pre-school child, and to work with the mother. It is clear from this transcript that these diaries, whilst perhaps being rather sparse by the standards of qualitative fieldwork, nonetheless did provide a potentially rich source of data, especially on parent-child interactions. This richness, however, does not really come through in the written report, where there is a clear sense that the team's quantitative work was more highly valued and perhaps that they felt defensive about the rest — as they indicate, they were aware that some people would not recognize their participants' evaluations as 'research' (p. 69).

Whilst there was some space for the development of qualitative research in these projects, therefore, it was accorded a very minor place. Meanwhile, the dominant mode remained as it always had been, fixed within a model of research which is essentially a sophisticated version of providing objective facts that can be generalized. This approach to research in fact significantly shaped the 'action' component also because, as Halsey acknowledges, the agenda of the researchers required that the action should be structured in such a way as to produce outcomes which could be measured, hence the emphasis upon educational attainment as the major focus, and the choice of the pre-school level as the major point of intervention which (quite apart from other considerations) meant that the researchers were in more of a position to control other factors than they would have been in formal schooling (Department of Education and Science, 1972, pp. 173–4). In relation to their major research strategies, the projects stayed with this model of research, despite a recognition that its goal of providing objective and uncontaminated facts was effectively unattainable in this kind of research.

All the major reports on education considered here have therefore concentrated heavily — often exclusively — on social research of a type which derives directly from the dominant tradition discussed in chapter 1; research which is quantitative in technique and positivist in orientation. Given that this *is* the dominant tradition it would be surprising if it were otherwise, especially at a time when social scientists in England were not themselves producing qualitative work which might have provided an alternative model. This was certainly true in the 1950s, although less so from the late 1960s onwards (see chapter 1). The important point is not so much that qualitative research was absent from these reports; rather that this absence left the committees without access to research appropriate to some of the tasks which they set themselves. This is the issue which I consider in the next section.

The Research Input to Educational Reports: Appropriateness to the Task

The dominant tradition of policy-oriented social research accords little place to qualitative approaches, and therefore the potential for them to complement or to replace quantitative studies is left unexplored. In this section, I shall argue that the educational reports under consideration provide examples which support the view that this is detrimental to informed policy-making and public debate. I shall suggest that these reports provide clear instances where the strengths of qualitative research could have been used to good effect, were it not for the overconcentration on statistics and surveys in the dominant tradition which left qualitative techniques grossly underdeveloped in social policy research. I shall offer three illustrative examples.

First, a dominant concern of all the Reports is with the outcomes of the educational system. Outcomes can to an extent be documented satisfactorily by quantitative methods, but the committees clearly wanted to move beyond simple documentation, towards explanations of how and why such outcomes occur. In developing such explanations, they were inevitably considering the processes through which educational outcomes are accomplished, and at this point their statistical and survey data are of only limited usefulness.

An example taken from the Crowther Report serves to illustrate this point. Among other things, the Committee wanted to consider the question: why do young people leave school at the minimum age? The surveys which they commissioned were able to tell them in some detail *who* leaves school at the minimum age, but the only data which they provided on *why* people leave came from questions asked of both young people and their parents about 'reasons' for leaving school. Their national survey, for example, provides a quantitative analysis of the 'main reason' given for leaving school at 15, and items which score highest are: saw no point in staying at school any longer; particular job was available; money short at home; fed up with school (Vol. II, Table 15). Several of these 'reasons' beg far more questions than they answer and in general, data of this kind cannot give a sense of how decisions are arrived at (or indeed whether the concept of 'decision' is even appropriate) because the individual is necessarily decontextualized, and social action divided into discrete items of behaviour (in this case 'reasons'). Similarly, in the Committee's social survey, there are questions designed to elicit the significance of parents in such decisions, but this is expressed as 'attitudes of parents' condensed to a four-fold classification: child did stay on at school; did not stay on but parents would have been willing; parents would not have been willing; parents doubtful (Vol. II, Table 8). To simply divide parents essentially into willing/not willing and to express this as a fixed 'attitude' — especially when questions are asked retrospectively about what would have been done in a hypothetical situation — comes nowhere near the kind of data needed to understand the dynamics of parent-child relationships in this matter, and how the final outcome is the product of interactions over time. Similarly, the Plowden Report's concern with the parent-child relationship, and how parents assist or hinder their children's learning (see previous section) raises the same kind of issues. In both cases, qualitative data is implied which can both capture the subtleties of parent-child interactions and examine how they relate to educational outcomes over time. The study of social processes of this kind is never easy, but qualitative methods have real potential here, as I shall argue in chapter 7.

Second, the reports in practice are all concerned not merely with the educational context of the home but also with the experiences provided in schools and colleges. The interaction between pupils and teachers is obviously a central feature of this, but it is an issue which survey data cannot satisfactorily address. When dealing with matters of this kind therefore, the reports tend to fall back on highly impressionistic data. The Rampton Report offers a useful illustration here. Their survey data enabled them to document the relatively poor educational performance of West Indian children, but essentially did not help them to explain how this occurs. The explanation which they offered was that one factor is that racism (much of it 'unintentional') is apparent in the educational system, and that this could account at least in part for the poor performance of West Indian children. But the nature of the evidence which they could cite for that important but very contentious conclusion is at best impressionistic; for example, 'there seemed to be a fairly widespread opinion among teachers to whom we spoke that West Indian pupils inevitably caused difficulties' (paragraph 6). The Committee — in the classic model of commissions of enquiry — had 'taken evidence' from a range of interested parties, in the sense of 'evidence' in a court of law. But what their approach does not enable them to do is to base their conclusions on 'evidence' in the sense which social scientists understand that term. To create that kind of evidence about teachers' racism and its effect upon West Indian pupils, one would of course need detailed studies of how teachers conceptualize different categories of pupils, and how those categorizations affect the way they act towards them. Again, detailed qualitative studies would be by far the most satisfactory way of exploring that systematically.

My third example is of a somewhat different order. I want to suggest that not simply did the overconcentration on statistics and surveys leave these reports without access to relevant qualitative data, but also that when qualitative data *were* available they were handled badly. The use of headteachers' unstructured reports by the Newsom Committee provides my illustration here. As I have already indicated, the Report does quote from these. However, the Committee's use of these documents was — so far as one can tell from the Report — in no sense systematic. Quotations from heads are strung together with no information about the basis upon which they have been selected so that, for example, one usually has no idea whether a particular quote has been selected because it is representative of others, or because it reflects a unique experience. Further, there is no apparent consciousness of the methodological issues entailed in interpreting documentary data of this kind (Platt, 1981b; Burgess, 1984b, pp. 123–42) rather, by implication, they are presented as straightforwardly 'true accounts' of the schools and children about whom the heads are writing. This means that, not only is the use of these data methodologically naive, but opportunities are missed which might have been taken if the headteachers' personal reports had been treated *as data* but data of a different kind to survey data, requiring different but equally systematic treatment.

The points made here can be illustrated by comparing two quotations which are used in the Report. The first comes from the Head of a Roman Catholic school in what is described as a Lancashire dockside parish, and concerns the community which the school serves:

> The people are decent and good-living; there are strikingly few broken homes and illegitimate children.... The parents are foolishly generous and quite inconsistent in their treatment of the children who are adept in evading consequences. The bad language shrieked from the top balcony of the tenements sounds appalling but appears to be rather a maternal safety-valve than a heart-felt threat. Indeed, the children are very much loved and secure in their family affection. (Paragraph 56)

This sympathetic, rather warm account of the local community and the homes from which the children come contrasts sharply with that of another Lancashire Head presented at the same point in the Report:

> there are many broken homes. Twenty-two per cent have no father, five per cent no mother; these figures may be higher in reality. At home corporal punishment (belting, a crack, a good hiding) is a common punishment. Some of it is severe and I have known a boy run away and sleep out for several nights for fear of the beating which he expected. (*ibid*)

These two very different comments are just presented without analysis or even comment about the discrepancies between them. If treated as qualitative data, one would then want to ask a range of questions which might well illuminate the dynamics of schooling and home-school relations in inner-city areas: for example, do the differences in the two heads' discussion of 'broken homes' reflect 'real' differences in the two areas, or differences in their interpretation of rather similar situations? The generally more hostile tone of the second account suggests that it may be the latter, and indeed that the two heads may be operating on different definitions of what constitutes a 'broken' home. Further, are there any consistent patterns in accounts which different heads gave in the apparent hostility or warmth to the children and parents with whom they work? Since the Committee also had extensive quantitative data on the schools, there are many possibilities here for comparing this with the qualitative accounts. However, the Report does not treat the headteachers' comments in this way, but rather uses them unproblematically as illustrative evidence.

For all these reasons, therefore, I would argue that the excessive concentration on statistics and surveys in the research input to these reports did mean that the committees were using research strategies which were in certain respects inappropriate to their task, and where qualitative methods (properly used) would have substantially strengthened the data available to them.

'Research' Reports from Her Majesty's Inspectorate

As is well known, since the middle of the nineteenth century, Her Majesty's Inspectors have been writing reports on schools based upon their inspectorial visits, and these reports themselves form important sources of documentary data, available for analysis by historians and others. It is beyond the scope of my purpose here to consider inspectors' reports as such and their relationship to policy. However during the past decade, HMI have increasingly produced reports on British education (as they did to an extent in the early part of this century) which move beyond the traditional model of a report on a single school, and have attempted to assess current practice in education, with a view to making recommendations, in ways which are much closer to a social research project. These reports are included here because they represent a different but important way in which there has been an attempt to feed social research into educational policy-making through the medium of official reports. Three illustrative examples of more recent reports will be considered here, asking the same questions as were applied to the previous reports, about the type of data which they use, the way in which it is used, and its appropriateness to the task.

The first report which I shall consider is *Primary Education in England* (Department of Education and Science, 1978). Published a decade after the Plowden Report and subtitled 'A survey by H M Inspectors of Schools', the design of the research is clearly based upon a survey methodology. Specific schools, and then specific classes within those schools, were selected by a stratified random sample and three different types of data were created about them: the 'main survey' entailed questionnaires completed by teachers and headteachers about the classes selected for study; 'objective tests' of performance in reading were administered to the children in those classes by researchers from the National Foundation for Educational Research; and finally, observational reports on those classes were compiled by HMI who visited them for the purpose (p. 2).

The particular interest from the point of view of my discussion is the third element — inspectors' written observations, being used here as part of a larger research project and in combination with survey data. In the report, no sharp distinction is made in the presentation of these different types of data, and indeed, some of the findings which must have come from the observational element are themselves presented in quantified and tabular form. All the data are, in other words, treated as 'facts' about the schools studied, and it is worth therefore looking at how the observational data were generated.

The inspectors' visits to the schools were undertaken by two HMI who spent $1\frac{1}{2}$–3 days in each school. Inspectors were matched to schools outside their normal districts where possible, but where their expertise was appropriate, and there was some circulation in the team of inspectors taking part in the survey. The purpose of these arrangements was to minimize 'the results of any individual bias' (Appendix C, p. 137) — a classic consideration in survey research, stemming from the presumption that researchers must be totally objective. The type of observation used by the team was neither the kind of systematic observation commonly used for example by psychologists, nor the ethnographic techniques used by qualitative researchers, but something in between those two (see chapter 1 for a discussion of these contrasting types of observation). Observations were written up according to an agreed schedule of items (given in the Report as Annex B), but there appear to have been no specific instructions about *how* to observe in order to arrive at comments under each heading. Indeed, there is a clear expectation that the normal procedures of HMI inspections would be followed, that is, that inspectors would make qualitative judgments of what they saw based upon their professional expertise, as they do in the normal course of their work.

This 'survey' therefore mixes qualitative and quantitative elements in a rather curious and distinctive way. On the one hand, there is overt concern with issues of objectivity and bias, and the overall context is a stratified random sample survey. On the other hand,

HMI are acting *as researchers*, but as researchers who are making qualitative judgments based upon professional opinions. However, those data are quantified in the same way as the survey data, and their character as qualitative judgments (and indeed qualitative data) is not thereby taken into account. This curious mixture can be seen by examining the schedules which HMI used and comparing them with the data presented. For example, one item which proved important in the final report concerned an alleged mis-match between work which children were doing, and that which they were capable of doing. The former of course could be simply recorded as an observation; the latter, however, depended upon the Inspector making a judgment in the classroom about what work he or she considered specific children were capable of doing — to an outsider, a formidable task on the basis of a couple of days in a classroom. The schedule used asked the 'match' to be recorded in a five-fold classification: considerable overexpectation; slight overexpectation; good match; slight underexpectation; considerable underexpectation. The inspectors were therefore working solely upon their qualitative *judgments* of children in the classroom but, unlike qualitative *research*, evidence for the judgments made is not presented in the Report. Instead, data based on these judgments are presented in quantified form (Tables 30–32, pp. 86–7), and used to support the important conclusion that, with the exception of PE 'there was a widespread tendency to underestimate the capacities of all groups of children, particularly the most able' (paragraph 6.21). Whatever one thinks about the validity of HMI procedures as the basis for inspection, as research one must have serious doubts about them.

The second HMI report which I shall consider is *The Education Welfare Service in Eight LEAs* (Department of Education and Science, 1984). This represents an exercise on a much more modest scale than the substantial research and large-scale inspections which produced the report on primary education. It is based on HMI visits to eight local education authorities, four in 1980 and four in 1982. As these visits are described in the Report, it is clear that the methods employed to collect data were mainly observational, with some data arising out of conversations, although there is no indication that either of these were conducted in a systematic way, as was the case in the primary education report. Indeed, the Report is hazy on a number of basic matters, including the number of education welfare officers who were involved. HMI apparently 'met more than 120 EWOs' and 'worked with' forty-six of them 'for at least half a day and in all but a few cases a day or more'; visited 107 primary, secondary and special schools; and attended case conferences in clinics and schools. On their school visits they 'met' headteachers, teachers and school secretaries — the latter getting a rare mention in this Report, which in itself indicates something about how the Education Welfare Service operates (paragraph 4).

What this study is based upon therefore is HMI operating within their normal model of professional inspections, but in a coordinated way within a limited number of LEAs, which then enables them to produce a report which reflects a 'snapshot' of the service. The authors of the Report are careful to underline the limited nature of this exercise and make the point that they cannot claim that it is in any sense representative, especially since they allowed LEA officers to select the EWOs whom they would meet (paragraph 11). There is not, therefore, an attempt to claim this as a piece of 'research' in the sense that this is claimed for the report on primary education; and, although the same criticisms of the methods used to generate data can be made in this instance, it could be argued that these are appropriate to an exercise which was essentially a professional inspection and not a piece of research.

There are, however, two reasons for considering this kind of HMI report in the context of a discussion of research methods. First, there is a certain confusion contained within the Report itself about whether it claims to be research. The section of the Report which describes what HMI did is entitled 'The Nature of *the Survey*' (paragraphs 4 and 5, my emphasis) and the phrases 'the survey' and 'the inspection' are used more or less interchangeably in the Report. Despite the qualifications about the limited nature of the undertaking, at the very least this is misleading and the unwary reader might very well think that she or he is reading a report based on research. Second, the reader might also be forgiven for reading into the Report a more authoritative analysis than can really be claimed for it from the very clear nature of the policy recommendations at the end. There has been a continuing debate about the proper location for the Education Welfare Service since the early 1970s, when the Ralphs Report recommended its development as a social work service in the education field, and the Seebohm Report recommended full integration with Social Services Departments (see Finch, 1984a, for further discussion). The HMI report comes out very firmly in favour of confirming the position of EWS as part of the education service and under the control of local education authorities (paragraph 63). This is an important intervention in that debate, given the status of HMI, but also because it is a recommendation which is based on empirical study of the operation of the service, in an area of education where there is very little other research which might offer an alternative interpretation.

Thus in the case of this Report — which is more characteristic of HMI's work than the rather special primary and secondary surveys — we see a kind of 'research' put to a purpose which is not really appropriate to the task. On the one hand, the empirical study undertaken is referred to as a 'survey' when the methods employed make it much closer to qualitative than quantitative research. On the other hand, the qualitative methods employed — like those in the primary survey — lack the systemmatic and open characteristics which would justify a claim that they constitute qualitative research. Policy recommendations arise from the study in some way, although the nature of the link between them is not spelled out. One could see a case for properly developed research of either a quantitative or a qualitative nature designed to study the institutional location of the Education Welfare Service, but the HMI report is neither.

Finally, *Ten Good Schools* (Department of Education and Science, 1977) is more modest again in scope and less is claimed for it, with its overt purpose being to provide 'material for discussion' rather than to be an authoritative assessment of current practice (p. 6). Its aim was to 'test whether generalizations can be made about the factors that contribute to success in secondary education' (p. 5), and this is done by focussing on ten schools which HMI considered to be successful, and trying to identify whether they shared common features. This was done on the basis of special inspections by a team of about five inspectors, visiting the school for between two and four days (p. 5).

In some ways, one can see the validity of such an exercise if its aim is to provide material for discussion. However, the way in which the Report is presented rather precludes that since, like other HMI reports, it is based on qualitative judgments, but no data are presented to show how those judgments were formed, nor what criteria were used. Therefore, the material provided for discussion is actually very limited. For example, one well-known 'finding' of this study is that the headteacher was a crucial figure in the success of all ten schools; but we are not told upon what basis HMI came to a judgment about the common characteristics of these heads. This information really is needed to evaluate their claims, which reads like a eulogy:

Without exception, the heads have qualities of imagination and vision tempered with realism. . . . Their sympathetic

understanding of staff and pupils, their accessibility, good
humour and sense of proportion and their dedication to their
task has won the respect of parents, teachers and taught.
(p. 36)

This Report is the furthest removed of those considered in this
chapter from the model of social research, and in a sense it is therefore
perhaps less appropriate to evaluate it in those terms. However, it
provides an illustration of how the boundaries between research and
professional assessment have become very blurred in the work of
HMI, with the consequent danger that reports such as this one will be
treated as having an authority which derives from a status as a
research study which they do not really possess.

Conclusion

In conclusion, I would like to highlight several points which have
emerged from the review of a rather varied range of official reports in
this chapter. First, looked at from this particular angle, the view of
the dominant tradition of policy-oriented social research which I
presented in chapter 1 is confirmed and strengthened. The various
reports about education considered here all see research as a fact-
gathering exercise in the positivist mode where 'facts' can be directly
used in policy-making, and also as the provision of administrative
intelligence in a particular form which relies principally upon statistics and social surveys. The official reports on research itself also
predominantly endorse that view.

Second, as I argued in chapter 1, such an approach leaves very
little space for qualitative work, and its use in these educational
reports is minimal. Indeed, rather less use is made of qualitative
techniques here than was made in some nineteenth-century work,
including Booth's surveys. This has remained the case in the educational reports despite the fact that two official reports on research
itself — Heyworth in 1965 and Rothschild in 1982 — whilst not
directly endorsing qualitative techniques did challenge the underlying
positivist epistemology of the dominant tradition by acknowledging
that 'fact-gathering' is not the same thing as 'research', and by
accepting that very little social science knowledge is produced in a
form which can be directly used by governments. These more
sophisticated perspectives appear to have made no impact on the
educational committees of enquiry, who have continued to use and

present social research in the terms set by the dominant tradition. Where some qualitative work is available, either it is not used (as appears to be the case in the Warnock Report) or it is presented in an apologetic manner, as a poor second-best to quantitative data (as in the EPA Reports).

Third, I have argued that the educational reports provide evidence that supports the argument that the view of social research promoted and perpetuated in the dominant tradition is detrimental to informed policy-making and public debate because it effectively excludes the possibility of qualitative research in particular. As there are certain kinds of issues which can most effectively be studied through qualitative techniques (for example, social processes and social interaction), policy debates about such matters are left uninformed by relevant social research data.

The dominant model of policy-related research is therefore clearly very limiting in relation to the reports discussed here. At the same time, it is also potentially highly misleading, as I argued in relation to the HMI reports, where the dominant model of 'scientific research' has been partly incorporated into HMIs normal activities, giving their recommendations an apparent additional authority which the quality of the evidence does not support.

The limitations of the dominant model identified here lead to the conclusion that there is much underexplored and unexploited potential for qualitative research to be used in policy-oriented studies. In the second half of this book, especially in chapters 7 and 8, I shall discuss how I believe some of that potential can be realized.

3 Social Research and Social Policy: An Alternative British Tradition

The material discussed in previous chapters suggests that in the development of policy-related research in England the dominant models of research were essentially quantitative in technique and positivist in epistemology and at best they accorded qualitative research a secondary place. It is possible, however, to identify an alternative tradition in both the nineteenth and twentieth centuries which, at the level of methods, appears to make much more use of qualitative techniques and at the level of epistemology, is concerned with uncovering and understanding the subjective reality of the people being studied (see Introduction for a discussion of these contrasting types of research). In this chapter, I shall discuss the key examples of research which I am placing in this 'alternative tradition' and clarify their main features. In the following two chapters, I shall consider questions about why these alternative approaches never came to challenge seriously or replace the dominance of the kind of research which I have discussed in chapters 1 and 2.

An Alternative Tradition? Mayhew's Investigations

My first example of an alternative approach to social research dates from the mid-nineteenth century and has its roots in what we would now call investigative journalism. In Marsh's view (1982, pp. 12–13), it represents a parallel to the survey tradition in the nineteenth century and is much closer to qualitative research. The essence of this writing is that the authors travelled about the country, immersed themselves in the conditions of the poor, and produced accounts of what they saw for the consumption of the more privileged. Marsh includes in this tradition the early work of writers like Cobbett in his

Rural Rides (1830), of Mayhew in the mid-nineteenth century, and later of Engels (1892). Investigative journalism is not the same thing as social research, and many journalists writing in the second half of the nineteenth century were producing pure sensationalism, for consumption through the middle-class press which was expanding rapidly in the 1870s and 1880s. These accounts capitalized on the public appetite and used the poor as 'grist for the literary mill' (Yeo, 1973, p. 66; see also Golding and Middleton, 1982, p. 21). It was partly in reaction to such accounts, and in an attempt to judge their veracity in a more systematic way, that Booth began his study (see chapter 1).

Whilst most nineteenth-century investigative journalism could in no way be considered as social research, out of this activity did come some writing which was much closer to serious investigation: the writers mentioned by Marsh, in particular, represent a serious attempt to document and understand the conditions of the poor. In the mid-nineteenth century Mayhew's work was of particular importance. His work also has conventionally been regarded as investigative journalism not social analysis (Dyos, 1967–68) but its re-evaluation by Thompson and Yeo (1973) has established Mayhew's work as social investigation of a serious kind, linked to a concern for social reform (Bulmer, 1982, p. 9; Marsh, 1982, p. 12; Golding and Middleton, 1982, p. 22). It also develops methods based upon journalism perhaps, but reflecting a rigorous and systematic approach to the collection of data, a respect for evidence, and an attempt to place findings within the framework of analytical argument. Mayhew's work is considered in detail here therefore, because it does represent an alternative 'tradition' in the nineteenth century: or at least, an example of a serious attempt to develop qualitative research targeted upon the same kinds of issues of social policy and social reform with which research in the dominant statistical and survey tradition was concerned.

Mayhew's own account of what he set out to do is given in the preface to his first collection of his investigative writings (Mayhew, 1851). His aim was to study the people of London, people of whom the public (the middle-class public, one presumes) 'has less knowledge than the most distant tribes on earth'. He saw himself as a pioneer, describing his work as:

> the first attempt to publish the history of the people from the lips of the people themselves — giving a literal description of their labour, their earnings, their trials, their sufferings, in their own 'unvarnished' language. (p. iii)

We see here some of the features which classically characterize ethnographic work in the social sciences: the use of the actors' own words and the intention to reflect faithfully the subjective reality of the people studied. Mayhew also espoused the classic ethnographic technique of observation: his was the first attempt, he said:

> to portray the condition of their homes and their families by personal observation of the places and direct communication with individuals. (*ibid*)

Of course in one sense it is not strictly true that he was the first to base his writing about the poor on personal observation: that was an important aspect of the work of the early statistical societies, and Kay-Shuttleworth's 1832 pamphlet itself incorporates a substantial amount of observation based upon his work as a doctor among the poor (see chapter 1). However, Mayhew's use of observation went beyond the people whom he happened to meet in the course of his job, and was undertaken specifically in relation to his investigations. There is also a distinctiveness in the way in which he used this material, which should become apparent. As Yeo puts it, Mayhew saw more of Victorian poverty than his contemporaries 'not just because he visited the poor but because he dared to acknowledge what he saw' (Yeo, 1973, p. 61).

Mayhew's investigations were originally published in regular 'letters' to the *Morning Chronicle* in 1849 and 1850, and subsequently in a weekly column in *London Labour*. Recent commentators argue that it is his earliest work which establishes him as a serious social investigator, not just a gifted journalist (Thompson, 1967–68; Yeo, 1973); and that in the *Morning Chronicle* letters in particular, for a brief period he was able to reshape middle-class consciousness of poverty, challenging the dominant political economy which held that the fate of the poor was in their own hands, and identifying poverty as an endemic condition over which the poor themselves had little control. This consciousness, argues Thompson, faded rapidly until poverty was 'rediscovered' by Booth forty years later (Thompson, 1967–68, p. 43).

The methods which Mayhew used in his investigations have to be reconstructed from his writings, since none of his original note-books have survived (Thompson, 1967–68). The core of his method, as has already been indicated, was direct contact with the poor themselves through observation and interview. His main focus was on workers in specific trades, and his writing contains vivid and detailed case-studies of different trades. He became interested very quickly in the relationship between poverty and low wages, and set about documenting the conditions of employment within each trade. In pursuing this, he used a range of methods including appropriate quantification: statements from employers (which he regarded as in need of checking), information from account books where he could get access to them, interviews with representative workers and, where he could, with trade union officials, and also more detailed interviews with working people in their own homes. Where appropriate, he supplemented these with other documentary evidence, such as the records of trade societies, or government statistics. His method entailed a mixture of methods (again characteristic of modern ethnographic work), which were used to provide careful cross-checking. He also called meetings of workers and others out of working hours, and used those meetings to invite people to tell their own stories, and sometimes to administer mass questionnaires (Thompson, 1967–68; Yeo, 1973, pp. 57–63). Mayhew also developed an early version of team research, working with a number of assistants, who were instructed and supervised by him. Yeo suggests that from a reconstruction of their interviews, it is possible to see that they followed more or less a standard interview schedule (p. 64).

Mayhew's work does seem therefore to represent an approach to social investigation which is thoroughly systematic, yet based upon detailed knowledge of cases. Like all qualitative work, it is open to the criticism that it cannot provide any indication of how representative these cases are (Bulmer, 1982a, p. 10). That criticism was made at the time, especially in the controversy between Mayhew and the Ragged Schools Union, when he was accused of bias in selection and misrepresentation of evidence, as well as his findings being generally suspect because of his reliance upon the direct testimony of the poor (Yeo, 1973, p. 62). This hostility is not surprising, since he had produced evidence to show that the schools were failing in their attempts to reform vagrants and cure delinquents of crime. If anything, he argued, they increased crime because a smattering of education made the boys more effective in their criminal activities, and also contact with each other enabled useful information to be shared (Thompson, 1967–68, p. 52). Interestingly, these are precisely the kinds of findings which criminologists have produced well over a century later (Thorpe, Smith, Paley and Green, 1980).

In presenting his work, Mayhew followed the ethnographic principle of giving verbatim accounts. The mechanics of recording the interviews appear to have entailed some editing of material but no paraphrasing, and when they were written up, Mayhew presented 'the informant's own words (in) a continuous monologue which enabled readers to see the world through the eyes of the poor' (Yeo, 1973, p. 64). When one reads these today, they present in a lively and interesting way which is strongly reminiscent of the modern ethnographic interview: allowing the interviewee to guide the conversation with occasional prompts from the interviewer, and a sense of the interview as a social interaction between two people. The following illustrative extract is taken from Mayhew's (1851) account of children as street-sellers, and from the section where he discusses their education and knowledge

> Another boy gave me his notions of men and things. He was a thick-limbed, red-cheeked fellow; answered very freely and sometimes, when I could not help laughing at his replies, laughed loudly himself as he entered into the joke.... He'd heer'd of the Duke of Wellington, he was Old Nosey.... Thought he had heerd speak of Buonoparte; didn't know what he was. Thought he had heer'd of Shakespeare, but didn't know whether he was alive or dead and didn't care.... Had seen the Queen but didn't recollec' her name just at the minute; oh! yes, Victoria and Albert. Had no notion what the Queen had to do. Shouldn't think she had such power as the Lord Mayor or Mr Norton as was the Lambeth beak, and perhaps is still. (p. 474)

The sense that Mayhew was an excellent fieldworker and — in marked contrast with many others who wrote about the poor in the nineteenth century — that he actually liked the people whom he interviewed, comes through strongly in this extract. This impression is also confirmed by accounts of the meetings he held which — as Yeo puts it — were not experienced as embarrassing or intrusive; rather, Mayhew's approach made it possible for people to share their experience with him and with others, and to give very frank accounts of their lives (Yeo, 1973, p. 63). Thompson (1967–68) also writes of his impressive capacity as a fieldworker, describing him in terms which might well be considered as a description of the qualities necessary to any good ethnographer:

> (he had) qualities of responsiveness, independence of judgement, and an unerring ear for significant anecdote. (p. 56)

As well as his investigative methods, the claim that Mayhew's work represents an alternative approach to policy-related research rests upon the perspectives employed in his work and his interpretation of his findings. There is a sense in which his work was indeed a direct challenge to the dominant statistical tradition, which rested upon orthodox political economy (see chapter 5). In reflecting the perspective of the poor Mayhew was, as it were, looking at orthodox political economy from the underside, and his methods enabled him to pose a direct challenge to the pure statistical work which supported the orthodox position:

> His method is ... anti-statistical and constructively so: by counterposing statistical generalities with actual life histories and individual witness he is both offering a running commentary — and criticism — of generalities, and offering a different frame-work within which they may be read. (*ibid*, p. 58)

Yeo makes a similar point in a rather different way: Mayhew, she argues, was able to capture the meaning of the social change taking place around him, and especially the changing relationships between capitalist and labourer (Yeo, 1973, p. 95).

Mayhew built his interpretations upon a comparison of his case studies, each of which was carefully constructed with a range of data. By focussing initially upon the conditions of employment, he was able to show that the availability of work and its organization structured the lives of the poor so that — rather than the Victorian orthodoxy that poverty is caused by bad morals and imprudent habits — irregular work and fluctuating wages made it impossible for the poor to organize their lives in a prudent, thrifty and regular way. His methods also made it possible for him to see economic change as it is experienced in a social context — as Yeo puts it, 'refracted though a cultural lens' (p. 84). This led him to identify sub-cultures among the poor, and the effect of these sub-cultures upon, for example, political attitudes. He was able, in fact:

> to see poverty in the round, as the product of an economic system, with devastating moral and social consequences yet varied cultural manifestations. (p. 88)

Even his enthusiastic defenders such as Yeo acknowledge that Mayhew fell far short of developing an alternative political economy, and that his skills were weaker in conceptualization than they were in investigation. He can also be criticized for his slipshod presentation of statistics at times, due largely to journalistic pressures to produce weekly copy (Thompson, 1967–68). Nonetheless, his capacity to see poverty 'in the round' was unrivalled at least until Booth's study, and Mayhew's view had the distinctive feature of being written from the 'underdog' perspective, as Becker called it very much later (see chapter 9). Unlike Booth, who for all the merits of his study still looked at the poor through middle class eyes to a great extent (see chapter 1), Mayhew was able to make 'imaginative leaps into the minds and hearts of the poor' (p. 95). He was concerned with the same issues of poverty as were the statistical and survey investigators and he looked to social reform to address those issues. But unlike them, he did not expect reforms to be aimed at changing the poor themselves or at least controlling them, but at changing the conditions under which they lived. As he states in the preface to his collection on London labour and the London poor:

> My earnest hope is that the book may serve to give the rich a more intimate knowledge of the sufferings, and frequent heroism under those sufferings, of the poor ... and cause those who are in 'high places' to bestir themselves to improve the condition of a class of people whose misery, ignorance, and vice, amidst all the immense wealth of 'the first city in the world' is, to say to very least, a national disgrace to us. (Mayhew, 1851, p. iv)

Mayhew's work, therefore represents in more than one sense an 'alternative' tradition in policy-related research. Its methods and orientation are different from the dominant statistical tradition and — unlike that work — it did not look at the poor from the perspective of government or administrators (see chapter 1 and chapter 5). It was perhaps inevitable therefore that it would not be taken up as the dominant mode of social policy research, since it essentially challenged the status quo as much qualitative work necessarily does — an issue which will be taken up in chapter 9.

The Alternative Tradition in the Early Part of the Twentieth Century

The approach to social research developed by Mayhew did not in any real sense form part of a continuing 'tradition', although there are other important examples in the nineteenth century of writers who were serious students of the conditions of the poor (as opposed to investigative journalists), who made use of direct questioning and observation and who reflected the subjective reality of the working classes, the most notable example being Engels' (1982) study of the condition of the working classes in England. An accessible introduction to some of this work is provided by Keating (1976). Marsh

(1982) considers that this alternative tradition survived into the twentieth century, and cites the work of Lady Bell, published in 1907 as an example (p. 13). This is indeed notable for its particular concern with the conditions of working-class women, a concern which was continued by the publication of reports based upon self-documented accounts by the Fabian women's group, and by Margery Spring-Rice (Pember Reeves, 1913; Spring-Rice, 1939).

Alongside these works, there was another movement in which many more people were involved, namely the community self-survey movement. In the United States, this took on something of the proportions of a mass movement and drew in — as Marsh puts it — large numbers of Christians, reformers and sociologists. Marsh cites an article published by E W Burgess in 1916 as offering a programmatic statement for the movement, and she paradies this in the following terms:

> The 'sociologist' is the football coach for a vast army of do-gooders who will survey conditions and then propose remedies. (Marsh, 1982, p. 153)

This description makes it clear that there were some continuities between the community self-survey movement and the ameliorist tradition in nineteenth-century Britain (see chapter 1), in that both drew in quite large numbers of people and both saw the use of surveys as a direct route to social reform rather than as an end in themselves. There are also significant differences.

In Britain, the intellectual origins can be seen as lying in the work of Patrick Geddes, and institutionalized to an extent through the Institute of Sociology (Wells, 1935, p. 15; Marsh, 1982, pp. 31–4). Geddes specifically rejected the use of universities as a base for these surveys, and used volunteers from among the local population (Bulmer, 1985, pp. 10–11). The main contemporary source for discussion of British community self-surveys especially in the interwar period is the work of Wells (1935), which has already been referred to in the discussion of the development of surveys in the twentieth century (chapter 1). At the level of methods, the studies discussed by Wells appear to be heavily quantitative, as is apparent from his definition of the local social survey as 'fact-finding studies of numerous aspects of social life in a restricted geographical area' (p. 11). However, the view of social reform embodied in these surveys is not the top-down version characteristic of the statistical and survey tradition and of the Fabian model (see chapter 1 and chapter 5), but looks much more like a view from below, in which the emphasis is upon public authorities formulating practical measures to provide a suitable environment in which people can live decent lives (p. 18; and see also the discussion of Mess' study of Tyneside in chapter 1). Further, these surveys used local volunteers not solely for pragmatic reasons, but also because the experience of taking part in such work was seen as an educational — in some senses a politicizing — experience (Marsh, 1982, p. 19). As Wells (1935) puts it, the aim of the local social survey was:

> the description of the social conditions under which the workers live and often also an attempt to arouse interest and action directed by the inhabitants of the locality studied towards their own social problems. (p. 50)

Wells notes that civic survey clubs were sometimes set up to conduct such investigations, and the findings were presented in an accessible form, for example in an exhibition held at the local library (p. 11).

There are, therefore, significant differences between these British inter-war community surveys and the ameliorist tradition. First, it is not so much a belief that the collection of new facts would lead directly to social reform, but rather a belief that the experience of undertaking research, and of putting together facts which already exist in a coherent and comprehensive form, would identify the areas in which reforms need to occur in a specific locality, and to demands that they should be undertaken. In this sense, research becomes a kind of political activity which people undertake on their own behalf. Second, there was a different emphasis upon the creation and ownership of data, which in these surveys was seen lying firmly with local people themselves rather than with those who wielded political and administrative power. In several senses, therefore, these surveys look much more like the view from below not the view from above. In the context of the analysis developed in this book, I would see the significance of this work partly in its espousal of elements of the alternative tradition which has some continuities with nineteenth-century work like that of Mayhew (whilst operating at the level of methods within the dominant fact-finding paradigm); and partly in the issues which it raised about the creation, ownership and use of data which move in the direction of seeing this process as properly left in the hands of the people who are studied rather than treating such people merely as objects of study who have facts extracted from them and then used by someone else. This position was most fully articulated in the work of Mass Observation from 1937 onwards, which is discussed in the next section.

Mass-Observation and the 'Alternative' Tradition

Mass-Observation: A Distinctive Form of Qualitative Research?

The organization called Mass-Observation, which was founded in 1937 and as originally conceived came to an end in 1949, provides an important twentieth-century illustration of an alternative model of social research, in that it explicitly espoused qualitative methods. It also offered a unique opportunity to assess what happens when governments seek to make use of such work directly, since Mass Observation did work for the government during the Second World War. This aspect will be discussed more fully in the next chapter.

There are clear affinities between Mass-Observation and some of the other movements within social science during the inter-war period, especially with the community self-survey movement discussed in the previous section. The emphasis in both was upon reflecting the direct experience of ordinary people — an aspiration which itself has similarities with ethnographic and other qualitative research in academic social science, which developed most obviously in Britain from the late 1960s onwards (see chapter 1). Indeed, Reynolds, writing of the popularity of naturalistic methods in the sociology of education during the 1970s, traces their origins partly to this tradition in the 1930s, which he describes as:

> a partially lost British tradition of 'tell-it-as-it-is' reportage of the 1930s when a wide variety of methods (embracing poetry, arts, novel writing and photography) were used to depict social complexity — mostly working class. (Reynolds, 1980– 81, p. 77)

In a sense, Mass-Observation was the organization which gave this inter-war tradition its most explicit expression although it also had distinctive features. Stanley, in his detailed analysis of the methods used by Mass-Observation draws parallels not only with the inter-war tradition but also with Mayhew and Engels in the nineteenth century. In all these studies, he argues, there was:

> the same conviction that once the victims of (poor social) conditions became aware of them they would be moved to demand a better life. (Stanley, 1981, p. 196)

The Mass-Observation organization was started in 1937 by Tom Harrisson and Charles Madge, who had very different backgrounds.

Harrisson had some experience of anthropological work but no formal qualifications and Madge was a journalist on the *Daily Mirror* who moved into social science through his involvement in Mass-Observation and eventually became the Professor of Sociology at the University of Birmingham (Calder and Sheridan, 1984). The organization produced a large amount of published work, being committed to a rapid feedback of their findings, and an anthology produced by Calder and Sheridan (1984) provides a good starting-point for readers not familiar with their work.

Madge and Harrisson set out to develop the 'science of ourselves' drawing upon the model of anthropology. Although professional anthropologists did not exactly universally welcome this development, eventually some at least were won over, including Bronislaw Malinowski, one of the most famous British anthropologists of the period who subsequently provided a lengthy final chapter in Mass-Observation's account of its first year's work (Malinowski, 1939). In this chapter, Malinowski explains how his initial suspicion of Mass-Observation had been replaced by an admiration for the concept of the 'anthropology at home', seeing it as a 'nationwide intelligence service' which in the long run 'will substantially contribute to greater national self-knowledge' (*ibid*, p. 83). This idea of using techniques based upon anthropology not only to study British society but to use that information to create a greater level of consciousness among the people was central to the ideas which Harrisson and Madge set out to promote, and they did so explicitly against the background of political developments in the 1930s in Europe, which they saw as duping the mass of the population by keeping knowledge in the hands of a few people in power. They make this very clear in their introduction to their collection '*Britain by Mass Observation*', published in 1939:

> we are cogs in a vast and complicated machine which may turn out to be an infernal machine which may blow us to smithereens.... We must have knowledge, at least enough to enable us to come to personal decisions. There is an alternative view of things ... according to which there can be only a handful of people who know the facts, it being their job to control the destinies of millions of other people.... It is because of this situation — the urgency of fact, the voicelessness of everyman and the smallness of the group which controls fact-gathering and fact-distribution — that this book came to the written.... To understand we must first have

> facts, and to get the facts a new kind of organization is needed, or rather a new attitude towards getting the facts and publishing them. (pp. 8–9)

It is clear from this extract that Madge and Harrisson shared an explicitly political concept of knowledge and its use, and set out to intervene in the political processes through which knowledge (and therefore power) is distributed. They aimed to do this through the medium of social research, and thus represent a highly distinctive development in the relationship between social research and social policy, far removed from the model of research as the tool of government, used to study problems which are defined by the perspective of those in power. The Mass-Observation view — like others which I am considering in the 'alternative' tradition — is very much the view from below.

The methods which were developed by Mass-Observation depended initially upon observation and self-reporting, both conducted principally by volunteers. The concept of 'observation' employed was a rather curious one, developed from Harrisson's previous experience as an ornithologist. It was, as Stanley puts it, the concept of 'observation' in its literal sense as used in the natural sciences, where it is presumed that the world can be directly perceived and unproblematically described. This contrasts sharply with observation as it is understood, for example, in the interactionist tradition in sociology which emphasizes such matters as the complexity of meanings and the negotiation of accounts (Stanley, 1981, pp. 16–17; see Woods, 1983, for a discussion of interactionist concepts in relation to educational studies). The topics covered by Mass-Observation were varied, not to say eccentric at times, and often not 'policy relevant' in the sense defined by the dominant tradition of policy research. The topics reflect an interest in how working people live their lives: in pubs, the workplace, the street, or on holiday at the seaside. Even when they touched on obvious 'policy issues' — such as mass unemployment — it was through personal, vivid and detailed accounts of experiences such as attending a Labour Exchange (Calder and Sheridan, 1984, pp. 23–8).

The observations were recognizably a modification of anthropological fieldwork techniques, where the observers were asked to note down things that they both saw and heard about a particular topic or event, the first coordinated study being of the coronation day of George VI in 1937, and what it meant to ordinary people (Jennings and Madge, 1937). When the two founders began the organization

Harrisson was based in Bolton, and this town was used as one of the two key localities where a substantial number of researchers were recruited, and where extensive observational studies were undertaken (Calder and Sheridan, 1984). Although in many ways these studies were akin to anthropological fieldwork, they were necessarily different in employing large numbers of people who had no prior training, who then produced data which was analyzed and interpreted by others, in contrast to the model of the professional anthropologist who undertakes his or her own fieldwork and regards the process of the collection and interpretation of data as deeply interwoven. Indeed, one of Malinowski's criticisms of the early work of Mass-Observation is that it was too unfocussed ('the inchoate observing of everything and collecting items on any subject-matter') and that to realize its potential, its methods needed to build in a distinction between 'the relevant and the adventitious' and to work towards an understanding of 'sociological laws of universal validity' (Malinowski, 1939, p. 85).

Self-reporting was the second major method developed by Mass-Observation and this was done by recruiting a panel of volunteers through newspaper appeals and then asking this panel for reports at regular intervals on certain aspects of their *own* lives. Initially, they were asked to keep a full day's diary of everything which they did on the twelfth day of every month for a year and later, to report on days such as bank holidays, or upon more specific events (Calder and Sheridan, 1984, p. 5). In this self-reporting part of Mass-Observation's work, the fact that these reports were necessarily subjective accounts was seen as a positive virtue, since Madge and Harrisson saw such accounts as giving a snapshot of real life as ordinary people live and experience it. The weaknesses of relying upon subjective accounts from self-selected (and therefore unrepresentative) volunteers became apparent when Mass-Observation faced challenges about its 'scientific status' (see chapter 4). But the use of volunteers in this way also had its parallel in anthropological fieldwork techniques, in the use of informants. Malinowski certainly saw Mass-Observation volunteers in this light, and regarded their recording directly of their experiences and feelings as of great value:

> The expression of sincere, simple Mass-Observers upon an issue which affects them deeply in an emotional and therefore a practical manner, will become a collective act on a nation-wide scale. (Malinowski, 1939, p. 120)

In drawing upon anthropology and adapting it, the founders of Mass-Observation were seeking tools which would enable them to generate and use data upon their own society in a way consistent with their aspirations to spread knowledge about ourselves more widely, and therefore put the mass of the population in a position to challenge the decisions of governments. They specifically rejected direct interviewing as of only limited value in this exercise, because of the difficulties of getting people to be open and honest in an interview. In a discussion of Mass-Observation's methods in 1941, John Ferraby (who worked for the organization during the war) spells out the belief within Mass-Observation that there is a difference between people's private and their public opinions and beliefs: their task was to develop methods for studying the private as well as the public, and they turned to qualitative methods as the most appropriate means for doing this (Mass-Observation, File 550, 1941).

Qualitative methods also seemed to commend themselves from the perspective of that key feature of the Mass-Observation concept — the democratization of knowledge. In a very real sense, Harrisson and Madge saw direct reporting of one's own feelings and actions, and direct reporting of the observation of other people, as a way of 'giving a voice' to ordinary people:

> Much lip service is paid to the Man in the Street — politicians and newspapers claim to represent him, scientists and artists want to interest him in their work. Much of what they say is sincere but it must remain ineffective while the Man in the Street has no medium through which he can express with equal publicity what *he* thinks of *them*. (Madge and Harrisson, 1939, p. 11)

Qualitative methods may be most appropriate to reflecting the view from below, but the political use of those views is something which Mass-Observation also concerned itself, and at this point it begins to look less like social research and more like a political movement (Summerfield, 1985). The most obvious articulation of the democratization of knowledge was in Mass-Observation's firm commitment to the role of the amateur in social research, building upon the approach of the community self-surveys. Stanley, in his assessment of this element in their work, argues that this in some ways was methodologically naive, but nonetheless represents an important attempt to 'introduce onto the sociological agenda proper ... the world of everyday experience, and experienced by actors not abstracted by professionals' (Stanley, 1981, p. 273). In so doing, they introduced the concerns of the Chicago school of sociology (see chapter 5) to Britain and developed innovative forms of social investigation techniques. In particular, in Stanley's view, their use of a volunteer panel represents a genuine attempt to provide an actor's perspective on events and represents Mass-Observation's greatest achievement which has 'never been reproduced' (p. 271).

An Illustration: Children, Education and the War

The material in the archive of Mass-Observation (deposited at the University of Sussex) offers a wealth of data of various kinds on a whole range of topics. To illustrate its variety and character, I shall discuss briefly some of the material generated during 1939–40 on children's views of the war, and on its effect upon education especially of the policy of evacuation. This discussion is based upon Mass-Observation file 299, dated 1940 and entitled *Children and the War*, which is a composite report based upon material from both observers and panellists.

The general theme of this report is: in what ways and to what extent have children been affected by the war? The conclusion of the report is that children had been comparatively little affected: that they are on the whole busy and active with the same kind of pursuits in which they would in any case be engaged, that the toys they play with and the books which they mostly read are not preoccupied with the war, and that their ideas about the war arise principally from what adults say, and from those very specific items which impinge directly upon them (for example, their dislike of having to carry gasmasks, and of being evacuated).

It is difficult to see how issues of this kind could be studied effectively through the use of survey methods, especially with children. However, Mass-Observations observers and panellists employed a range of imaginative techniques which enabled them to document the impact of the war upon children. Panellists who were teachers wrote of specific experiences and specific children in their schools, and of their own experiences of teaching under war-time conditions. Observers held informal conversations with groups of children in and out of schools, watched them in the street to see what kind of games they played, and reported overheard conversations (a classic Mass-Observation method). Use was also made of creative work which children produced. Children's essays were analyzed for their content about the war from sources as varied as Roedean and an elementary school in Huddersfield. More limited use was made of children's drawings, although one observer in a London school specifically explored this method. The analysis of essays and drawings, among other things, make it very clear that boys were much more positively identified with violent activities associated with war than were girls. Finally various unobtrusive measures were employed: evidence about the kind of games and toys on sale at Woolworths and what proportion concerned war; analysis of all children's comics aimed at a variety of age-groups for a specific two-week period; and analysis of the content of school magazines produced by some grammar schools (these latter were deemed rather unsatisfactory as data, as they did not appear to reflect 'individual feeling' and adopted a rather official tone).

Simply at the level of documentation, therefore, the data provided by Mass-Observation's methods was undoubtedly much richer than anything which quantitative methods could produce, although it was always liable to be criticized on the grounds that it was not systematic or representative (see chapter 4). Similarly, material contained in this file documents in a very vivid way, through the comments of both children and teachers, the negative feelings and consequences which were generated by the policy of evacuation. The chaos which this policy subsequently caused in schools, is captured by this comment to an observer from the headteacher of an elementary school in Stepney:

> Oh dear, I couldn't give you anything like that (figures). I'm so disorganised. It's a terrible muddle at the moment.... We are very badly under-staffed. The children evacuated have one teacher to twenty while we've got as many as 88 to one. I can't get any figures because we simply don't have any. We've got both sexes, all ages, from all schools. It's very difficult to re-organise.

One important aspect of documentation of this kind therefore is that it is capable, through the very quality of the detail which it generates, of reflecting the real impact of government policy upon the lives of people to whom it is addressed. On occasions, such data may have the potential to directly challenge 'official' interpretations: a point which is well illustrated by Mass-Observation's data on evacuation. The conventional account of the war-time evacuation, still being found in text-books of social policy several decades later (Marshall, 1965, pp. 75–89; Bruce, 1968, pp. 291–325), is that, whilst it caused various kinds of disruption, one lasting effect was that it helped to create the conditions under which universalist social policy could be implemented after the war, by bringing many of the more privileged sections of society into direct contact with the poor (or at least the children of the poor) for the first time, and therefore demonstrating the extent of social and economic divisions in a way which most people found unacceptable. Thus, it is conventionally argued, bringing together the 'two nations' led to post-war social reform. Mass-Observation's data seriously challenge that view. As it is expressed in the report on children and the war:

> (Evacuation) has left behind more new antagonisms than friendships. Many of the upper classes have come into contact with the workers for the first time and have been horrified. The minority ... has determined that the appalling conditions which the evacuee children reflect shall be swept away, and very soon; the majority have turned their horror into fear and even hatred, seeing this level of humanity as an animal threat, that vague and horrid revolution which lurks in the dreams of so many super-tax payers. (Mass-Observation, File 299, 1940)

The language is clearly 'unscientific' and the material has been interpreted from a specific political stance; the use of phrases such as 'minority' and 'majority' claim more for the data in terms of representiveness than can be justified; but there remains here clearly reflected a view of evacuation from a range of people which challenges the blandness of the official rhetoric.

The illustration of children and the war demonstrates some of the weaknesses but also the potential of Mass-Observation's approach, including its potential in relation to social policy. It appears quite consistent with the basis of Mass-Observation's work that the data which it generated should not only be relevant to policy but in many instances was likely to challenge the official view — that indeed was the express intention of the organization's founders. It is appropriate therefore to see it as an alternative and an oppositional social science.

However, only two years after the organization was founded the war began, and this occasioned the use of Mass-Observation directly by government. On the face of it, this seems curious, since its stance against knowledge being confined to the powerful would seem to be inconsistent with assisting in knowledge creation precisely for those groups. Problems indeed arose precisely by that tension, inter alia, and these will be discussed in chapter 4, where the use of Mass-

Observation by government during wartime will be compared with the government's use of statistical research through the setting up of the Wartime Social Survey: the use of the two parallel organizations in the early years of the war offers a unique opportunity to assess the comparative position of quantitative and qualitative research in relation to government policy, and to observe the consequences of the incorporation of social science in an alternative, oppositional tradition into the structures of government.

Conclusion

The work of Mayhew in the nineteenth century, and community self-surveys and Mass-Observation in the twentieth, do not constitute an alternative 'tradition' in anything but the weakest sense. There is not the same sense of building upon past work (or reacting to it) which one finds in the dominant tradition. Nor indeed is the research discussed in this chapter always sharply distinguished from the dominant tradition, in terms of either its methods or its epistemology. In some ways, therefore, it is artificial to separate it and label it as a different 'tradition'.

It does, however, contain elements which are sufficiently distinctive, in my view, to warrant its identification as 'alternative', in the sense that it contains the germs of what could in principle become a quite different approach to social research oriented to social policy. In particular, the range of methods utilized have much clearer qualitative elements; the approach to data-creation goes beyond concepts of unproblematic fact-gathering; there is a more explicit recognition of the process of undertaking research as a political activity in the broadest sense, and the knowledge thereby created as intrinsically political; and there is an approach to policy-related research which reflects the view from below, not the view from above. All of these issues are important when one considers how qualitative research related to social policy might develop in the contemporary context, as will become apparent in the second part of the book (see especially chapters 7 and 8). The reasons why this 'alternative' approach has never seriously challenged the dominant tradition are considered in the next two chapters.

4 Qualitative Research Used by Government: A Comparative Case Study of Mass-Observation and the Wartime Social Survey

The theme of chapters 1 and 2 concerned the dominance of survey and other quantitative methods in social research oriented to social policy, supported by an epistemology which emphasizes providing neutral facts. At the same time, in chapter 3 I have argued that there has been a discernable 'alternative' tradition of social research oriented to policy issues, which has made much more use of qualitative methods, which has sought to reflect the view from below in terms of political structures, and which — at least in certain instances — has seen the data which it generated as intrinsically political, not neutral fact.

In this chapter, I shall focus upon this alternative tradition, and pose the question: *can* qualitative research be used by governments? This question is addressed in a different way in chapters 6 and 9, but here it will be considered in relation to a specific example in the past of the use of qualitative research by government, namely the use of Mass-Observation by the Ministry of Information during the early years of the Second World War. Although concerned with social research generally rather than education specifically, this is an important example whose utility for the purposes of this discussion is further enhanced by the fact that the Ministry was simultaneously encouraging the development of the Wartime Social Survey. It thus provides the opportunity to compare directly the use of quantitative and qualitative methods by a government department. Since the Social Survey survived and expanded well beyond the demise of Mass-Observation, this example provides both an opportunity to examine what happened when a government department did attempt to use qualitative research of a type which was likely to challenge the official view (see chapter 3 for a discussion of Mass-Observation's methods), but also it offers a case study of how the dominant position of quantitative methods was secured.

The discussion in this chapter is based on the records of Mass-Observation which are available as a research archive at the University of Sussex library, having been deposited there by Tom Harrisson in 1970. Details of the contents of this archive can be found in Calder and Sheridan (1984, chapter 8). For the purposes of this book, I have used two sections of the archive. First, the File Reports. These are summaries of the work of Mass-Observation according to topic and were produced regularly, and they also contain drafts of articles and broadcast scripts written by members of Mass-Observation, a number of which include discussions of methods. The File Reports are also available in microfiche form (Tom Harrisson Mass Observation Archive, 1983). Second, I have used the Mary Adams Papers. Mary Adams was a personal friend of Tom Harrisson and his main contact in government. She deposited her personal papers in the archive in 1976. I have used that section of her papers which covers the period 1939–41, when she was Head of Home Intelligence at the Ministry of Information, and responsible for recruiting Mass-Observation to work for the government. This section includes both her internal correspondence and external letters from the Ministry.

Mass-Observation was first employed by the Home Intelligence Division of the Ministry of Information in the spring of 1940, the contact coming directly through the friendship between Tom Harrisson and Mary Adams, who was in charge of the Division. In a memo of 5 March 1940, Mary Adams expresses herself as well satisfied with Mass-Observation's first report for the Ministry, a study of public opinion in Silvertown at the time of a by-election (Mary Adams Papers 1/B). Although the friendship between Harrisson and Adams clearly goes some way to explaining the links between the two organizations, it still seems curious that an organization committed, as Mass-Observation was, to challenging the official view of the world and making knowledge widely available (see chapter 3) should have been prepared to work for the government. However, there is evidence that Harrisson was pressing for this as soon as the war began, arguing that in war-time the government needed reliable information and this could only be obtained by the use of proper social research (Mass-Observation, File 10, 1939). His views were not shared, however, by Charles Madge, who believed that Mass-

Observation should retain its independence of government in order to be able to maintain a critical stance — a disagreement which ended in Madge's leaving the organization altogether. There was therefore from the beginning a tension between the kind of research to which Mass-Observation was committed and its work for the government.

The kind of work done by Mass-Observation and the way in which it was received and used within the Ministry are well documented for the early years of the war through Mary Adams' papers, until she left the Ministry in April 1941. It is clear from the internal memos especially that Adams was frequently in the position of having to defend her use of Mass-Observation and the reports which they produced, with one of the most persistent criticisms concerning the alleged unreliability of their methods. From the early days, however, she thought it prudent to ensure that Mass-Observation was not the sole source of the Home Intelligence Division's information, as she made clear in a memo of 12 March 1940, that is four days after the first report had been produced (Mary Adams Papers, 4/E). She was indeed already negotiating with the London School of Economics to cooperate in setting up a statistical survey under the direction of Professor Arnold Plant, and a letter to Plant of 29 April 1940 formally confirms that the Ministry will sponsor the work of this new unit, the Wartime Social Survey (Mary Adams Papers, 2/E).

For a while, both organizations seemed to be on the same footing with the Ministry, that is to say, both were seen as external organizations with some funding from the government, but essentially independent agencies from whom the Ministry would commission various pieces of research — this is the situation as it was explained, for example, in a memo from Adams to the Minister dated 29 May 1940 (Mary Adams Papers 1/B). However, the comparative status of the two organizations changed rapidly and an exchange of memos in late September 1940 indicates that the Director General wished the Wartime Social Survey to be brought more directly under the control of the Ministry whilst Adams was asked to 'think out some plan for retaining certain of the services rendered to us by Mass-Observation'. The change in the status of the Social Survey proved unacceptable to the LSE academics who were involved in it and they withdrew, and the Ministry decided to appoint a permanent Director of Survey Work (Mary Adams Papers 1/B). Thus within six months, the status of the two organizations had changed dramatically, with the Wartime Social Survey being set up as a quasi-independent organization but rapidly taken directly into the structures of government, not only for use within the Ministry of Information — it was soon being offered to other ministries as a facility which they could use (Mary Adams Papers 2/E).

The Ministry continued to use Mass-Observation, although there is a very interesting letter from Harrisson to Adams dated 9 January 1941 in which he details his growing dissatisfaction with the way in which the relationship between Mass-Observation and the Ministry had developed. He was concerned that his relationships with civil servants were poor, and he wanted to restore direct communication between himself and Adams as the basis of his relationship with the Ministry; he felt that the Ministry was making insufficient use of Mass-Observation's reports; and further, that he was getting little positive feedback on them, only criticism. As his letter puts it:

> it would be a great help to have some constructive criticism of the reports we send in. Lately there has been much criticism of reports, as always, but practically no indication of anything good in the work we have done, or of it being put to any purpose or used in any way. For instance, this morning, you picked me up on several small points in the Liverpool report — points which would have been masked if I had taken the superficial and easy way of writing a one-paged report, which would have sufficed. But you did not in any way indicate that the report was interesting, significant or useful. . . . I don't want praise, but I do want leads and definitions. (Mary Adams Papers 4/G)

The points which Harrisson makes here make it clear that the information which they were providing was (for whatever reason) not the kind of information which the Ministry felt able to use, and that their feedback to Mass-Observation was, by the beginning of 1941, almost wholly negative. Some of this may be accounted for by the fact that Mary Adams felt that the work of the Home Intelligence Division itself was marginalized and undervalued in the Ministry — a point she made forcibly after her departure in her evidence to a parliamentary Select Committee in December 1941 (Mary Adams Papers 6/E). Nonetheless, it remains clear that the use of Mass-Observation's work by the Ministry was limited and short-lived; meanwhile the Wartime Social Survey flourished. The Survey's enhanced position is all the more remarkable because it was involved in the 'Cooper's Snoopers' press campaign in the summer of 1940, when various newspapers raised objections to the work of the Home

Intelligence Division, accusing it of spying on the population. Press reports said that 'Cooper's Snoopers' (named after the Minister, Duff Cooper) were official nosey parkers asking people impudent questions on their doorsteps (Mass-Observation, File 325, 1940). This was a direct consequence of the Ministry's desire for surveys of 'morale', which it commissioned from the Wartime Social Survey in its very early days (Mary Adams Papers 1/B). Reports in the press appear to have referred to the Survey and to Mass-Observation interchangeably, as if they were the same organization (Mass-Observation, File 325, 1940). However, when the situation was defended publicly by the Minister, Duff Cooper, in a House of Commons debate, the discussion was focussed almost entirely upon the Wartime Social Survey, whose position in government by that time was clearly assured (House of Commons Official Reports, Vol. 363, No. 98, August 1940). Bringing the Survey more closely under the control of the Ministry was clearly one consequence of these events — but the interesting point is that politicians and civil servants did not react by abandoning survey work but by, in effect, strengthening its position within the government. Meanwhile, Mass-Observation was further marginalized.

What general points can be drawn from the experience of Mass-Observation about the use of qualitative research by government? First, at the level of methods, it is clear that Mass-Observation was constantly vulnerable to criticisms informed by a view of quantitative and survey work as the standard against which all research should be measured. Those criticisms were tempered, at least initially, by a recognition on the part of some that there was positive value to government in the use of qualitative methods. For example, a report to the Ministry by R H S Crossman in October 1939 saw the strength of Mass-Observation as lying in its in-depth knowledge of specific localities (Mary Adams Papers 4/E). Mary Adams defended her own use of the organization on the grounds that there were certain tasks for which statistical methods were not suited and where 'qualitative not quantitative study is necessary' (Mary Adams Papers 1/B). So, for a brief spell in 1940, qualitative and quantitative methods (as represented by Mass-Observation and the Wartime Social Survey) were apparently seen as complementary in their usefulness to government. Mary Adams saw the strengths of Mass-Observation specifically as: incisive observation, good at giving the 'temperature' of a problem; works flexibly and speedily. The Social Survey, meanwhile she argued, had methods which had been tried and tested; methods which were open to constant scrutiny by external advisers; was 'always objective'; but its work was limited to topics suitable for statistical treatment (Mary Adams Papers 2/E). This position of complementarity was never secure, however, and Harrisson was soon having to defend his work against unfavourable comparison with the Wartime Social Survey, which he did by stressing the difference of function and emphasizing the qualitative/quantitative distinction (Mass-Observation File 455, 1940 and File 572, 1941). The key dividing line between the two methods seemed to be, in his view, reliance upon direct interviewing, and he set out very clearly the limitations of this method in a variety of places (Mass-Observation, File 1133−4, 1942 and File 1212, 1942).

This defence, however, did not stick. The kind of criticisms made of Mass-Observation's methods are perhaps best summarized by a considered discussion offered by Mark Abrams in 1951 which reflects in a more systematic form the kind of comments which can be found throughout the archive material. Abrams argued that their use of quotations from individuals without any knowledge of their representativeness was insupportable; that the recording of overheard remarks was dubious without an accompanying account of the social context in which they occurred; that indirect and in-depth interviewing is viable only if it is grounded in a theoretical understanding of the social relationship or institution being studied; that observation of everyday life is a skilled job and again needs to be grounded in theoretical understanding; and that the analysis of the materials generated by observers and panellists was not undertaken in a systematic way (Abrams, 1951). Many of these criticisms make points with which contemporary qualitative researchers would undoubtedly agree. Criticisms made at the time echoed Abrams' views but largely in a less well-informed way, concentrating principally upon issues of objectivity and representativeness, and objecting to Harrisson's flamboyant, publicist style (Stanley, 1981, p. 192). Increasingly Mass-Observation responded to these criticisms in the terms set by their critics, attempting to stress the objective, neutral and factual nature of their findings, and indeed making increasing use of compiling techniques and direct interviewing. This amounted to a significant departure from the original basis of its work and caused some dissent within the organisation. For example, John Ferraby was arguing in 1943 that Mass-Observation was going too far in its search for accuracy and quantification (Mass-Observation, File 1886, 1943).

By giving way to this kind of criticism, Mass-Observation was moving onto territory where it could never successfully compete. The Wartime Social Survey, by contrast, was able to satisfy demands for scientific methods in the collection of objective facts. Indeed, the grounds upon which the Home Intelligence Division argued for an expansion of its work are set out in a paper dated 1st March 1941, and make this abundantly clear. They argue that technical competence and expertise in statistical methods is the basis of its work; that the Ministry must have what she called 'objective fieldwork'; and that the details of questionnaires can be agreed in advance and controls built into the process (Mary Adams Papers 6/A). The concept of facts (underpinned by positivist epistemology) which can be collected by researchers and then used by government was well established in the nineteenth century, and was now powerfully reasserting itself at the point where there was at least some opportunity for a different type of social research to be used by government. The close alignment between survey methods and the needs of government (see chapter 5) was powerfully confirmed and — as Mary Adams put in her evidence to the Select Committee — 'survey methods represent a new instrument of government' (Mary Adams Paper 6/E). Although not new in conception, there was indeed a new departure in setting up a social survey organization within the government. This served to consolidate the dominance of statistical methods as essential to the machinery of running a complex state — as the Clapham Committee noted in 1946 (Report of the Committee on the Provision for Social and Economic Research, 1946, paragraph 8).

The second lesson which can be learned from the experience of Mass-Observation is related to the first: that research of this type is always vulnerable in that it has a tendency to challenge the official view, and therefore cannot be straightforwardly incorporated as administrative intelligence — a model which has been dominant in policy-oriented research, as I have argued already (see chapter 1). The original concept of Mass-Observation, that it should be an organization which democratizes knowledge and therefore power (see chapter 3) meant that it was likely to produce research which ran counter to what people in power wanted to hear, as indeed Tom Harrisson had suggested shortly before the war began when he wrote that the 'high-ups' had reason to fear research because they wanted to believe that all the people were united behind them. He referred to this again in 1940, suggesting that the nature of work which the 'high-ups' do cuts them off from contact with and knowledge about the 'low-downs' (Mass-Observation, File 10, 1939 and File 446, 1940).

Such an unequivocably oppositional stance was bound to be uncomfortable once the organization was incorporated into government, and as early as March 1940 Mary Adams was having to defend

Mass-Observation within the Ministry against the accusation that their work was 'subversive'. She argued that its results were naturally critical of events, but that criticism is not the same thing as subversion:

> What does one mean by 'subversion'? The results of Mass-Observation are, not unnaturally, *critical* of certain social happenings, and I do not think that criticism is subversion. The use to which criticisms are put may lead to subversive actions. But it is our business to acquaint ourselves with criticisms and direct the attention of those in authority to the causes of discontent. By doing so we hope to prevent unfortunate consequences. (Mary Adams Papers 4/E)

Adams' attempts to argue for the positive virtue of critical research findings was not successful, however, as she made clear subsequently in general terms in her evidence to the Parliamentary Select Committee on the work of the Wartime Social Survey. She indicates that it was never properly understood within the Ministry that an analysis of tension and criticism was an essential basis for government action, but that reports which contained such items were 'regarded as supplying undesirable forms of pressure' (Mary Adams Papers 6/E). Whilst it is certainly possible for the results of social surveys to contain critical material, the kind of qualitative work which Mass-Observation undertook, with the stance it adopted on the political nature of knowledge, led in this direction almost by definition. Small wonder therefore that work of this type met with a cool reception within the Ministry. This particular example therefore supports the position which I argue in chapter 5, namely that qualitative social research aligns badly with the perspectives of politicians and especially of administrators, and is far less likely than quantitative work to meet their research needs as they define them.

Third, there is an interesting lesson to be learned from the Mass-Observation experience concerning the role allocated to research and researchers within the structure of policy-making. Essentially, this lesson is that officials tried to relegate the researcher to the role of technician who simply provides facts and hands them over to others to use — a role which had already become the dominant one but which fits much better with quantitative research (see chapters 5 and 8 for further discussion). From the earliest memos in the Mary Adams collection it is clear that from the beginning the view from the Ministry was that the government department would decide the nature of the enquiry, Mass-Observation would collect the data and hand it over, then the government would interpret the results (Mary Adams Papers, 1/B). This clear statement of the research organization as technician, with limited input into the design of the research and no part in its analysis, is repeated throughout the years covered by this collection, and used by Adams as a defence of her use of the organization. The emphasis is upon the supervision by the Ministry, which would ensure the reliability of the results. Indeed, Adams suggests that it is necessary to exclude Tom Harrisson from the interpretation of the results, since he is a person with his own ideas and opinions. In a memo dated 12 March 1940, she wrote:

> It is for us to use his *findings* and not his opinions. I believe, with supervision, we can do this. (Mary Adams Papers 4/E)

That distinction between fact and opinion is not one which can be applied very easily to qualitative work, but it is easy to see how the Wartime Social Survey commended itself more readily on those criteria.

Finally, the experience of Mass-Observation's use by government highlights some important ethical issues. The split between Harrisson and Madge raised overtly the question of whether an organization committed to making research an activity which both involves and is addressed to ordinary people can properly make its services available to a government department. The immediate practical problem created by that disagreement was resolved by Madge's departure, but the questions which he raised did not go away, and the experience of Mass-Observation's involvement with the government led Harrisson in particular into some situations which, from a distance, look highly dubious.

Specifically, Harrisson agreed with Adams that both parties would remain silent in public about the fact that Mass-Observation was working for the Ministry of Information — an agreement which Harrisson wanted because he wanted to maintain the public posture that Mass-Observation was an independent organization, and to be free to publish and broadcast in their own right (Mary Adams Papers 2/E). This meant that Mass-Observation's observers and panellists were not to be told that they were working for the Ministry when they sent in certain reports, and Mary Adams made a virtue of this arrangement in an internal memo in March 1940, by using it as one piece of evidence that the organization was merely providing neutral, factual information (i.e. that the researchers were technicians) (Mary Adams Papers 1/B). It appears that the arrangement also suited the Ministry, in that it did not have to defend publicly its use of an organization whose methods were widely criticized. It is a very interesting feature of the parliamentary debate on the Cooper's Snoopers affair that the Minister made no mention of his department's use of Mass-Observation (but said plenty about the Wartime Social Survey), and when pressed by several questioners to say whether the Ministry was employing the organization, he gave an answer which seems not wholly consonant with what was actually happening:

> Mass-Observation is, I understand, privately run and controlled. We have once or twice applied to it for statistical information on certain subjects which it has been able to furnish, information which it was not worthwhile setting up a special inquiry to obtain. (House of Commons Official Reports, Vol. 363, No. 98, 1940, Col. 1552)

The tension inherent in employing an organization committed to research as the democratization of social knowledge in the service of government led in this instance to secrecy about their involvement, as the way of maintaining publicly a stance which in fact was being undermined; and that secrecy included outright deception of volunteers who were collecting data. Whatever one's moral stance on such matters, the experience of Mass-Observation provides an important warning about the path down which others in similar circumstances may be tempted to travel.

A further ethical issue concerns the kind of data which Mass-Observation was able to supply to the government. Although ultimately its services were not greatly appreciated, it was recognized, at least by Mary Adams', that the kind of research which they undertook could be of great value. To put it crudely, the observers *were* capable of spying on the population in a way which a social survey never could, because its methods were unobtrusive and its researchers well integrated with the social life of ordinary people. Several of Mary Adams memos hint at this, most interestingly a memo of 12 April 1940 addressed to Col. Harker at MI5, informing him of the Ministry's decision to use the organization:

> (Mass-Observation) agrees to undertake certain researches on our behalf. These investigations will be mainly of a qualitative nature: by means of overheads, direct conversations and interviews Mass-Observation will supply us with information

about public opinion and about the state of feeling during crises. Mass-Observation will also undertake certain other enquiries on our behalf, e.g. a study of non-voter attitudes during by-elections, observations of picketing by anti-war bodies at Labour Exchanges etc. (Mary Adams Papers 2/E)

The last example in particular is in stark contrast to Mass-Observation's own commitment to challenge the status quo, and it is all too clear just how useful such studies might be to the Home Intelligence Division. Tom Harrisson was indeed alert to this in his initial negotiations with the Ministry, and his letter of 8 April 1940, stating the terms upon which Mass-Observation would continue to work for government, he indicates that they will do 'special studies on any subject provided it does not involve "espionage"' (Mary Adams Papers 4/E).

The special circumstances of war-time, of course, have to be taken into account in commenting on the experience of Mass-Observation. Nonetheless, the potential is clear for qualitative research — precisely because it is unobtrusive and studies natural social situations — to be drawn into government intelligence in the political, not just the administrative sense. Indeed there is some evidence that MI5 disliked Mass-Observation precisely because the latter appeared to be attempting to invade its own activities (Stanley, 1981, p. 14). The Mass-Observation experience therefore does highlight some very important issues in the use of qualitative research in relation to government policy, which will be taken up in more general terms in chapter 9.

The experience of Mass-Observation suggests therefore that qualitative research *can* be used by governments, but that its position is likely to be far less comfortable and more constantly open to challenge than is survey work. Moreover, when it *is* used, this occurs on terms set by government which reflect the dominant research paradigm and the dominant structural position accorded to research; and this leads to situations which are ethically and politically difficult to manage. In the intervening forty years, there has been some official recognition that research and fact-finding are not the same thing, and that research which challenges government should nonetheless be encouraged (see the discussion of the Heyworth Report, and the Rothschild Report on the SSRC, in chapter 2). To some extent it can only be a matter for speculation as to whether this means that in the circumstances of the 1980s it is much easier to challenge the dominant paradigm, and thus make qualitative research targetted upon government policy more intellectually and ethically viable. The discussion which follows in chapters 6–9 takes up that issue from a variety of angles.

5 Why Has Qualitative Research Had Little Impact on Educational and Social Policy in Britain?

In this final chapter in Part I, I shall draw together a range of issues explored in the previous chapters and pose the question: why have quantitative methods achieved and maintained their marked dominance and conversely, why has qualitative research had such little impact on the study and practice of social policy?

In chapters 1 and 2 (where I have documented the dominance of quantitative research) I have hinted at some explanations, and in chapters 3 and 4, which are concerned with the 'alternative' tradition that highlights qualitative research, I have suggested some others. In this chapter I shall consider these in a more systematic way by focussing on three different but interlinked explanations: first, the utility of statistics and politically neutral 'facts' from the perspective of governments; second, the dominance of the Fabian model of the research-policy relationship; third, the way in which different disciplines have developed in British social sciences, and the type of research orientation associated with each. The discussion of each of these focusses on a specific historical period and, although the argument concerns social research in general rather than education specifically, examples drawn from education are used where appropriate.

The Utility of Statistics and Surveys to Governments

The first explanation which I shall explore for the dominance of quantitative methods centres on the argument that the data provided and the processes through which they are generated make such methods much more useful to governments than anything which qualitative alternatives can offer. I shall focus my discussion here on the early Victorian period, when the relationship between social research and social policy was being shaped (see chapter 1). At that time, it can be argued, quantitative data provided by social investigators were politically useful to governments in their task of managing a developing industrial economy. Further, the character of those investigations themselves was shaped by the Victorian intellectual climate in which positivism was a dominant force, thus favouring a particular concept of 'facts' and allegedly objective methods of collecting them. I shall examine each of these features in turn.

Commentators upon the major problems faced by governments in the first half of the nineteenth century note that these were generated by the changing size and distribution of the population and the change from an agrarian to an industrial economy, creating both urban concentration and an industrial labour force. Developing new mechanisms for managing this urban population was an urgent necessity, and the result was an administrative revolution in government during this period, which brought about much greater centralization and created the character of the modern British state (Lubenow, 1971, pp. 15–17; Macdonagh, 1977, pp. 1–3). The same problems demanded the systematic collection of data about the population, since this developing administrative apparatus needed statistical information in order to be able to expand and refine its capacity to manage an industrial economy (Lubenow, 1971, p. 16; Shaw and Miles, 1979, pp. 32–5). This view — that statistical information about the population is vital to the management of an industrial society — can be supported from primary sources well into the twentieth century. The Clapham Report on the provision of economic and social research, for example, noted the improvement of government statistical service during the Second World War, and saw these partly as a result of the 'exigencies of war' but also of 'a gradual enlargement of views as to what is essential as the basis for running the complex machinery of a modern state' (Report of the Committee on the Provision for Social and Economic Research, 1946, paragraph 8).

Lying behind this interpretation that statistics are necessary to the management of an industrial economy is the view that the state aims to create a stable, hierarchical society in which that economy can flourish, and therefore needs to develop mechanisms of control over the mass of the population. Shaw offers a strong — if somewhat crude — account of this, when he argues that the early social surveys (including censuses) which documented purely descriptive characteristics of the population served the needs of the state and the ruling classes by providing the kind of information which they needed to develop more effective mechanisms of control (Shaw, 1975, pp. 36–41). Some non-Marxist commentators also note the importance to the Victorian middle classes of creating a stable, hierarchical society and regard this as a major motivation for social investigations leading to social reform. McGregor (1957) in his discussion of social policy and social research in the nineteenth century sees the impetus for social reform as deriving from the anxieties of the professional middle class who wished to maintain social stability. Defining social problems was seen as the first step to solving them, and therefore measuring the consequences of economic and social change became central to the enterprise of social reform:

> the essential feature of social policy is the growing capacity to measure, and hence to express in politically constructive ways, the economic costs of unregulated individualism. (McGregor, 1957, p. 146)

A further refinement of these arguments concerns the importance of *classifying* the population. The argument here is that the Victorian approach to social policy in general and to the management and the relief of poverty in particular required administrative measures to be developed which would divide the population into different 'grades' of pauper. Increasingly during the nineteenth century this became the basis upon which poor relief was administered, as a central issue became the removal of certain classes of pauper from the workhouse to alternative provision designed to meet more specialized needs (Corrigan and Corrigan, 1978, pp. 11–16; Golding and Middleton, 1982, p. 20). In the later part of the century, Golding and Middleton argue that the work of Booth and Rowntree (see chapter 1) which systemized the study of urban poverty had precisely the same roots. Research, like policy, was about classification, they argue, especially about distinguishing the 'residuum' (those who 'from shiftlessness, idleness or drink are inevitably poor') from the respectable working class ('decent steady men, paying their way and bringing up their children respectably') (Golding and Middleton, 1982, pp. 23–4). Certainly evidence can be found in the work of Booth and Rowntree to support that conclusion, especially in the classification which they themselves used for identifying different categories of the population. As I noted in chapter 1, classification was a strong theme in Booth's work, including the classification of elementary schools according to the 'type' of children who attended them.

Within the developing strategies for managing the industrial, urban population, education can be seen as having a key role. Marxist commentators commonly emphasize the controlling role envisaged for education at this time. For example, Corrigan and Corrigan (1978) argue, in relation to the 1834 Poor Law reforms, that the object was to create 'new kinds of people' and that:

> the 'educational solution' was the paradigm for social policy, as long as we recall that by 'education' far more than merely reading and writing was to be undertaken. (p. 11)

Certainly support for this view can be found in the writings of Kay–Shuttleworth (see chapter 1) who saw the long-term solution to the problems of control as control over the minds of the people; as he put it, 'moral subjection, which has hitherto been the only safeguard of England' (Kay, 1839, p. 228). Whether or not education is actually efficacious in this regard, the mid-Victorian pioneers of state sponsorship in education do seem to have seen it, at least partly, in these terms. Education was therefore closely bound into other measures which at that time were concerned with developing mechanisms for managing the population, using as their base statistical data which monitored, described and classified the condition of the poor.

Alongside these arguments about the political utility of statistical data about the population, one needs to consider a somewhat different set of arguments which again point to the significance of the nineteenth century origins of social research for understanding how the dominance of quantitative methods was established. These arguments concern the Victorian intellectual climate, specifically the prevailing concept of facts, the meaning of facts and how facts are generated and used, highlighting the themes of scientific objectivity and neutrality. Bulmer argues that one of the main reasons for the particular character of social research as it developed in Britain was 'the enduring strengths of empiricism and positivism in British intellectual life' (Bulmer, 1982a, p. 28). This view is echoed by Russell Keat, who argues that the positivist conception of social science has provided an important basis for the role of statistics; the key links being, first, the concentration upon observable phenomena as the basis for scientific enquiry; and second, the emphasis upon social science as value-free. Acknowledging that the term 'positivism' can be used very loosely (see Introduction), he defines it as, first, the belief that the basic features of social sciences can and should be modelled upon natural sciences; second, a specific conception of science itself, which is concerned with establishing general laws based upon observable phenomena (Keat, 1979, pp. 75–8).

The position which Abrams adopts in his work which is centrally concerned with this issue is somewhat different. He argues that to say that nineteenth-century social scientists were all positivists is true on one level, but obscures the important differences between them. His own analysis separates the three categories of political economy, ameliorism and social evolution each of which has a strong positivist orientation, but takes on a distinctive colour. In all three traditions, he argues, there is a history of controversy about facts and the meaning of facts, and collectively they represent the intellectual structure within which British sociology was formed (Abrams, 1968, p. 7). Of course, collectively they also provided the intellectual structure within which concepts of the relationship between research and policy were formulated. A central theme of Abrams' discussion is that the dominant position of statistics in the nineteenth century derived from a strong view of political economy, which held that it was possible to uncover the natural laws of society, and that government intervention was proper to secure the optimal conditions in which those laws could operate freely. Thus there was a need to collect factual information which would uncover the laws, and a faith that the facts would unambiguously 'speak for themselves' (pp. 8–10). As I argued in chapter 1, this concept of facts was dominant even in the most sophisticated and important of the nineteenth century quantitative research. In fact, as Abrams argues, it became increasingly difficult to sustain the distinction between fact and opinion, as more and more 'facts' of a patently ambiguous nature were uncovered (p. 22).

A further feature of this intellectual tradition is the relationship which it implies between the researcher and the policy-maker or administrator. If the dominant conception of social research is that it should provide 'facts' which specify the dimensions of a particular social problem which the government has identified, then this casts the social scientist in the role of a technician, with decisions about what facts are relevant and how they are used lying firmly with the policy-makers (Cherns, 1972, pp. 16–17; Bulmer, 1978b, p. 43). An extreme version of that relationship is Rothschild's customer-contractor principle, although it must always be remembered that he himself did not apply it to the social sciences, even if others have attempted to do so (see chapter 2). The implications for the researcher of being cast in the role of technician are discussed further in chapter 9, in relation to the prospects for developing a stronger link in future between social policy and qualitative social research. But as far as the past is concerned, it seems clear that the division between providing facts on the one hand, and interpreting them and using them on the other has fitted quantitative methods more comfortably. Quantitative methods also provide more opportunities for the policy-makers to control and scrutinize the 'technician's' work. As Payne *et al.* put it, 'hard facts' are:

> more easily scrutinised and therefore controlled by the spon-
> soring body than the more intangible sociological activities
> occuring . . . in the 'softer' techniques of participant observa-
> tion and depth interviewing. (Payne, Dingwall, Payne and
> Carter, 1981, p. 151)

As I noted in chapter 4, this was one reason why the Wartime Social Survey rapidly came to be preferred to Mass-Observation by the Ministry of Information in the early 1940s.

The enduring strength of these concepts of facts, objectivity and neutrality goes a considerable way to explaining not only why the work of someone like Mayhew (see chapter 3) did not become part of the dominant tradition of social research, but also why contemporary researchers doing qualitative work still have difficulties in making their work seem credible to policy-makers. An interesting contemporary example which concerns education is provided by Shipman (1985), writing specifically in relation to ethnography and policy in the field of education, where he argues that ethnographers face a special problem among social researchers because their activities appear on the surface to be very like those of advisers or inspectors. Even if the methods are reported in detail the distinction may be lost on the lay person. He cites a specific instance arising from his own experience in the ILEA Research and Statistics Group, where the results of an ethnographic study in primary schools were not published because the inspectors claimed that their own observations led to very different conclusions, and there was no way of adjudicating between the accounts. More generally there is a common strand running through much contemporary writing on research and policy, which emphasizes that policy-makers want 'description or "surveys" — using administrative rather than social scientific categories — rather than general causal theories', and that quantitative work is looked on more favourably because it appears to provide the kind of neutral description which they see as the function of research (Blume, 1979, p. 320). The more sophisticated understanding of social science research contained for example in the Heyworth Report (see chapter 2) seems to have made little impact.

In conclusion therefore, I would argue that the character of policy-related social research as it was formed in the early Victorian period has been of lasting importance. At that time, the collection of quantified, descriptive information arranged in administrative categories was politically urgent, and the early social investigators set about providing this. Since the people (mainly men) who undertook such investigations were themselves part of or closely identified with the governing classes, their interests were both represented in and reflected by the work of these early social investigators, which made them lean towards methods that would accommodate the concerns of those who governed, not of the powerless who were the subjects of their work. Qualitative methods tend to sit uneasily with this arms-length, top-down approach because by their very nature, as they get close to the subjects of their research and necessarily reflect social reality from the bottom upwards — a point which I shall take up again in chapters 8 and 9. Quantitative methods, by contrast, can generate administrative intelligence about the poor whilst at the same time keeping them at arms length, in the sense that statistical surveys give little opportunity for direct experience of poverty to be reflected, or the voice of the poor themselves to be heard. This was especially true in the nineteenth century, when the poor themselves were not questioned (see chapter 1). There is a marked contrast here with the work of Mayhew during the same period who — using different methods and having far less impact upon government — demonstrated how the developing industrial society operated from the perspective of the poor.

As well as the urgency of generating administrative intelligence about the poor during the early Victorian period, the prevailing intellectual climate at that time further reinforced the tendency to adopt statistical and other quantitative methods because of their appearance of scientific objectivity. Although, as I argued in chapter 1, there is no automatic and necessary alignment between positivist epistemology and quantitative techniques, nonetheless qualitative methods can much less easily be accommodated within a prevailing climate of positivism in relation to policy-oriented research, as is demonstrated by the experience of Mass-Observation in its work for the government (see chapter 4).

These two features — the need for administrative intelligence and the intellectual dominance of positivism — represent the conditions under which the dominant tradition of policy-oriented social research was formed in the mid-nineteenth century. Whilst I would not claim that this can explain in fine detail the characteristics of every piece of policy-oriented research either then or subsequently, I do see these as the major forces shaping the dominant tradition at that time. Subsequent developments — as I go on to argue — seem to have consolidated rather than undermined them.

The Dominance of the Fabian Model of the Research-Policy Relationship

In the previous section I discussed the reasons for the dominance of particular research methods in the nineteenth century. Here, I shall argue that in the early years of the twentieth century the work of the Webbs in particular was important in articulating and consolidating a particular model of the relationship between social research and social policy. This model has formed the basis for the development of the research-policy relationship during this century. The model which the Webbs established incorporated many of the concerns of the dominant tradition in the nineteenth century. Further, in terms of methods, although Beatrice Webb in particular was interested in qualitative as well as quantitative techniques, the former were nonetheless accorded a secondary place within the Webbs' overall concept of research, which also drew upon a positivist conception of 'facts' (see chapter 1). Nonetheless, this Fabian version of applied social research has had an important influence subsequently.

A major reason for the significance of the Fabian approach lies in its political location within socialist politics. It can, of course, be argued that very little social research can be clearly shown to have been used by governments, and indeed that to expect this to happen is an unrealistic aspiration (Blume, 1979) — an issue which will be taken up in chapter 6. On the other hand, where research *has* had an impact upon social policy in Britain, there is a good case for arguing that this has come principally through the Labour party, whose social policies have been influenced by research when the party was in opposition, and some of them translated into reforming action when the party was in government. This applies particularly to the period when the Labour party held power after the end of the Second World War, when the structures of the contemporary welfare state were laid down. The measures introduced then can be seen as importantly deriving from debates within the party during the inter-war period, and especially in the 1920s, when the policies subsequently implemented were developed (Marwick, 1967). Again, during their period of government in the 1960s, the Labour party can be seen as implementing a range of policies developed during their period in opposition and with a substantial input from social research. Education was a particularly prominent feature of that process, as I indicated in chapter 1. Donnison and Halsey have both given fascinating accounts which derive from this period, of the importance of a small group of social scientists, London-based and mostly with LSE connections, in the formulation of Labour's social policies (Donnison, 1978; Halsey, 1982; see also Banting, 1979).

The approach of the Labour party in developing their social policies during these periods can be characterized as social engineering (Finch, 1984, pp. 114–44). This concept implies that governments can intervene 'from the top' to change social structures and the character of social relations in substantial ways, thus bringing about changes in the nature of a society, but through peaceful and democratic (as opposed to revolutionary) means. It can of course be used in principle with the aim of creating either a more just or a more unjust society. But as far as the Labour party is concerned, the dominant goal has been greater social justice especially between social classes. Education has been seen as a key area through which this goal of greater social justice could be achieved, and this has variously meant: changes in education designed to create more just outcomes specifically in the educational system itself; changes in other social policies (child health services, family support services, urban policies, and so on) which have the long-term aim of creating more just outcomes in education; and changes in education which would produce changes in other aspects of social life. This latter aim has been characterized by Halsey as the central theme of educational discussion in the twentieth century, with its underlying question of 'whether and in what circumstances education can change society' (Halsey, 1972, p. 3).

Both the social engineering model itself, and the place which research is accorded within it, have their roots in the Fabian tradition as far as the Labour party is concerned. The reform of social and economic relationships rather than a more radical transformation of them has its origins in the Fabian theme of 'the inevitability of gradualness' (see chapter 1). The importance of research in developing reforming measures again follows the theme developed by the Webbs in particular: that objective research and expert opinion based upon it should determine the direction of policies, which would then be implemented by sensible and humane administrators.

It is important therefore to examine the Fabian model of the research-policy relationship, as a basis for understanding how certain approaches to research have come to be favoured within the social policy sphere. The Fabian model of the research-policy relationship was established in the early work of the Fabian Society, consolidated above all by the Webbs, and then continued in the establishment of the Fabian Research Department in 1912, and subsequently (after the Society was formally merged with the Labour Party in 1919) the New Fabian Research Bureau was started in 1931 by G D H and Margaret Cole (Cole, 1974).

The Fabian research tradition shares some common features with the earlier statistical survey work discussed in the previous section. In particular, the model of unproblematic 'facts' was essentially the same. Abrams argues that the Webbs were in fact the direct inheritors of this tradition — represented in the nineteenth century by the statistical societies — which relied upon the belief that facts, properly gathered, would speak for themselves (Abrams, 1968, p. 23). At the same time, there were differences. The idea that the facts themselves are politically neutral, and that the researcher is merely a technician who hands the facts over to policy-makers to do what they will with them, is replaced in the Fabian tradition with the idea that the researcher should be actively involved in promoting his or her work with those who can make use of it. Moreover, because the Fabian tradition always looked to socialism as its political inspiration, and eventually became a full part of the Labour party, Fabian researchers did not approach their work with an open mind about what it might demonstrate — rather, they had a confidence that the facts would demonstrate the need for policies of reform of a broadly socialist character. The facts would — as it were — inevitably speak with a socialist voice.

The particular characteristics of this approach to research are set out well by Margaret Cole (1974), on the basis of long experience in the tradition, working first as a researcher in the Fabian Research Department from 1917 to 1926, and subsequently as a founder member of the New Bureau. She uses the phrase 'tendentious' research to describe this approach, a category somewhere in between 'pure' research and 'propaganda'. In this 'tendentious' model, the researcher does have a view before the research begins but — unlike propagandists who only present those facts which support their own case — there is no suppression of evidence which does not support that view, even if more prominence is given to the supporting evidence. Since the Fabian position was a version of socialism, this would typically mean that researchers expected to find supporting evidence for socialist measures:

> the Fabian belief was that by *proper presentation* of actual, verifyable facts capitalism could be convicted so to speak out of its own mouth, and the necessity of socialism established. (Cole, 1974, p. 149)

This model of research, therefore, combines an approach which in some senses is partisan with a respect for evidence and a rigorous approach to collecting it. In describing her early experiences of working in the Fabian research department, Cole describes the Webbs' firm commitment to accuracy and adequate knowledge which was, she says, strictly observed (p. 162). The actual methods employed by the Webbs were discussed in chapter 1.

The Fabian tradition is also the inheritor of the Webbs' strategy of behind-the-scenes manoeuvring. As Hobsbawm puts it, the Webbs speciality was contact with actual and future policy-makers, and they moved in the highest circles of government, opposition and the civil service (Hobsbawm, 1964, pp. 251–2). For them, there was no contradiction between doing research and developing — even administering — policies, and in this sense the Webbs were the inheritors of the nineteenth-century ameliorist tradition, with its belief in the direct connection between the collection of facts and social reform (Abrams, 1968, p. 52). In fact, their efforts saw comparatively little immediate success (Hobsbawm, 1964, p. 265) and, somewhat disillusioned with their non-partisan attempts to influence policy makers, the Webbs turned increasingly to the Labour party as the vehicle through which a socialist reformist programme could be developed and implemented. Cole sees the setting up of the Fabian Research Department in 1912 as part of the change of emphasis. The Webbs decided that what was needed was:

> a Socialist body to work out afresh, by careful and detailed study, plans for the transformation of Britain into a Socialist country — plans which would in due course be implemented by a Socialist government. (Cole, 1964, p. 151)

The model of the researcher embodied in this approach is far from the concept of the technician — in this model, the researcher is the professional expert and adviser to those in power, or potentially in power. The characteristics of that model were set down clearly by the Webbs, initially in their attempts to be independent advisers to the powerful of all persuasions (Mackenzie and Mackenzie, 1977, p. 297), and subsequently within the Labour party. Once they threw in their lot unambiguously with the Labour Party, Sidney Webb in particular rapidly became, as the Mackenzies put it, the party's 'adviser-in-chief ... its intellectual leader' (p. 398). This Fabian model of the researcher as expert who provides the intellectual input into Labour policy-making in particular remained strong well into the twentieth century.

Another important feature of the Fabian model of the research-policy relationship should already be apparent from the above: the close links between research, policy and administration. The administrative perspective is a characteristic feature of the Fabian approach: that is, the researcher does not only provide an intellectual input into the formulation of policies, but may on occasion be directly involved in administering them. Again, the Webbs set down the parameters. As Bulmer puts it, their approach to research was 'severely practical': they believed that research into social institutions should be combined with active participation in their operation (Bulmer, 1982a, p. 18). Beatrice Webb did acknowledge that there are potential dangers to the quality of scientific investigation if the researcher is temporarily operating behind the scenes, but she regarded her partnership with Sidney (where one was predominantly the investigator and the other predominantly the administrator, but with cooperation on both activities) as providing the perfect balance (Webb, 1948, pp. 17–18).

Even when the researcher is not actively involved in implementing policies, it is the perspective of the administrator — perhaps more than the politician — that informs this approach. As Abrams puts it, the Webbs saw 'administrative intelligence and action as the pivot of effective policy' and characteristically their prescription for all ills was, 'government-sponsored empirical investigation to measure the problem and government machinery to deal with it' (Abrams, 1968, p. 27). The view of research as administrative intelligence, which should then be rationally and humanely put to practical application, is apparent in the report of the Haldane Committee (see chapter 2), of which Beatrice Webb was a member. The essentially administrative, rather than political, approach of the Webbs is brought out well by the Mackenzies when they write of Sidney Webb:

> trained as a civil servant, (he) was much better at writing
> briefs for policy-makers and devising administrative means of

applying them than he was at making political decisions himself.... He thought that men of intelligence and goodwill should be able to implement policies which were self-evidently sensible and with which, to his knowledge, they agreed. (Mackenzie and Mackenzie, 1977, p. 214)

The Webbs' work in the field of education provides a good illustration of the research-policy relationship which they established: careful study leading to widely-read publications which contain specific proposals for reform, lobbying of administrators and politicians, plus direct engagement in the policy-making process.

The Webbs (like early nineteenth century social investigators) saw education as part of a broader social policy strategy. Its importance for them was its key role in developing 'national efficiency', especially in fostering efficient administrators to run the country and the empire (Brennan, 1975). They were central figures in the development of education in London especially. Sidney Webb was elected to the London County Council in 1892 and soon became Chairman of its Technical Education Committee. He was actively involved in promoting substantial changes in London schools and colleges. In higher education, the Webbs' major life project was the founding of the London School of Economics, and subsequently they were involved in the reorganization of the University of London.

Thus in a variety of ways, the Webbs carried their interest in educational policies directly into the political and administrative arena. A specific example of how they did this relates to the reforms introduced in the 1902 Education Act, which created local education authorities. In 1901, Sidney Webb had published a pamphlet called *The Education Muddle and the Way Out* based upon his and Beatrice's studies of the local administration of education — a characteristic concern of theirs. In this pamphlet he argued for reforms which would create an 'administrative unity' in education, and took the view that elected local authorities were proper bodies through which this would be achieved. When the Bill which resulted in the 1902 Act was published, it proposed precisely that kind of reform but excluded London from these proposals. The Webbs were greatly displeased at this and worked very hard at having that clause struck out. They used their contacts in central and local government, they wined and dined the Prime Minister, they lobbied professional associations, they colluded with sympathetic MPs, and they tried to manipulate the climate of public opinion by writing articles in newspapers. These efforts were unsuccessful in relation to the 1902

Act but the following year the London Education Act 1903 was passed, which laid down the principle that London was to be treated in the same way as the rest of the country (Brennan, 1975, pp. 53–5).

This activity in the field of education is a successful illustration (or at least partially successful) of how the Fabian version of the research-policy relationship 'ought' to operate. In fact, many of the Webbs' other attempts to operate it were conspicuously unsuccessful, despite the fact that they represent a particularly strong version of the aspiration to feed social research into policy. This can be interpreted as indicating a weakness in their strategy which in principle could be remedied, or as an indication that their approach was fundamentally flawed, an interpretation offered by Hobsbawm (1964), who is unsympathetic to the Fabian position. He describes them as essentially a body of intellectuals, strong on public relations but basically composed of new salaried professionals for whom the enemy was not capitalism per se, but the mid-Victorian laissez-faire version of it. They established a version of socialism which subsequently became dominant and which had affiliations with government administration and the political right. They were nearly always at variance with others on the left. As for the Webbs, Hobsbawm regards them as fundamentally middle-class socialists and isolated from contact with the Labour movement. Moreover, in his view, they lacked political judgment in their dealings with Liberal politicians in particular.

A similar criticism which can be levelled at all work in the Fabian tradition takes an essentially administrative perspective. Martin Shaw argues that this development of reform-oriented social research, with its emphasis upon social researchers as expert devisers and administrators of policy based upon state-sponsored research, is itself a product of the developing capitalist and bureaucratic state, and the state's need to accumulate more subtle forms of social regulation (Shaw, 1975, pp. 28–31). Certainly the Fabian model of the research-policy relationship is essentially part of a top-down model of social reform — which in Bulmer's view — was able to flourish in its early days because of the close connections between the intelligensia and politicians in Victorian and Edwardian society (Bulmer, 1982, p. 28). Its continuation is perhaps more difficult to explain except that, as already indicated, the connections between the Labour party and sympathetic social scientists have remained close and significant at least until the very recent past. Indeed, Reynolds has drawn a specific parallel between the early Fabians and those academics involved in the sociology of education in the 1960s when he writes that in both cases they:

believed that the water of an empirical, truthful knowledge, if filtered down by intellectuals by themselves through a political conduit, would eventually succeed in wearing down the stone of ignorance that prevented the capitalist class from seeing that social reform was in the interest of *all* social classes. (Reynolds, 1980–81, p. 79)

The significance of the Webbs' model of social research and social reform for my argument here can be summarized as follows. They consolidated and promoted a version of the research-policy relationship which subsequently became very influential and in which research is fed into policy-making at the highest level and is used to formulate policies which are then implemented. The whole process is confined to a small, elite group of people and is antithetical of concepts like the democratization of knowledge and therefore of power, which were promoted by an organization like Mass-Observation (see chapter 3). The essentially administrative orientation of the Fabian model, coupled with its positivist conception of facts, meant that at the very least it was unlikely to challenge the emphasis on quantitative research established in the nineteenth century, for the same reasons which I discussed in the previous section. Despite the fact that Beatrice Webb was interested in qualitative techniques, the potential to develop them in relation to policy-oriented research was not realized, as I argued in chapter 1. Thus the Fabian version to policy-oriented research, whilst in certain ways modifying the nineteenth-century approach, nonetheless in practice consolidated the dominance of quantitative work in the twentieth century.

The Separation and the Character of Disciplines in British Social Science

My third explanation of why qualitative research has had relatively little impact upon the study of social policy concerns the particular character of disciplines — especially sociology and social administration — in British social science. Again, I shall suggest that the study of education, which is to be found within each discipline, needs to be understood in relation to the development of the discipline as a whole. I shall argue that a series of linked developments has produced a situation which has crystallized in the last twenty years, where the two disciplines have become sharply separated. When qualitative research developed subsequently in sociology, it was mostly without a policy focus, as I demonstrated in chapter 1 in relation to education. In this chapter, the reasons for and the consequences of this separation of disciplines will be explored, and I shall consider whether one can envisage a significant breaking-down of this separation. To aid that aspect of the discussion reference will be made briefly to the American situation, where a separation of this kind has not occurred.

Sociology, Social Administration and the Study of Social Policy

Although sociology and social administration are now recognizably separate disciplines with separate institutional bases in higher education (sociology being much the larger), this is a development of the period since the Second World War, consolidated by the expansion of social science within the general expansion of higher education in Britain since the 1960s. Significantly for my argument in this book, both disciplines trace their origins in a way which encompasses the work of the nineteenth-century statistical societies, the poverty studies of Booth and Rowntree and the work of the Webbs; although sociologists would add to this the rather separate traditions of nineteenth century social philosophy and the work of Marx (Abrams, 1968 and 1981; Townsend, 1981; Taylor-Gooby and Dale, 1981). The two disciplines, however, were increasingly disentangled from each other during the 1950s and 1960s, for reasons which were quite centrally to do with the kind of empirical research associated with policy-related studies. Husbands has summarized the position well in his discussion of sources of anti-quantitative bias within sociology:

> It is incontrovertible that in the 1960s empirical research, even if it claimed to be theory-based, ceased to be a high-status activity within (sociology). Its claims for policy relevance were seen as often disingenuous, or even sinister, by many of the practitioners of a discipline whom external events had made increasingly suspicious of the alleged ideological functions of much of the immediately proceeding legacy of their subject. Even empirical research whose liberal policy relevance could be much less easily gainsaid (for example in the field of education) was none the less of low status within the dominant hierarchy of values within the profession. This sort of work, it was felt, would best be left to the likes of social administrators. (Husbands, 1981, p. 97)

The linked developments to which Husbands alludes, and which I shall consider here can be specified as: (i) sociology and social administration became clearly separated as social science disciplines; (ii) the study of social policy was assigned to social administration and specifically rejected as inappropriate for sociology; (iii) sociology also rejected empirical research, defining it as a low-status activity, partly because of its association with social policy studies; (iv) social administration continued to develop principally the kind of quantitative, policy-oriented work which sociology had rejected; (v) subsequently, there was a growing interest in qualitative research within the discipline of sociology, but by this time policy-orientations had already been rejected. I shall now consider each of these developments briefly.

The institutional separation of the disciplines can be documented by the establishment of different departments in the expansion of higher education, with social administration departments frequently providing the institutional home for social work training, along the lines of the first department at the London School of Economics. A general discussion of the reasons for the institutional separation (taking into account such factors as the expansion of social work as a profession in the 1960s) is beyond the scope of my purpose here. However, it is important to note that such a development at the very least was encouraged by a growing distaste within sociology for its links with social reform, a distaste which has already apparent in the 1950s. This was noted in general terms by Simey in 1957, who saw current developments as moving away from the traditional concerns of 'problem-centred' empirical research — a change which he regretted (Simey, 1957, pp. 127–8). In the same year, but specifically in relation to education, Jean Floud confirmed the growing distaste among sociologists for dealing with questions of social policy, especially as a reaction to Mannheim, whose work has been influential in the years following the Second World War in the growth of the sub-discipline of 'education sociology' although several decades later, his influence does not appear decisive (Szreter, 1984, pp. 14–15). In 1957 however, Floud was able to note that 'more recent years have seen a growing distrust of his particular emphasis upon social engineering' (p. 172). This 'distaste' led eventually to an overt rejection of the 'political arithmetic' tradition of educational research in the 1960s — a change which is documented in chapter 1. So far as sociology in general is concerned, the rejection of a policy (especially a reformist) orientation to the discipline appeared conclusive in the 1970s; so that in 1981, Philip Abrams was able to write, on the basis of interviews which he had conducted with fifty 'fairly senior' sociologists that:

> I have not come across a single professional sociologist in Britain who now believes in the sort of direct relationship between knowledge and action which inspired the monumental labours of Booth as a serious possibility of our own contemporary social order. (pp. 60–1)

So far as most sociologists were concerned in the 1970s at least, social policy research linked in any way to social reforms was off-limits, but the discipline of social administration did not follow the same path and became effectively not only the direct but also the sole inheritor of the empirical, reformist tradition in British social science. As one commentator described it, social administration is 'the science of reformism and piecemeal social engineering, underpinned by the values of compassion and justice as well as efficiency' (Mishra, 1977, p. 5).

Thus in the decade when qualitative research was developing within British sociology (including importantly within the sociology of education: see chapter 1), the discipline had explicitly rejected policy links. It is hardly surprising, therefore, that qualitative researchers did not target their work specifically on issues of social policy in most cases. There are some exceptions, perhaps most importantly in the field of deviance, where qualitative research studies made some impact upon the policy-oriented study of criminology, and upon the training and practice of social workers, principally through developing the concept of labelling theory (Wiles, 1977). However, in the field of education, qualitative work developed within the discipline of sociology on the whole insulated from social policy concerns, as was documented in chapter 1. Part of the reason for the rejection of policy links concerned suspicion about the incorporation of social scientists into the structures of the state, so that their work is used to serve the interests of the powerful, as Husbands indicates — an issue which has also been raised more recently within social administration (George and Wilding, 1977; Taylor-Gooby, 1981). Further, within sociology, there was a substantial redefinition of the concerns of the discipline following the impact of Marxism in the late 1960s. This redefinition concentrated upon theoretical concerns (Abrams, 1981), leaving little space for empirical, policy-oriented research, and setting qualitative researchers the task of justifying their work vis-a-vis theory rather than in terms of its policy relevance. In fact, they were not notably successful in this defence, and ethnography was bracketed with other empirical work as inappropriate to a radical, theoretical discipline (Payne, Dingwall, Payne and Carter, 1981, p. 109). Finally, the challenges to the kind of positivist epistemology which is represented by the British tradition of policy-oriented research removed the intellectual basis for undertaking it and, as Abrams puts it, sociologists failed to 'work out a relationship between ourselves and the domain of public action which could satisfactorily replace the lost innocence of positivism' (1981, p. 61). That rejection of positivism particularly affected the kind of quantitative, empirical research which had always been associated with policy-related studies, introducing a strong anti-quantitative bias into British sociology (Husbands, 1981) and providing a further reason for rejecting policy-oriented work. Proponents of naturalistic and interpretivist styles of research of course were prominent among the critics of the quantitative, especially survey work (p. 92), a development which is well illustrated in the field of education, as was shown in chapter 1.

For a variety of reasons therefore, social policy was rejected as an unsuitable orientation for sociological study at precisely the time when British sociology was developing qualitative research studies, in the field of education especially; and the reasons for the rejection of a policy-orientation made it very unlikely that qualitative researchers would challenge this, if only out of self interest. As Shipman has put it in his discussion of ethnography and policy in the field of education, in research and academic careers critical challenge and demolition of other people's conceptual frameworks is the most praiseworthy activity, and critical theory-building is now a high status task even for ethnographers. Meanwhile, policy-makers want research which provides good description, stable conceptual models, and is confirmatory of other work on which policy is based — in other words, demands which are incompatible with the self-interests of sociologists defined in terms of the discipline (Shipman, 1985).

Meanwhile studies of social policy, being assigned in the academic division of labour to social administration, continued to be promoted within the context of a discipline with very different orientations, as I have already indicated. In particular, those orientations were unlikely to promote the development of qualitative work. The discipline of social administration continued to pursue its studies of social policy in ways recognizable within the traditions of statistical and survey work, with its concentration on fact-finding, and within the Fabian model of the research-policy relationship, in which gathering facts is linked to specific political or value commitments — a blend which many commentators would argue has proved effective

(Pinker, 1971; Mishra, 1977). However one explains the persistence of this model, so long as it reigned supreme in social administration, it was unlikely that there would be a substantial development of qualitative research studies within the discipline, since — as I have already argued in the earlier sections of this chapter — the traditions upon which it draws are far more hospitable to quantitative work. As Mishra puts it when discussing social administration in the 1970s:

> Given the concern with reform and intervention, it is natural that quantification of the dimensions of a problem remains central to the subject.... The tradition of piecemeal reformism within a consensual framework also encourages a strategy of exposure and publicity, of dramatic revelation of facts in order to shock public opinion out of complacency. (Mishra, 1977, pp. 15–16)

It seems clear, therefore, that the linked set of developments within social science in the late 1960s and the 1970s ensured that where qualitative research was developing, it was unlikely to be oriented towards social policy. In the mid-1980s, however, the situation looks a little different, and it seems to me that more recent developments within the disciplines have produced a situation which is much more conducive to the development of policy-oriented qualitative work. First, within social administration, the discipline has been opened up since the late 1970s most especially by the intervention of Marxism and of feminism. Marxist, and other, critics have challenged specifically the 'empiricist' orientation of the discipline (Mishra, 1977; Taylor-Gooby, 1981; Taylor-Gooby and Dale, 1981), producing a situation in which theoretical issues have become much more prominent and a discipline which now contains a more diverse range of concerns and approaches. It seems to me that this opening up of the discipline in itself creates space for promoting a different approach to research, including research which has a very different epistemological basis. Second, the discipline of sociology, in part at least under pressure from public expenditure cuts, seems to have become somewhat less hostile to social policy. This change is difficult to document, since — like the shift in the late 1960s which privileged theory over other kinds of sociology — it is a matter of partially hidden messages about what kind of work has status within a discipline. One can point, however, to pressures upon sociologists to demonstrate the 'relevance' of their work, most explicitly in the reorganization of the Social Science Research Council, which grouped all its work into committees, each of which was to pursue specific policy areas (SSRC, 1981). Third, some important recent developments in both disciplines bring a different kind of policy focus unto both. I refer here specifically to the development of feminist research and scholarship, much of which — whilst not necessarily focussing upon social policy in the narrow, conventional sense — is concerned not only with documenting what the world is like, but also in evaluating how it could be changed. This is not the Fabian model of policy research, seen from the perspective of the administrator and 'taking' the problems of government, but it is concerned with government policy in much the same sense that the work which I have placed in the 'alternative' tradition of research; that is, seeing the world from the perspective of the powerless and disadvantaged. Interestingly, many (although not all) feminists have actively promoted the merits of qualitative research as being more appropriate to their purposes (Oakley, 1981; Graham, 1983; Stanley and Wise, 1983). There is a sense therefore in which feminist research provides a possible model for the development of qualitative work on social policy issues. Feminist research is certainly a growth point within both sociology and social administration (including feminist work on education) which introduces both qualitative empirical work and a policy-orientation which, I am arguing, is a helpful development within social science, although of course it will not necessarily be readily taken up by policy-makers any more than other kinds of empirical work.

My suggestion that the situation is now more auspicious within social science disciplines for developing qualitative work on social policy depends upon an assumption that there is no incompatibility in principle between the two. Although I see some problems in pursuing such work, nonetheless I believe that in principle it is possible to envisage such a development — a view which is reinforced by consideration of the rather different situation which pertains in the United States.

The American Contrast

The development of social sciences in the United States presents a contrasting picture, which helps to illuminate some features of the academic context which appear to be more favourable to qualitative research oriented to social policy issues.

Rist (1984), writing specifically in an educational context, highlights the rather different character of policy-related research in the

United States when he argues that 'two remarkable and interrelated developments have occurred in policy research in the last ten years'; the first is the collapse of the natural science model as the pre-eminent model in policy studies; the second is the 'retreat' of quantitative methods into an intellectual cul-de-sac, leaving a vacuum which has been filled 'by a growing and vigorous interest in qualitative methods' (p. 159). In terms of the discussion being pursued in this book, there has been a shift towards qualitative research both at the level of epistemology and of techniques. Rist attributes these developments to a constellation of reasons, partly concerning the same kinds of intellectual challenges to positivism and empiricism which occurred in Britain in the same period (see previous section). But in contrast to the British situation, in the United States social scientists did not thereby abandon policy-related studies, and policy-makers also be-came dissatisfied with existing modes of research and open to alternatives. As Rist puts it, the antagonism of both practitioners and policy-makers to the 'sterile empiricism of much current research' led, inter alia, to a recognition that it is inappropriate to focus constantly on measures of policy *outcomes* when relatively little is understood about the *processes* entailed in implementing programmes (p. 161). Consequently, research of a qualitative type began to find a niche in policy-related studies, along with its 'different way of knowing — one based on experience, empathy and involvement' (p. 160).

A much fuller analysis than I am able to offer here would be necessary to properly account for these developments. But I am using the American contrast for two reasons. First, it demonstrates by example that there is no necessary incompatibility between qualitative research and studies related to social policy. Second, it offers an opportunity to consider what made American soil more fertile for these developments than British.

I shall suggest briefly three reasons why American soil was more fertile, concentrating on the development of academic disciplines rather than the wider social and political context of social research. The first reason is — as it were — a negative one. The separation of the disciplines of sociology and social administration has no direct parallel in the United States. Indeed, the intellectual and research tradition upon which social administration is based — the inheritance of the great poverty studies and of the Fabian society — is very much a British tradition. Work of this type did make some impact in the United States at the turn of the century, but it quickly diverged from academic sociology (Faris, 1970, p. 7). Therefore, where developments in policy-oriented social research have taken place, this has been under the general disciplinary framework of sociology or of a multi-disciplinary 'area', such as education, but not within a hostile discipline.

Second, and running to some extent in parallel with developments in sociology, the United States has a tradition of applied anthropology which has had no real equivalent in Britain, and which — in the field of education — has produced qualitative, ethnographic work with something much closer to a policy focus than in the British case (Wilcox, 1982; Fetterman, 1984). The comparison between the two traditions of ethnographic work in education has been reviewed and discussed by Delamont and Atkinson (1980), who argue that British educational ethnography principally draws upon sociology as its frame of reference, whereas in the United States, educational ethnography has more often defined itself as part of anthropology, and has been more clearly an 'applied' discipline than has the British equivalent. Indeed, when ethnographic work took root in Britain, most researchers looked to American sociology for their models, and not to British anthropology (Payne, Dingwall, Payne and Carter, 1981, p. 95). An exception to that general rule is the development of applied anthropological work on British society in the 1960s under Max Gluckman in Manchester (Frankenberg, 1982). Some important examples of this work have been in the field of education, especially the studies of Hargreaves (1967), Lacey (1970) and Lambart (1976) (see chapters 1 and 8 for further discussion). On the whole, however, mainstream anthropological work in Britain has continued to define its focus as the study of non-British societies (Kuper, 1983, pp. 188–90).

In the United States, the existence of a different style of anthropology which legitimated studies of one's own society with an applied focus, has been more conducive to the development of policy-oriented, qualitative research. The subject-matter of the educational studies reviewed by Delamont and Atkinson (1980) is substantially concentrated on 'problem groups', that is 'groups who are a "problem" in educational terms because they are seen to be "failing"', which in the US context usually means ethnic minorities (pp. 143–4). Although such studies do not necessarily amount to research which is intended to produce a list of policy recommendations in any straightforward way, their choice of topic and the way it is pursued and written up are clearly related to policy issues in the broader sense. The existence of work which is defined as applied anthropology in the United States has therefore provided a source of support for policy-oriented qualitative work separate from the discipline of sociology.

Third, the development of empirical research within American sociology has a rather different history than its British equivalent, which has made it both more varied and more theoretically sophisticated at an earlier date. From the point of view of policy-related studies, this has meant that it has not been so comprehensively dominated by a crude empiricist conception of 'the facts', although American sociology certainly went through a period in the 1940s and 1950s where this model achieved substantial dominance, as is evidenced by C Wright Mills' famous attack upon it in his discussion of 'abstracted empiricism' (Mills, 1959). However, the earlier and separate research tradition associated with the University of Chicago meant that American social science encompassed from an early stage an understanding of social research which was qualitative in orientation and characteristically concerned with aspects of social life which constitute the terrain of social policy.

The University of Chicago established the first sociology department in the world in 1892. This meant that the discipline was institutionalized in the university sector much earlier in America than in Britain and as a consequence, as Bulmer has argued, empirical research was brought much more quickly into contact with theoretical ideas, with the urban studies of the 1920s being a high point. At that time,

> 'much empirical research was carried out which fitted a more general theory or urban structure, despite being very matter-of-fact in its character. Such an intellectual nurturing was absent in Britain'. (Bulmer, 1982a, p. 28)

Other commentators attribute the consolidation of research as central to the sociological enterprise in the Chicago department to the initial enthusiasm of Albion Small, who founded the department, and subsequently to the lengthy influence of Robert Park, who defined research in a specific way, based upon active investigation, with students being urged to constantly observe, record and organize their observations, that is to draw on their own experience and to understand it systematically (Faris, 1970, p. 129; Payne, Dingwall, Payne and Carter, 1981, pp. 98–101). This department — as is well known — has made a major contribution to the development of empirical research using qualitative techniques, not only observation (although this was used extensively) but also life history studies and documentary analysis, following the pioneering work of Thomas and

Znaniecki's (1918–20) study of the Polish peasant in Europe and America, based on autobiographical materials, letters, newspaper files and institutional records (Bulmer, 1984, pp. 90–3). In its early days, it built specifically upon anthropology and, although a separate department of anthropology was established in 1924, as Faris says (writing as an insider) the habit of both reading and using ethnographic materials was never lost (Faris, 1970, p. 16). Further, this department not only nurtured ethnographic methods of study, but it also produced some of the most important contributors at a theoretical level to the development of the perspective known as symbolic interactionism, which is adopted by many who pursue qualitative research (Rock, 1979; Kurtz, 1984). In ethnographic studies of education in Britain, this perspective has been particularly important (Woods, 1983; and see Introduction for discussion). G H Mead, who provided the social psychological underpinnings of this theoretical position taught in the department as did W I Thomas, whose development of concepts such as the definition of the situation has been especially important. As Faris makes clear, Thomas was developing these ideas specifically in relation to issues raised by empirical research:

> To scholars who were troubled by the problem of whether personal statements could be of use in science in view of the unsolved question of the truth or reality of such statements, Thomas provided the dictum, 'If men define situations as real, they are real in their consequences'. (Faris, 1970, p. 18)

The Chicago department was therefore central to the development of qualitative work, both at the methodological and the theoretical level, although it also encompassed an interest in quantification (Bulmer, 1981 and 1985). But what of its relationship to social policy and welfare? Albion Small, who was the founding Professor in the department, is on record as seeing very clear links between ethnography and social reform, especially in the education of students. He believed that in educating undergraduates one is training citizens and that an education in sociology — that is, training in empirical research based on observational methods — would produce citizens who were politically aware. This experience was likely to make students into reformist citizens because 'it instructs students in the complexities of the social process, complexities which utopians, and amateurs and agitators, leave out of view' (Dibble, 1975, p. 34).

These perceived links between ethnography and social reform

were not applied in a direct way, however, and the Chicago department as a whole did not straightforwardly espouse social policy studies. Indeed, they rejected a directly reformist approach to social science of the kind that developed in Britain; that is, they rejected the direct link between knowledge creation and social change. But at the same time, the kind of work which they developed did characteristically have a 'social problem' focus of a much more sophisticated type (Hughes, 1960, p. vii). The studies in the Chicago locality, developed on the basis of concepts of social disorganization formulated by Park and Burgess, concentrated precisely on social groups and social actions which are commonly the focus of social policy: delinquency, crime, suicide, family disorganization, mental illness. As Bulmer argues, these researchers engaged directly with the social circumstances in which they lived, and saw themselves using the city of Chicago as a sociological laboratory (Bulmer, 1984, pp. 92–3). Their approach to their studies was not as social problems to which they wanted to find solutions, but as social phenomena which they wished to understand as a product of both personal and social disorganization. In so doing, the work which they produced had direct policy implications but not of a kind which could be straightforwardly applied within the dominant political framework. Rather these studies, by their very nature, challenge dominant conceptions incorporated in social policies, because they are committed to reflecting a view of the world as the participants see it — the 'view from below' which has formed much more of a minority tradition in social policy studies in Britain (see chapter 3).

The development of Chicago sociology represents an American tradition which has not only stimulated empirical research of a qualitative kind, but which also has long pursued a kind of policy-oriented work which is much closer to the 'alternative' than to the 'dominant' tradition in Britain. Indeed, Mass-Observation did specifically try to emulate it (Stanley, 1981). I am suggesting that when one puts this long-standing approach to research within sociology alongside the rather different division of labour between the academic disciplines of sociology, anthropology and social policy which has developed in the United States, one can begin to see why American soil has proved more fertile than British in nurturing qualitative research with a policy focus. At the same time, the prospect of greater cross-fertilization between disciplines in Britain — perhaps even a blurring of the boundaries between them — will place British social science in a situation more analogous to its U.S. counterpart, thus giving some grounds for optimism about the future development of qualitative, policy-oriented social research.

In conclusion, I shall not attempt to summarize the range of answers which I have suggested to the question: why has qualitative research had little impact on social policy in Britain? I have suggested three sets of reasons, each of which is rooted in a different historical period, but I would not claim that this is necessarily an exhaustive account. I hope however, that the material presented here does make the limited impact of qualitative research understandable given specific historical circumstances, whilst at the same time demonstrating that it is not inevitable that its under-use should continue. On this basis, Part II of this book moves on to consider how the under-used potential of qualitative methods can be developed in relation to policy-oriented research.

Part II

6   Models of Policy-making and The Research Input

In this second part of the book, there is a shift of focus away from the use of different types of research in the past and towards a discussion of the potential in the present and the future for the development of qualitative research concerned with educational and social policy issues.

This chapter focusses specifically upon different models of the policy-making process, and their implications for the input of research. Previous chapters have explored this issue historically in relation to Britain, and emphasis has been placed upon the concept of fact-finding and upon the Fabian model of the research-policy relationship. My purpose in this chapter is to consider that relationship not so much as an historical phenomenon (although I shall draw upon previous chapters) but to consider in principle the questions: on what basis can we expect to feed research into policy? At what points of the policy-making process is research likely to make an impact? To pursue those questions, it is necessary to consider some contemporary evidence about the actual use of research, and also about the nature of the policy-making process itself. In the course of this discussion, the question of what methods are appropriate will necessarily be raised, but these are taken up in more detail in subsequent chapters. This chapter therefore sets the context for subsequent discussion, where the use of qualitative methods specifically is addressed.

Research Potential: Unused and Underused?

Faith in the utility of social research in policy-making has been an important theme in the past in Britain, as I indicated in earlier chapters. Indeed, all the work which I have placed within the 'dominant' tradition of policy-related research demonstrated faith in a rather straightforward and rationalist model of research input to policy, where empirical data can be fed in at appropriate stages to guide the course of policy-making: to document the existing state of affairs, to assess the feasibility of alternative outcomes, and to design the mechanisms for bringing about change (Platt, 1972, p. 78). The reports on education which I discussed in chapter 2 represent that kind of aspiration.

This dominant tradition of course implies that the use of research necessarily improves policy-making and that an increase in its use is always desirable — a position which was challenged specifically in the 1960s and 1970s, both in sociology generally and within the field of education in particular (see chapter 1 and chapter 5). The grounds of that challenge concern the use of research in supporting and legitimating the political status quo, but there are also other grounds for rejecting a naive enthusiasm for the use of research in all possible circumstances. As Weiss and Bucuvalas argue, emphasis on the use of research can direct attention away from central policy issues which research cannot deal with into more marginal areas which it can; further, the effect can be to centralize power at the point where research is available and used (1980, p. 1). The well-known use of research as a delaying tactic, where governments do not wish to take any decision, is another obvious example where increased use of research should not necessarily by welcomed (Merton, 1973, p. 80).

These reservations, however, have not been significantly reflected in the dominant tradition of policy-oriented research, with its enthusiasm for the utility of research. Accordingly, disappointment is expressed when evidence comes to light that rather little research is actually directly used in policy-making. Even where research is specifically designed to influence the course of policy, and where researchers are careful to cultivate contacts with the powerful, it is difficult to find evidence of the utilization of findings and recommendations on a scale which comes anywhere near to matching the amount of such work produced (Payne, Dingwall, Payne and Carter, 1981, p. 148).

The work of the Webbs is the prime illustration of the failure of policy-oriented research to make a direct impact on central government policy, as I noted in chapter 5, although dissatisfaction with the lack of use of research has continued to be a theme, both in Britain and elsewhere. Wagenaar, writing in 1982 and reviewing developments internationally over the previous decade in the impact of social science research, was prepared to describe the situation as a 'crisis' in which there has been disillusionment among all parties both about the content of research and about its use (Wagenaar, 1982, p. 23). More recently still, and specifically in relation to education, Sir James Hamilton, former Permanent Secretary at the Department of Education and Science, speaking as the President of the National Foundation for Educational Research, described the impact of research on policy over the previous decade as 'pathetically small', despite the advances in both the quality and the quantity of educational research during the period (reported in the *Times Higher Education Supplement*, 7 December 1984). The disappointment felt by researchers that their work is usually ignored seems to be mirrored by a dissatisfaction on the part of policy-makers with the usefulness produced. Lord Rothschild, in his report on the SSRC (see chapter 2) noted that the reputation of social sciences stood fairly low with policy-makers (Rothschild, 1982, paragraph 4.11). In relation to education specifically, there is some evidence that this disillusionment stems from what Husen calls the 'golden years' of educational research in both Europe and the United States: the 1960s and early 1970s. Hopes were raised perhaps unrealistically high about what educational research could achieve in relation to social policy and social reform, and when those hopes were not realized, disillusionment and disenchantment set in on all sides (Nisbet and Broadfoot, 1980, pp. 2–3; Husen, 1984).

Apart from instances of unrealistic expectations, how can the apparent underuse of policy-oriented research be explained? Accounts offered by writers on the topic fall broadly into two kinds of explanation: those which concentrate upon the differences between researchers and policy-makers and between the worlds in which they operate; and those which concentrate upon the intrinsic character of the research process and research findings.

First, there is an explanation which highlights organizational gaps; that is, differences in the way in which research and policy are organized, such differences making utilization of research unlikely. One obvious example is that the timescale of research is frequently much longer than policy-makers are prepared to wait before coming to a decision (Weiss and Bucuvalas, 1980, pp. 17–21). A classic educational example is the question of whether pre-schooling ultimately makes a difference to children's educational performance and life chances: an issue which necessarily requires longitudinal study over a twenty-year period if research is to be used to settle the question authoritatively. Research questions of this kind are almost bound to require a longer period of study than the dictates of the policy-making timetable will allow. In consequence, the methods employed may be dictated by a fore-shortened timescale rather than by the research questions, and are therefore very likely to favour the cross-sectional survey rather than more detailed, ethnographic methods, especially if a longitudinal element is essential to the latter. Commissioned research and evaluation is especially likely to be constrained by the timescale of decision-making, and therefore it is not surprising that — as I indicated in chapter 2 — the kind of research commissioned for major official educational enquiries in Britain has focussed on the outcomes of the education system (which are amenable to cross-sectional analysis) rather than the processes which produces those outcomes (which usually is not) (Blume, 1979, pp. 318–20). Indeed there is evidence that, at least in the case of the Plowden Report, the research programme had already been set up even before the Committee had set about defining the questions which it needed to answer (Acland, 1980). These questions of time-scale are therefore bound in a sense to make the input of research to policy a very hit-and-miss affair, with only a proportion of research undertaken actually able properly to address the issues which policy-makers need to consider.

Another different kind of organizational gap concerns the relative status of the researcher and the policy-maker. This varies, of course, in different circumstances, but certainly in relation to central government policy, researchers are likely to be relatively low-status in relation to those whom they wish to influence. Or, to put the same point in a different way: it is not simply the nature of the research findings, but also whose name is attached to them, which is likely to have some bearing upon whether they are taken up. This is partly but not solely a matter of status within the academic hierarchy. It also concerns influence within specific circles. As I noted in chapter 5, there is evidence that the most important occasions upon which social scientists have influenced the course of social policy in Britain came about through the personal connections between an LSE-based group of academics and the Labour party at a high level (Donnison, 1978). The influence of A H Halsey on the development of the Educational Priority Area programme is an important example of this, which I discuss later in this chapter. In relation to the group whom Donnison discusses not only were the academics people of appropriate status, they also shared the political views of those whom they advised: a coincidence of interests which is not always present, and which sometimes opens up another kind of organizational gap, where research is rejected because of the political commitments of the researchers, or because policy-makers simply rule out certain courses of action, or because researchers simply cannot get near enough to the real locus of power in the policy-making process (Merton, 1973, p. 93; Rossi, 1980, p. 897). Further evidence of the great significance of pre-existing personal contacts between researchers and powerful individuals in the policy-making process is provided by Patricia Thomas (1983) on the basis of her small study of twelve British projects funded by SSRC or charitable foundations. Of these, four had 'brushed shoulders with the policy-making process', and in all four cases the researchers were personally known to senior officials or their Ministers. On this level at least, the Webbs seem to have got the strategy right (see chapter 5).

The second kind of explanation for the underuse of policy-oriented research sees the gap between researchers and policy-makers in cultural rather than organizational terms. This is the 'two communities' thesis, which holds that policy-makers and social scientists live in different worlds conceptually as well as spatially, and cannot communicate with each other very easily. Husen (1984, pp. 8–12) discusses this argument in relation to educational policy, suggesting that researchers, especially those who work in universities or research institutes are oriented to valuing research for its own sake, to the independence and autonomy of the researcher, and to judging research products for their intrinsic qualities rather than their utility. By contrast policy-makers, at whatever level of educational administration, see research almost entirely in instrumental terms; that is, in terms of its usefulness for planning how many school places are needed in a given locality, whether curriculum content should be changed, or whatever.

Expressed in more general terms, the idea that the two groups 'speak different languages' is common, although frequently not spelled out. Caplan and his colleagues, however, subjected this explanation and others to empirical test, in a study of policy-makers in the United States federal government, and found the 'two communities' theory to be the most plausible. They concluded that the relative under-utilization of research findings is largely a consequence of 'differences in values, language, reward systems, and social and professional affiliations', as well as simple mistrust (Caplan, Morrison and Stambaugh, 1975, p. 27).

These first two explanations imply that there are gaps which are unfortunate but explicable and in principle one could imagine how they might be bridged. The third explanation, whilst also formulated in terms of differences between the worlds of the researcher and the policy-maker, implies that the gap could not necessarily ever by bridged. This is the explanation which holds that policy-makers and researchers have different sets of interests and concerns in relation to any research project. 'Interests' means here not so much that their intellectual predilections differ but that their approach to the use of research findings reflect the material interests of their own position in the social order. This rather challenges the view implied above that research utilization could be improved simply by better communication. Joan Higgins puts the point graphically in her discussion of the poverty 'demonstration' projects in Britain and the United States in the 1960s and 1970s, including the British EPA projects. Lack of effective mechanisms for communicating the results of research was a problem in these projects, but this was not accidental in Higgins' view, since the fundamental wish to eradicate poverty was missing from governments concerned, and therefore they had no real interest in research which indicated *how* that could be done (Higgins, 1978, p. 141). The interests of the two groups were diametrically opposed in this instance.

This account of different interests, it seems to me, offers the most convincing account of the gap between researchers and policy-makers. The question of the time-scale of research, for example, is not simply a matter of how governmental bureaucracies happen to be organized, but also of the imperatives which derive from the real situation in which decisions are made, and which may indicate that it is politically dangerous to delay. The pragmatic response on the part of researchers is to recognize that sets of interests *are* different, and to try to work within the constraints imposed. Thus, for example, one should not be shocked to find that policy-makers want to use one's research not because of its great intellectual contribution, but because it legitimates something which they were going to do anyway. For example, the Robbins Committee on higher education in Britain, which commissioned extensive quantitative research (see chapter 2), used research data to support the case for the expansion of higher education, when this policy had in practice already been accepted within government (Silver, 1980, p. 127). Again, research may be used because it makes actions look as if they are planned rationally when actually they are not, or because a smokescreen is needed to deflect public attention from the most contentious issues. All of these have been identified as uses of research (Merton, 1973; Higgins, 1978, pp. 132–3). Equally, researchers ought not to assume that policy-makers share their own basic commitments. MacDonald and Norris make this point forcibly in their discussion of educational evaluation based on fieldwork, in which they argue that it is naive in the extreme to adopt the assumption that many researchers hold, namely that people involved in government are essentially liberals like themselves, who want research because they see informed executive and legislative action as the key to creating greater social justice (MacDonald and Norris, 1981, pp. 277–8). The implication of this pragmatic response is that one goes into policy-related research — if one goes in at all — with caution and cynicism, and looking for ways to turn an essentially hostile situation to some nobler purpose.

The alternative response is to openly challenge the subordination of research to the interests of policy-makers. This response perhaps itself sounds somewhat naive, but it has been interestingly reflected in the views of official commentators. Certain government reports on research in Britain (see chapter 2)have explicitly endorsed the value of research even when it does not accord with the interests of government, as defined from within. The so-called Haldane Principle indicated that there should be a government research department separate from other ministries precisely because this is the only way to ensure that the results of research could be properly assessed and used: when research is located in separate ministries, decisions about its use are always subordinated to administrative interests (Haldane Committee, 1919). Something of the same desire to ensure that administrative and political considerations are not always paramount is apparent in Lord Rothschild's report on the SSRC, in which he acknowledges that, although ministers cannot be expected to fund research which is likely to be highly critical of their departments, governments do more generally have a duty to sponsor social science research which challenges prevailing orthodoxies (Rothschild, 1982; and see chapter 2 for further discussion). There is a sense therefore in which the relationship between the researcher and policy-maker *ought* to be characterized by conflict rather than consensus in a democratic society (Rein, 1976, p. 116). This case has been made strongly by Sir Douglas Wass, a former senior British civil servant, in one of his Reith Lectures, when he argued that it is essential for democracy that government themselves should not be the only (or even the primary) source of information and analysis on policy-related topics, and that independent research makes an important contribution to the democratic process (Wass, 1982). A contemporary educational example of that point can be found in research studies of the various youth training programmes introduced by central government since the mid-1970s, each of which can be shown to diverge substantially in practice from the claims made by government (Rees and Atkinson, 1982; Gleeson, 1983). I shall return to this example in chapter 8.

All three explanations considered so far for the underutilization of research have concerned the apparently different worlds of the researcher and the policy-maker. I shall now briefly consider two further explanations, both of which are concerned with the nature of social science research itself.

A number of writers have suggested that the nature of social science knowledge makes it not actually very useful to policy-makers. Essentially, this amounts to the argument that social science knowledge is necessarily imprecise, inconclusive and complex, whereas policy-makers can only use knowledge if it is precise, gives clear guidance, and is formulated in sufficiently simple terms to be directly applied. Merton, for example, emphasizes the problems caused for policy-makers by the essential indeterminacy of social scientists' findings, and Lindblom and Cohen highlight the fact that conclusions are seldom authoritative or even conclusive (Merton, 1957; Lindblom and Cohen, 1979). This can be problematic even when research is closely allied to policy, as it was for example in the British EPA action-research projects (see chapter 3). Halsey's own conclusion from that experience was that:

> Action-research is unlikely ever to yield near and definitive prescriptions from field-tested plans. What it offers is an aid to intelligent decision-making, not a substitute for it. Research brings relevant information rather than uniquely exclusive conclusions. (Department of Education and Science, 1972, p. 179)

Rist, in making a case for qualitative methods in educational evaluations commissioned by policy-makers, argues that the conventional concentration upon quantitative methods itself has led to misunderstanding of the nature of social science knowledge. It offers, as he puts it, 'artificially created "clean" data in a complex and messy world' (Rist, 1981a, p. 39). Thus Rist, whilst accepting what other writers say about the indeterminate nature of social science knowledge, turns this round into an argument in favour of using qualitative methods in educational evaluations because they can reflect the complexity of social reality — a point to which I shall return in chapter 7.

A final explanation for the underuse of research is offered by Cohen and Weiss. This is not so much on the knowledge produced by social scientists, as the nature of the research process itself. Writing in relation to the issue of schools and race in the United States, they argue that it is unrealistic to expect that an expansion of social policy research is likely to produce a more direct and effective input to policy-making. If anything, the reverse is more likely. The aspiration of social scientists and policy-makers is that, as research multiplies, knowledge will converge, and will produce authoritative and cumulative findings, but in fact the opposite happens. As research on social policy matures, they argue, the terms of the problem tend to shift, the angles of vision multiply, and advances in research methods increase divergence in the treatment of evidence: 'the net result is a more varied picture of reality, but such results do not lend themselves to straightforward policy guidance' (Cohen and Weiss, 1977, p. 89). To expect more than that, they argue, is to misunderstand the research process, and the pluralistic and divergent character of social policy research (p. 91).

The argument presented by Cohen and Weiss seems to me to present an accurate picture of the research process, and added to the argument about the different interests of researchers and policy-makers it leads to conclusions which are relatively pessimistic from the perspective of those who want to foster the direct utilization of research. Looked at more positively, however, this analysis suggests, rather than abandoning the exercise, we may need to redefine the parameters of the possible relationship between these parties, finally abandoning the aspirations of the dominant paradigm. The terms upon which such a re-definition should occur are suggested by some empirical studies of the research input to policy, conducted in the United States.

Evidence About the Use of Research

American researchers have undertaken large-scale studies on the use of social science by policy-makers, of a kind which have not really been replicated in Britain. One needs to be somewhat cautious about using evidence from one country to interpret the situation in another since it is clear that the contexts do differ significantly in this instance: the involvement of social scientists in policy-making has been more extensive in the United States, a phenomenon which Sharpe attributes to the different structure of government and their associated bureaucracies in the two countries (Sharpe, 1978). Substantial cuts in funding for social science in President Reagan's term of office have of course changed that situation somewhat (McCartney, 1984). Nonetheless, it is useful to consider this comparative evidence, because it suggests how research is likely to be used in a situation which is somewhat more open to it, and also the likely points of resistance.

Rein has distinguished between three different ways of finding out about the relationship between social science knowledge and governmental action, all of which have been used in American studies: first, studies of usability, which focus upon what knowledge policy-makers believe to be useful; second, studies of direct use, which implies in-depth study of officials in a specific policy area, to find out what actual use they have made of research findings; and third, studies which focus on the diffusion of knowledge, which take a longer timescale, and which try to trace the use of social science knowledge to its use at different times and in different settings from where it was initially generated (Rein, 1980). I do not intend to discuss such studies in detail, but to highlight some of the findings which bear upon questions of how we can realistically expect research to be used. These findings are interesting, because they do to an extent challenge received wisdom about the use of research, and certainly shed a different light on discussions of its underuse, considered in the previous section.

First, there is the question of the political process, and the argument that research use will always be subordinated to political considerations, by both politicians and officials. There is evidence from the study by Caplan, Morrison and Stambough (1975) that this is indeed the case. This study covered 204 senior policy-makers in the United States federal government, which confirmed that the political implications of research findings will override all other considerations about their use, and that most policy-makers think that social scientists are naive about this issue (p. 49). On the other hand, in more general terms, these policy-makers showed a clear willingness to use research within those specific constraints (p. 26). In another study by Weiss and Bucuvalas (1980) concentrated on decision-makers in the mental health field, and the researchers found a willingness to use research which challenges rather than confirms prevailing views, and to use research in situations which are politically controversial — presumably as a weapon to be wielded in favour of one specific course of action. The major consideration to the policy-makers was not whether the research findings accorded with their own views, but the quality of the research itself, as they perceived it (pp. 87–91).

Second, it is not at all clear that the only kind of research which policy-makers are interested in is quantified and apparently objective facts. In the study by Caplan *et al.*, it certainly was the case that the kind of research methods used in studies seen as most useful were predominantly of a quantitative type: survey research, demography and social statistics accounted together for 41 per cent of studies regarded as particularly useful, and studies based on participant observation, by contrast, accounted for only 4 per cent (Caplan, Morrison and Stambaugh, 1975, p. 11). However, when asked to identify the social science disciplines regarded as most frequently found useful, sociology ranked the highest 'largely because respondents associated (it with) higher amounts of conceptual, but less specific, knowledge' (p. 10). These results must be used cautiously, since, as I have already indicated, policy-oriented research is more varied in the United States than in Britain (chapter 4). However, it is interesting to note that American policy-makers do appear to value policy-oriented work which focusses upon concepts and not just upon facts.

Third, this conclusion is further supported by evidence from a number of studies which suggest that we ought to expect research to be used in a diffuse, not a direct way in most cases. In the study by Weiss and Bucuvalas, two-thirds of policy-makers interviewed said that they definitely had made use of social science research. However, most of them were not able to give specific examples of its usage, but simply to state in general terms that they had been influenced by it (Weiss and Bucuvalas, 1980, p. 154). This finding indicates just how important it is to uncover whether a specific piece of research actually has been used, rather than, for example, simply to assume its use because a policy has been developed which is consonant with the research findings. Premfors has given a very good illustration of that in relation to higher education policy in Sweden, where there has been a history of close liaison between researchers and policy-makers. That, however, is not in itself evidence that research as such has made an independent impact. As Premfors puts it:

> I have observed no *major* instances of policy change where research made the difference, or instances where similar, if not identical, policy measures could not or would not have been taken in the absence of research. (Premfors, 1984, p. 237)

The example of Swedish higher education policy is a single, if very significant, illustration of the importance of Weiss and Bucuvalas' finding that, whilst research was thought generally to be useful, policy-makers were unable to cite concrete examples of its use. Rather its influence was much more diffuse and non-specific. The type of use which respondents in this study cited was: general guidance rather than specific input into individuals' decisions and orienting one's perspectives when moving into a new policy area. That conclusion is also supported by a small study of the impact of educational research in Britain conducted by Nisbet and Broadfoot, where they interviewed nineteen 'leading researchers' who have written on research policy and administrators who were 'well placed to express views'. Their conclusion was that research is most likely to make an impact on policy in an indirect way, by 'creating an agenda of concern' (Nisbet and Broadfoot, 1980, p. 49).

Weiss and Bucuvalas, on the basis of their study, conclude that research is rarely used instrumentally in individual decisions, but it *is* used in these diffuse and general ways much more widely than many writers on the topic have supposed (pp. 167–8). This finding is clearly supported by the Caplan *et al.*, study, where the researchers found it very difficult to trace specific effects of research on policies; but looked at in more general terms, they found many more examples of research being influential than most people suppose (Caplan, Morrison and Stambaugh, 1975, p. 46). The finding that social science knowledge affects policy-makers in a diffuse rather than a direct way was further confirmed in this study by the fact that the most frequently cited *source* of useful knowledge was newspapers (p. 12). The authors comment in fact that policy-makers do seem to use research rather like the news, as a way of keeping up with professionals and the informed public in their awareness of dominant concerns in their own policy areas. This means that they are eclectic in their use of sources, assimilate such evidence as they deem relevant, and may well not put it to immediate use (p. 190). As Weiss puts it, reviewing a number of studies of research utilization, it appears that 'ideas from research filter through (and) officials test them against their own standards of judgement. . . . If it "makes sense", if it helps them to organise . . . their earlier knowledge, and impressions, they tend to incorporate it into their stock of knowledge' (Weiss, 1982, p. 291). The effect of this, as Weiss points out, is that social science is merged with other kinds of knowledge, and that officials may actually not be aware that they are using it.

The picture which emerges from these studies, then, suggests that social scientists who have wanted their policy-oriented research to be used by policy-makers have in a sense been unnecessarily discouraged. Direct use of findings is certainly very limited, but concentrating upon that rather obscures patterns of usage which do occur. In failing to appreciate the diffuse ways in which research findings do filter into policy-making processes, social scientists have tended to misunderstand the influence that their work can have (Weiss and Bucuvalas, 1980, chapter 11). It also means that the timescale over which one should look for such an impact should be much longer, since the most significant effect of research is likely to be a modification of conceptual framework, rather than the direct application of findings (Rein, 1976, pp. 111–23). This pushes us towards a very different model of the research-policy relationship from that represented in the dominant British paradigm, and a redefinition of the relationship along the lines indicated is further supported by considering the nature of the policy-making process itself.

Models of Policy-Making and the Research Input

The dominant tradition of research-policy relationship reviewed in earlier chapters embodies a simple and straightforward notion of both the policy-making process itself and of the potential input of research. The ameliorist tradition, for example, was interested in research only insofar as it could be of direct practical use in bringing about social change, and the Webbs' position, although somewhat more sophisticated, still emphasized the direct utility of research in formulating measures for social reform, and the capacity of researchers to promote these directly with politicians (see chapter 5). This dominant tradition represents a version of what Weiss has called the 'knowledge-driven' and the 'problem-solving' models of research utilization: in the former case, based on the natural science analogy, the sheer fact that knowledge exists compels its use; in the latter, research provides specific information which is used to solve some discrete policy problems (Weiss, 1979).

I have already suggested that these models do not accord with available evidence about how social science research is actually used. They also misunderstand the nature of the policy-making process itself. The key contrast here is between 'rationalist' and 'incremental-ist' models of policy-making (Blume, 1979; Wagenaar, 1982; Rist, 1984). The rationalist model of policy-making sees it as a series of discrete events, where each issue to be decided is clearly defined, and decisions are taken by a specific set of actors who choose between well-defined alternatives, after weighing evidence about the likely outcome of each. This model has been challenged by Lindblom (1968) who argues that policy-making is in fact an incremental not a rational process and moreover one which is quite disjointed. His analysis has been widely taken up by writers on research utilization. Weiss argues that each component of the rationalist model can be challenged and that 'Policies, even policies of fateful magnitude, often taken place by jumbled and diffuse processes that differ in vital ways from conventional imagery' (Weiss, 1982, p. 295). The incrementalist model emphasizes that there are seldom specific 'decisions' taken by a clearly defined set of actors choosing between alternatives. Rather 'policies' are shaped by previous actions taken by a range of people, which have the effect of closing off certain options and encouraging others in ways which are not apparent to the actors. Another way of expressing the same point is to contrast the concept of 'decision-making' with 'policy-making'. The former implies that discrete decisions are taken and can be identified, whilst the concept of 'policy-making' can cover a longer-term process, in which change occurs cumulatively through a series of small-scale decisions. Examples which could be cited in relation to educational policy-making in Britain derive from the fact that education is a locally-provided service in Britain, so that policy change can develop gradually and separately in different local education authorities. Even major policy changes have developed in this way. The comprehensive reform of secondary education, for example, was not a policy that was 'made' by a group of people in the Ministry of Education at a single point in time, but was part of a process which included long-standing debates within the Labour party, the actions of several different governments and experiments within separate local authorities (James, 1980). The most obvious single 'act' of policy-making, the issuing of Circular 10/65, was only one event in a much more complex process which had begun long before in a number of different places, and continued long afterwards.

The difference between the rationalist and incrementalist models of policy-making is important in relation to research, since each model implies a somewhat different type of research input. The rationalist model implies that research provides knowledge which can be fed in at a single point and will be considered in a series of logical steps by a 'decision-maker'. There is a strong case for suggesting that social scientists will continue to be disappointed about the use of their research if they continue to operate on that model (Cherns, 1979; Lindblom and Cohen, 1979). The model of research input implied by the rationalist concept of decision-making is a linear one. Interestingly, this appears to be the model which some of the key official reports on social science were assuming. The Haldane and Clapham Reports both appear to have assumed this linear relationship, in which research findings lead to policy formulation directly. However the Heyworth Report departed from this, by accepting that policy issues do not usually present themselves in such a way as to show clearly how social scientists could make a direct input (see chapter 2 for further discussion).

The linear conception of the research input to policy has been challenged by a number of writers (Lindblom and Cohen, 1979; Rein, 1980; Wagenaar, 1980; Weiss, 1982). Most of them point to the evidence of studies of research utilization which demonstrates that in practice the input of research is diffused, not linear. The alternative, 'diffuse' model therefore emphasizes that the potential for research input comes at many different points in the policy process; that there are different parties to the policy-making process (most obviously making a distinction between officials and politicians) and that they may be differently influenced by research; that the impact of research is more likely to be indirect than direct and to be effective in a range of policy areas, not only where it were originally targetted.

The point about linear and diffuse models can be further reinforced by considering the experience of the British EPA projects. The concept of the Educational Priority Area entered educational policy throughout the Plowden Report, and was subsequently implemented in a modest way, with associated action-research projects encouraging and monitoring developments (see chapter 2). In the end, however, this policy made relatively little impact on policy and provision in the longer term because — as Banting puts it — it was always an idea looking for, but ultimately failing to find, a major political constituency (Banting, 1979, pp. 116–22). The 'idea' had in fact originated with social scientists, in particular with the influential group associated with the Labour party in the 1960s, especially Donnison and Young who were both on the Plowden Committee, and Halsey who directed the EPA research projects. All three had access to both politicians and officials at a high level, and actively promoted their ideas in those circles. The circumstances were therefore exceptionally favourable for social science knowledge to be translated directly into policy but — like the Webbs before them — these contemporary Fabian social scientists ultimately failed to make a direct impact. They did succeed, however, in shifting the terms in which the debate about educational achievement was constituted, and that has had a more lasting effect (Banting, 1979, pp. 137–40). In other words, the aim was a linear input of research to policy in the short term; the effect was a diffuse input in the longer term.

This alternative diffuse model of the research input to policy clearly accords with the evidence of research utilization, in the sense that it de-emphasizes the fact-finding and intelligence gathering functions of research and accepts that the potential for that kind of input is limited, while recognizing that there is nonetheless real opportunity for research to influence the conceptualization and the frames of reference of those who are involved in the policy-making process. As Weiss has put it, research:

> influences (policy-makers') conceptualisation of the issues with which they deal . . . it widens the range of options which they consider; it challenges some taken-for-granted assumptions. . . . This kind of conceptual contribution is not easy to see. It is not visible to the naked eye. (Weiss, 1982, pp. 289–90)

The kind of research-policy relationship which is 'not visible to the naked eye' stands in sharp contrast to the model incorporated in the dominant tradition of British policy-oriented research. If social research is to be principally oriented to this alternative model the pressure to be immediately relevant in practical terms is released, and this means that there is less room for disappointment about the products of applied social research. In this context, it is interesting to note that some American social scientists have been advocating a repudiation of the old-style applied, policy-oriented research in favour of prioritizing 'basic research that ultimately may prove useful', as a strategy for regaining some of the lost ground in social science funding under the Reagan administration (McCartney, 1984).

The diffuse model also has the merit that it recognizes much more clearly the political nature of the situation into which research is being fed, again in contrast with the dominant tradition, which saw rational administrators as its target more than politicians (see chapter 5). The rationalist model of policy-making of course itself underestimates the importance of value-judgments and partisan considerations in the policy-making process (Carley, 1980, p. 6). Husen makes this point strongly in relation to educational research precisely because of the value elements in policy decisions:

> the crucial thing is that research and development *cannot provide the answers to value questions* with which social

issues, including educational ones are imbued. (Husen, 1984, p. 12.)

So far as social science research in general is concerned, there is clearly a sense in which it cannot ever be regarded as politically neutral — a case which is made strongly by Rothschild in his report on the SSRC, where his acknowledgement of that led to a specific rejection of the consumer-contractor principle in relation to applied social research. I shall take up some further implications of seeing the knowledge produced in social research as intrinsically political in chapter 9.

Engineering Versus Enlightenment

The range of issues which I have been considering in this chapter have mostly frequently appeared in recent writing on policy-related research in the context of a discussion of 'engineering versus enlightenment', originally formulated by Janowitz (1972). These discussions are well summarized by Bulmer (1982a). The engineering model (or 'social engineering' model, since the two terms seem to be used interchangeably) encompasses the approach to policy-oriented research which I have characterized as the dominant British tradition: a linear relationship, with research feeding into specific 'decisions' by providing the missing facts. The enlightenment model, on the other hand derives from the evidence about the actual use of research which the American studies discussed above have uncovered, emphasizing intellectual and conceptual contributions rather than the provision of facts, and seeing both the policy-making process itself as diffuse and the relationship of research to policy as usually indirect (pp. 43–5). Further, as Lindblom and Cohen put it, the engineering model demands the production of knowledge which makes authoritative claims, but the enlightenment model sees a non-authoritative role for research (Lindblom and Cohen, 1979, pp. 73–4). Abrams (1985, pp. 181–98) has further subdivided both engineering and enlightenment into strong and weak versions. I shall return to his discussion in chapter 9, where I shall consider the role of advocacy, which Abrams considers to be the 'weak' version of enlightenment.

Should we all therefore entirely repudiate the social engineering model, which has formed the dominant tradition in British policy-related research, in favour of creating enlightenment, a position which is clearly the new orthodoxy amongst writers in this field? There is widespread agreement that the engineering model should be rejected, amongst social scientists both on the left and on the right. Kallos, writing about the Marxist tradition of field studies in education, rejects the view that educational researchers should seek to be 'improvers'; and Pollard writing from within mainstream educational ethnography argues that educational ethnographers should 'scrupulously avoid any seduction into forms of reproductive social engineering' (Kallos, 1981, p. 45; Pollard, 1984, p. 194). From the political right, Digby Anderson has argued that social scientists should not engage with 'social intervention' to bring about social change, largely because he believes that the knowledge which they produce is not adequate to the task (Anderson, 1980). Simply at a pragmatic level, it seems that far too much can be, and has been, expected from research by those who have espoused social engineering.

By contrast, the greater sophistication and complexity of the enlightenment model is bound to make it very attractive to many social scientists. The goals which it sets are much more modest and therefore seem more attainable, and in a sense are comforting, since it is acknowledged before we begin a piece of research that no single study is likely to have a major impact, and that in any case, we should not expect ever to know ultimately what influence our work may have (Cohen and Weiss, 1977, pp. 89–91; Rist, 1984, p. 168). Moreover, it enables us to get away from the policy agenda as set by policy-makers, since the aim of our work is to encourage reconceptualization and redefinition of the issues. As Rein puts it, in policy-related research, we should not simply be finding the answers, we should also be finding the questions (Rein, 1983, p. 212). Further, there seems a reasonable hope that the enlightenment role of research will be understood by those who make policy as a useful role, since it accords with their own use of research in practice; and something very much like this role has received official endorsement, in the Rothschild Report on the SSRC, in the argument that most applied social research does not have an 'end product' like research in the natural sciences. Its main purpose rather is to enable more informed debate to be conducted and thereby better decisions to be made (Rothschild, 1982, paragraphs 3.9–3.10). Finally — and importantly in the context of this book — the enlightenment model offers far more space for qualitative research, through its emphasis upon understanding and conceptualization, rather than upon providing objective facts. Indeed, Rist had made a strong case that qualitative research is vital to the endeavour of social enlightenment, since this kind of research is more able to provide appropriate data enlightenment must be based not on prefabricated or furtive encounters with the society, but on a long-term and intense familiarity. (Rist, 1981a, p. 493).

An example of the potential of qualitative research for providing reconceptualizations of a policy-related issue can be found in British studies of juvenile delinquency conducted in the 1960s and early 1970s. Building on American subcultural theories and Cohen's (1955) pioneering study of a delinquent gang, research of this period offered an alternative account of delinquent and law-breaking acts, portraying them as an understandable response to the disadvantaged structural situation of many young people, supported by dominant rather than deviant values. The collection of articles edited by Carson and Wiles (1971) provides a good introduction to this research, and includes an extract from Hargreaves' (1967) study, where these ideas were explored in the context of a secondary modern school.

A powerful case can be made, therefore, in favour of the enlightenment model and broadly I would endorse it. In my view, however, it would be wrong to dismiss totally the social engineering enterprise, especially if that means too naive an enthusiasm for the alternative of enlightenment. I take this position for several reasons. First, the intention that one's research will enlighten policy-makers may be little more than pious hope in many instances, and certainly cannot be legitimately used as an all-embracing justification for a range of disparate studies. Merely hoping that one's work will enlighten may well not be enough, since there is no automatic guarantee that policy-makers will hear about it through the very eclectic sources they use. Even if some do hear, the findings of a specific study may confuse rather than enlighten especially when, as I have already suggested, social science knowledge is not cumulative, but rather the increase of studies in a given area is likely to produce greater diversity of perspectives and analyses (see also, Wagenaar, 1982, p. 28). Second, if enlightenment means that one simply publishes one's research findings and hopes that they pass into the common stock of knowledge upon which policy-makers will draw, this then means that the researcher abdicates responsibility for the use of her findings, in a way which is actually rather similar to the role of the researcher as technician in the engineering model. I shall return to this issue of taking responsibility for one's own findings in chapter 9. Third, enlightenment aims at changing the way in which policy-makers think, but — as Weiss (1982) has pointed out — thinking differently is not the same as acting differently and *merely* to change the way policy-makers think is a very limited aspiration for policy-related research. This view is broadly shared by Blume, writing in the British context, who sees the enlightenment model as rather too pessimistic about what can be achieved in the shorter term (Blume, 1979, p. 330).

It seems to me therefore that, within an overall framework of the enlightenment model as the realistic goal for most policy-oriented social research, we should nonetheless be hoping to switch to the more direct, engineering mode on appropriate occasions. By this suggestion, I do not mean to imply a reversion to the linear model of research input based upon a rationalist model of decision-making. Rather that the researcher always needs to recognize and work within a diffuse and incrementalist policy-making process, and this means looking for opportunities to feed in social science knowledge at different times and with different people aiming at small changes, rather than expecting that a single input of research at a rational moment in the policy process will be effective. The position which I am arguing here is somewhat akin to Popper's famous discussion of social engineering. He distinguishes between 'Utopian' and 'piecemeal' social engineering: whilst rejecting the former, he puts up a spirited defence of the latter. He rejects the idea of a social engineering which seeks to remodel the whole of a society along the lines of a pre-defined blueprint, but he approves of the piecemeal approach, which seeks out and fights over the most urgent social evils, rather than pursuing the ultimate good, aiming rather to make a series of small adjustments (Popper, 1963, pp. 64–92). Whilst I would not endorse the general view of politics expressed here, in relation to the impact of research my point is it emphasizes modest aspirations as appropriate to the enterprise of feeding social research into the policy process, and also emphasizes a series of small changes, rather than the single big bang. Major political change does not come about through the use of research by policy-makers but by quite other means, as the whole history of the dominant tradition demonstrates. But well-targetted research may on occasion encourage small changes, which perhaps of themselves seem trivial. I would see these instances of piecemeal engineering as opportunities which social researchers might seize from time to time, but within an overall framework of research whose relationship to policy is enlightenment. Within that overall framework, qualitative research can make a very significant contribution — a topic which I consider explicitly in the following two chapters.

7 The Uses of Qualitative Research: Evaluating Existing Policies

In this chapter I shall consider some of the uses to which qualitative research can be put in studies of social policy, and its relative merits and defects in relation to quantitative alternatives. I shall be concerned in particular with the contribution of qualitative research to evaluating existing policies — an activity which, it can be argued, is a vital part of the democratic process (see chapter 6). The following chapter is concerned with the uses of qualitative data in relation to developing and changing policies.

To make the discussion more concrete, I shall concentrate my examples principally in two areas: research and policy on preschooling, and on aspects of juvenile delinquency related to schooling. In the next chapter, I shall draw on examples in a similar way. My purpose in using examples in this way is not to provide a comprehensive assessment of work in either field, but to illustrate the case for qualitative research without being too eclectic in the examples which I offer. Both preschooling and delinquency are areas where educational issues clearly overlap with wider social policy concerns, and where certain policies pursued within the educational system have been designed to secure wider social goals. The use of preschooling as envisaged by Plowden and as experimented with in the EPA projects was seen as a means ultimately to create a more equal society through changing the balance of educational opportunities (see chapter 2); and in the field of delinquency, educational failure has been seen as an explanation of the phenomenon, and education has sometimes been seen as the arena in which the 'cure' for this 'disease' would be administered (Reynolds and Jones, 1978).

One point which I need to clarify immediately is that in discussing the evaluation of policies I am not referring to 'evaluation' in the narrow sense, which I take to mean the direct commissioning of research on the effects of a particular policy. A case can also be made for using qualitative methods in this type of evaluation, although that is rare in Britain, more common in the United States (Patton, 1980; Fetterman, 1984). But I do not intend to discuss 'evaluation' in this sense specifically because it seems to be that insofar as it involves research, it entails the same kind of methodological issues which are raised by non-commissioned research. There are, however, additional questions about the control of data, which are taken up in chapter 9. It also raises problems about whether social science knowledge can ever be procured for direct use of the kind which I discussed in chapter 6. It seems to me, in other words, that 'evaluation' in this narrow sense, if it involves empirical research, does raise a range of questions which are common to other types of research, although the particular blend of issues may be unique to evaluation studies.

My purpose in this chapter is to consider how qualitative methods can contribute to the 'evaluation' of existing policies in the more general sense of that term: that is, to describe and understand the real effects of policies, to compare the assumptions upon which policies are based with social experience, and to assist in a considered assessment of their viability and appropriateness.

The Limitations of Quantitative Data

The case for qualitative data rests partly upon the limitations of the kind of quantitative research which has represented the dominant mode of policy-oriented research in Britain (see chapter 1). In chapter 2, I discussed some limitations as revealed in research undertaken for official reports on education; I shall now look at this issue more broadly.

Criticisms of quantitative research in general, and survey research in particular, are well known, and there is no need to elaborate them here in general terms (see, for example, Mills, 1959, pp. 60–85; Cicourel, 1964, especially, pp. 14–31). I shall, however, deal with some of those which are especially pertinent to policy-oriented research. My argument will be that in policy-related studies there are issues where qualitative research should be able to improve on the defects of the more conventional quantitative approaches. However, at the same time, one needs to recognize that there are certain features of quantitative and survey work which qualitative approaches cannot match and certain research tasks for which they would not be appropriate — for example the tasks which many of the committees of enquiry set themselves (see chapter 2), which essentially entailed documenting the extent of educational inequality and social experiences associated with it, across the whole population.

Jennifer Platt (1972) has usefully highlighted some of the weaknesses of using survey data in policy research, in an article which is generally supportive of this kind of work. She argues that the common use of the survey, that is, questioning the 'consumers' of a given service, can provide useful factual data but is limited in its scope, especially in relation to possibilities for change: the respondents may well not be able to envisage changes or provide relevant information about them, and those aspects of the situation about which they can give information may not be the most important ones. Further, she suggests that there are weaknesses in using surveys to develop theories which are policy-relevant, because of the common problem that surveys confuse attitudes and behaviour, because there is a temptation to take respondents' theories as theories rather than treating them as data; and because in survey research the data to be collected have to be specified in advance, so that only theories formulated in advance can be tested. Platt thus highlights some important weaknesses in survey research, upon which qualitative research can certainly improve. These are: a lack of flexibility in the research process once it is set up, and a series of problems arising from survey research procedures, which collect data via verbal or written responses to questions, thus removing the process of data generation from concrete social situations which the study seeks to explore.

A further but related problem is that the kind of statistical analysis and cross-sectional survey data which was characteristic of much of the research discussed in chapter 2, can document the outcomes of policy and practice in a way which is generalizable (a considerable strength) but can say little about the processes which produced those outcomes. I illustrated this point in chapter 2 with reference to the research undertaken for the Crowther and Newsom reports, and it is a problem with a good deal of the work undertaken within the framework of 'political arithmetic' research in education (see chapter 1). The same problems can be identified with similar — and equally influential — educational research in the United States. Trow (1984, pp. 271–5) has argued this point in relation to the Coleman Report (1966), which was very influential in developing policies concerned with educational opportunities for black children. Trow argues that the Coleman research relied on measures of school organization and operation which were readily quantifiable (such as pupil/teacher ratios or the quality of buildings) and this led to the report's central conclusion that the characteristics of schools have little or no relationship to educational outcomes, by comparison with the overriding significance of family background. This conclusion was wide of the mark, argues Trow, because the research methods adopted were not subtle enough to uncover the real differences between schools and the way children learn in them (p. 274). The problem that a survey is a rather blunt instrument for uncovering social processes is aggravated by the fact that most surveys are single, cross-sectional snapshots — a limitation which was identified by Beatrice Webb in relation to Booth's massive surveys. This difficulty can be overcome in surveys to an extent by building in a longitudinal element, either by the study of successive cohorts retrospectively, as was done with the educational element of the Oxford social mobility study (Halsey, Heath and Ridge, 1980), or best of all, in an ongoing cohort study such as that undertaken by Douglas (1964). The length of time required for a longitudinal study makes it very expensive and means that it is not a realistic option, except unusually.

A different set of problems is created by the over-concentration upon technique which characterizes certain quantitative studies. This can result in the production of virtually meaningless data — what Wright Mills (1959) called the 'abstracted empiricism' of American sociology of the 1950s. This approach to research, he argued, depends upon a philosophy of social science which is modelled on the natural sciences, and which allows methods to determine the problems to be studied. The resultant 'facts' are of little value in advancing social knowledge because 'social research of any kind is advanced by ideas; it is only disciplined by fact' (p. 82). The situation has of course moved on, but another American writer, considering the effect of research upon policy, has much more recently pointed to similar weaknesses, arguing that much research produced for policy-makers sinks quickly into obscurity because the researchers' obsession with technical adequacy is not matched by an equivalent concern for utilization (Rist, 1984, p. 154). In the British context, Edwards is highly critical of some of the research which was done in relation to urban deprivation and positive discrimination programmes (including EPAs). He argues that there was an excessive concern for technical niceties which produced an 'arithmetic of woe' that diverted attention away from questions about the causes of that woe (Edwards, 1981). These atheoretical aspects which make some quantitative work exceedingly superficial represent a key weakness, especially if one takes seriously the evidence that one can most usefully feed research into policy not by providing facts, but by suggesting conceptual reorientations (see chapter 6).

Finally, it is a common criticism of survey research that it focusses upon causal explanations derived from statistical correlations, but cannot deal with the social meanings of the action thus described. A number of examples of this were discussed in chapter 2, for example, the Plowden Committee's attempts to use survey data as a basis for understanding the dynamics of parental encouragement of their children's education. Again, the issues here are not unique to policy-oriented research, but derive from important underlying debates about the nature of social science knowledge, and especially the distinction between positivist and interpretivist frameworks, to which I referred in the Introduction. In particular, the issue being raised derives from Max Weber's important formulation that explanations of social phenomena must be causally adequate and adequate at the level of meaning. A common criticism of survey research is that at best, it can achieve the former but not the latter; and conversely it is argued that small-scale and ethnographic studies, conducted within an interpretivist framework, are centrally concerned with meanings, but cannot produce causal explanations. However Marsh (1982, pp. 98–124), writing from the perspective of a survey researcher, challenges that over-simple distinction between two separate and incompatible methodologies. Survey research, she argues, can go some way to uncovering meanings by asking actors themselves to supply them or better, 'reading them off' from the actor's behaviour, situation or from 'naturally occurring' speech. Even if we heed Marsh's warning not to draw too crude a distinction between quantitative and qualitative research, it remains the case that the relative weakness of the former — the exploration of meanings — is the great strength of the latter (see also Burgess, 1985c). A related issue is the 'macro' level of analysis attempted by survey methods, whereas characteristically qualitative studies are small-scale and aim at producing explanations at the 'micro' level. Again, this distinction can be overdrawn (Hammersley, 1984) but it reinforces the point that qualitative research does have specific strengths which focus on concrete instances of human interaction.

From this discussion of the limitations of quantitative methods, I take certain pointers to the kind of research at which qualitative studies should aim: flexibility in the research process itself; studies which place social life in its natural context; a concern with process as well as outcome; explanations which are adequate at the level of meaning, but which also are aware of questions of causal adequacy, even if they cannot be fully resolved. In policy-oriented research specifically, qualitative methods cannot provide — as quantitative methods can — descriptive documentation of the characteristics of whole populations or patterns of social phenomena which can be generalized to whole populations; that is, the kind of data which the dominant tradition of policy-related research has sought to provide. On the other hand, it should be well-placed to offer the kind of conceptual reorientations which may raise questions of a more fundamental kind about existing policies. The rest of this chapter is concerned with spelling out the specific strengths of qualitative research within this overall framework.

Arguments for Complementary Data

When making the case for qualitative research targeted upon social policy issues, probably the simplest and the least contentious argument is that it complements other types of data. Charles Booth's observation still holds good, namely that facts and figures are potentially misleading because of the 'lack of colour' (see chapter 1), and contemporary writers on policy research equally acknowledge that surveys are only suitable for certain types of data collection (Platt, 1972). It seems to me that there are two rather different grounds upon which we can argue this case for complementarity: first, that qualitative, especially ethnographic, research can provide the descriptive detail which makes a complex situation comprehensible; and second, that different kinds of data about the same situation provide a check on each other.

The capacity to provide descriptive detail is clearly one of the great strengths of ethnographic work which has been underused in the dominant tradition of policy-related research, although not entirely absent from it; the work in the 'alternative' tradition comes much closer to this, especially Mass-Observation (see chapter 3). Shipman (1985), writing about the relationship of ethnography to policy argues that producing good description can potentially be an important basis for practical action, since the policy-makers always lack details of what is actually happening, and always make decisions without adequate information. Similarly, James, writing of ethnography and policy in the United States context, argues that its great strength is that it can provide 'perspective, insight, understandable description' (James, 1977, p. 193).

Research on juvenile delinquency provides a good illustration of the value of qualitative research in providing descriptive detail which can help to clarify the impact of social policy upon its target group, and to evaluate the assumptions which underlie policy decisions, concerning the motivation to commit offences. Although invaluable quantitative work has been done which documents patterns of social experience which are likely to be associated with delinquency, including poor school performance (see, for example, West and Farrington, 1973, pp. 84–97), it is the ethnographies of juvenile groups based on participant observation, such as James Patrick's classic study in Glasgow (1973), which have led to understanding about how different ingredients of social experience blend together to produce a particular outcome. Interestingly, Mass-Observation also produced a study of juvenile delinquency, based on documentary evidence, case studies and observation, but this seems to have been little recognized (Willcock, 1949). In relation to understanding the dynamics of delinquency in the school setting, several important recent studies are also based upon ethnographic methods (Hargreaves, 1967; Hargreaves, Hestor and Mellor, 1975; Willis, 1977). More recent school ethnographies, although concerned with wider issues, have produced a good deal of 'understandable description' which makes the world of those who would be labelled as 'delinquents' more comprehensible (Burgess, 1983); and Lynn Davies has recently provided a detailed ethnography of school deviance focussing upon girls (Davies, 1984). Of course none of this work has been produced with the principal aim of feeding it into policy-making; but my point is that it has the potential to be used for that purpose. Simply the detailed descriptive material which it provides can be used to challenge any approach to social policy which is based on the assumption that the actions of young delinquents are basically *in*comprehensible.

Second, the case that qualitative research can complement quantitative data can also be made on the grounds that any social research is likely to be more convincing if different kinds of evidence have been brought to bear, and qualitative studies do commonly use a range of methods for data collection. The most common version of this case of course concerns Denzin's concept of the triangulation of data; although, as I have argued elsewhere, one does not have to argue that multiple sources of data will bring one nearer 'the truth' about a given situation, but simply that different kinds of data will provide a more rounded picture (Denzin, 1970; Cain and Finch, 1981). Rist, specifically arguing the case for qualitative data in policy-related research, points out that frequently it contains different kinds of evidence within a qualitative project. This is particularly important, he argues, as a check upon statistical portrayals because statistical data can 'often lead to mathematically correct but socially ludicrous conclusions' (Rist, 1984, p. 164). A good example of an ethnographic case study which uses different kinds of evidence (including some quantitative data) is provided by Davies' (1984) study of gender and deviance, where she uses observation; unstructured interviews and conversations; semi-structured, taped interviews; and structured questionnaires. In a study of this type, different facets of social reality are uncovered by different methods, and a rounded picture is built up.

Building on Strengths: The Naturalistic Perspective

The argument about qualitative data being a useful complement and supplement to other kinds perhaps appears relatively modest and uncontentious. I want to move beyond that, however, and argue that there are other grounds for promoting policy research with a qualitative orientation, which imply that qualitative research is in some ways superior. In this section, I shall suggest that a good case can be made for building on those strengths of qualitative research which derive from what is usually called the 'naturalistic' orientation. In particular, qualitative research can yield data which are superior to quantitative data because first, it studies social processes and social actions in context; and second because it reflects the subjective reality of the participants. In chapter 3, I identified these as among the major strengths and distinguishing marks of what I called the 'alternative' tradition of policy-related research, which includes the work of Mayhew, community self-surveys and Mass Observation.

First, policy-oriented research can capitalize upon the capacity of qualitative methods to study social life in its natural context, rather than the decontextualized and artificial settings in which data are generated in social surveys. In general terms, the case for this is well-known; and in relation to policy research in the education field, Rist has strongly endorsed this case, emphasizing that the capacity to study beliefs and behaviours in context means that qualitative research has 'a respect for diversity' and can articulate the multiple ways in which people understand their world and react to it (Rist, 1984, pp. 162–4). Rather than the world of the participants being transmitted to the researcher at second hand, through the medium of question-and-answer, qualitative research attempts to study the social world directly and therefore provides contextualized data, although probably about a much smaller number of individuals than the average survey would cover. A strong version of the case for qualitative research is put by Jack Douglas, who argues that direct experience is the most reliable form of knowledge about the social world, but researchers often compromise this because policy-oriented work seems to demand a big picture of society; in consequence we make do with less reliable forms of truth (Douglas, 1976, p.7).

Douglas' point about the reliability of different forms of knowledge certainly seems to have some force in areas of study such as delinquency, where the definitions of what behaviour and which individuals 'count' as delinquent can only be understood in relation to the context in which particular actions occur. Lynn Davies demonstrates this very effectively in relation to her own study of gender and deviance in school. She shows that survey methods, which take terms like 'delinquency' or 'disruption' out of context almost inevitably mean that different types of behaviour will be included by different individuals; in other words, there is a real problem with definitions, not in the formal sense, but in the sense that the meaning accorded to an item of behaviour will vary between individuals and between social contexts (Davies, 1984, p. 211). This is not a matter simply of teachers having different 'attitudes' to deviance in the sense of fixed views which guide individual's actions in a consistent way, but that the same individual may respond differently in different circumstances even on such basic matters as whether a particular act is treated as deviant or not. The net result is that the researcher's capacity to understand the social processes which result in either deviant or conforming behaviour is limited by variations in definitions, to which survey data give only limited access. Similarly, in Davies' view, charting 'rates' of delinquency and their correlates in social experience through such apparently objective measures as court appearances can also be misleading, especially in relation to gender differences, since it is well known that the police decision-making processes (through which young people must pass before they end up in court) operate differently for boys and girls. In her view, only a detailed case-study methodology can overcome these problems of meaning and definition by giving access directly to the contexts in which they operate (p. 212).

Developing Davies' arguments in the social policy context, it seems clear that a reliance upon quantitative research as the basis for understanding how deviance occurs in schools (a necessary prerequisite for developing policies designed to cope with it) will inevitably be inadequate because it cannot satisfactorily take account of the way in which different contexts produce different outcomes — at best can only express such variations as teacher 'attitudes'. It also will tend to focus upon the characteristics of individuals who have been identified as delinquent rather than upon the interpersonal processes which produce this identification. This focus on what actually happens in concrete situations is of course very likely to challenge the status quo as, for example, did Mayhew's study of what Ragged Schools were actually like (see chapter 3). It does not allow the unruly sectors of society simply to be counted and categorized as the basis for controlling them which, it can be argued, has been one reason for the dominance of quantitative methods in policy-related research (see chapter 5). Rather, a great strength of qualitative study in natural settings is to reflect the view of the participants — a point which I shall take up shortly.

So far, my argument about studying behaviour in context has simply referred to 'qualitative research' without distinguishing between qualitative methods and interpretivist epistemology, and the examples which I have used implied that I am referring to a style of research which encompasses both. It is however quite possible to study social behaviour in natural settings in a different way, adopting a positivist epistemology and using techniques which depend upon quantification. The contrast here is, for example, between the two different styles of observation which I discussed in the Introduction. Does observation which adopts a positivist framework and applies quantified techniques for studies in natural settings have the same potential strengths as the kind of research strategy that I have been describing as 'naturalistic', that is, participant observation drawing upon an interpretivist framework?

It is beyond my scope here to discuss that question in general terms, but in relation to policy-oriented research, it seems to me that such methods do potentially offer an advance on the social survey in that they give direct, not second-hand, access to social behaviour. On the other hand, much of the potential of naturalistic fieldwork is missed, because items to be studied do have to be decided in advance, and the observers' capacity to understand social processes and social meanings by becoming part of the setting is severly curtailed. An illustration of this can be drawn from the preschool field, from one of the studies undertaken in connection with the major Oxford preschool research project. I refer to Sylva, Roy and Painter's (1980) study of children in playgroups and nursery schools, where observers in the groups recorded children's activities at regular intervals on a structured recording schedule (see also, Bruner, 1980 chapter 5). This study was carefully conducted, and in a sense quite appropriate to its purpose, which was to study individual children and the development of their learning, rather than interpersonal interactions. However, when the authors are interpreting their data, there are points where they lean towards a different mode, in a way which is reminiscent of the Newsom report's presentation of quantitative data in a more qualitative form (see chapter 2). In this case, the researchers really want to know what their observers 'made of' the groups in a more qualitative sense, which would help them to understand the differences which they documented between playgroups, nursery schools and nursery classes. So they write:

> Hypothesis after hypothesis can be found. What did our observers think? It was their strong impression that the organisation and ethos of the various types of centre affected the children. (Sylva, Roy and Painter, 1980, p. 126)

They do, therefore, need to understand something of what they call the 'ethos' of the individual nursery, and their data do not give them access to this, so at this point they are left to fall back upon the unsystemmatized 'strong impressions' of their observers. Qualitative methods, utilized within an interpretivist framework and conducted rigorously can advance upon this considerably. Indeed, I have argued that my own study of preschool playgroups, which was on a much more modest scale and attempted to capitalize upon the naturalistic aspects of qualitative research, is the only kind of study which can demonstrate what preschool playgroups are 'actually like' (Finch, 1984c and 1985). To know what playgroups are actually like is of profound importance in evaluating the effect of current social policies and assessing their viability, since policies have increasingly emphasized this voluntary form of provision over statutory services, including the nursery school (Finch, 1984b).

The second, and related, area in which the naturalistic orientation of qualitative research has particular benefits for social policy studies concerns its capacity to reflect the subjective reality of those people who are the targets for policy decisions. The value of this was recognized by Mass-Observation, and reflected in the methods which the organization employed. Tom Harrisson believed strongly that the people in power were out of touch with ordinary people and needed to have their view of social reality directly challenged (Mass Observation, File 10, 1939 and File 446, 1940). It was of course, as I argued in chapter 3, a distinctive part of the 'alternative' tradition of policy-related research that the view from below was given much greater prominence than the view from above. Again, this is likely to lead to research which questions and challenges current policy and practice through offering alternative definitions of those situations which policy is designed to address. On the other hand that very feature can be seen as a strength if one takes seriously the arguments and evidence which I presented in chapter 6, which indicate that research is in any case most likely to make an impact upon policy through the conceptual reorientation which it provides.

This aspect of qualitative research is firmly rooted in the interpretivist approach to the creation of knowledge and of course may have to be defended on those grounds. However, as I argued at the beginning of this chapter, producing explanations which are adequate at the level of meaning is one of the clear ways in which qualitative studies can advance on survey research. An illustration from the field of delinquency serves to show how important this can be in relation to policy issues, in particular the question of truancy, a topic which has long exercised the minds of policy-makers and social policy researchers. The appropriate response to truancy depends very much upon one's analysis of the motivation to truant, and I have argued elsewhere that there have been two dominant analyses with rather different policy implications: the one sees truancy as wilful delinquency, the sign of an incipient criminal career which must be firmly stamped out; the other sees it as a symptom of personal or family disorganization, to which the appropriate response is a therapeutic one (Finch, 1984a, pp. 167–71). A school-based ethnographic study in which truancy features significantly is Corrigan's (1979) study of working class boys in Sunderland schools. This study, by providing ethnographic data which reflect the meaning which truancy has for these boys implicitly challenges both those explanations by showing that it is an understandable response to a situation in school which they find oppressive and pointless (Corrigan, 1979, pp. 18–44).

Building on Strengths: Studying Processes over Time

Qualitative research often — although not invariably — involves sustained contact over a period of time with an organization or a particular social setting which is being investigated. It therefore routinely builds in a longitudinal element which is usually prohibitively expensive in survey research.

Qualitative research therefore is particularly suited to studying social processes over time, and there is an obvious application here to the study of policy changes as they are implemented, which I shall discuss in the next chapter. However, it also has much to offer in the study of settings which have long been the target of social policy. My own study of preschool playgroups was conducted over a three-year period, the first two years consisting only of participant observation, and in the final year I also conducted semi-structured interviews. My focus was on what I called 'working class playgroups'; that is, playgroups run in inner city areas or on council estates, by local women on a self-help basis. I began studying five such groups all recently established, but by the end of the three-year period of study only two remained open, so a major focus of my study became an attempt to understand why working class playgroups apparently have a tendency to collapse after a short life-span. I have discussed this in detail elsewhere, but broadly my conclusions were that collapse of such groups is very likely because policies which have encouraged women to set up self-help preschool groups have — in the case of economically deprived areas — encouraged women to take on an inherently middle class model which they have neither the economic nor the cultural resources to sustain (Finch, 1983, 1984a and 1984b). The points about methods which I want to make here are first, that in studying the groups at close quarters over three years I was able to document in some detail the processes which led to their collapse, whereas a large-scale survey about the reasons for playgroup collapse would have to rely substantially on the retrospective accounts of participants; and second, this major research question emerged during the course of the study itself, but qualitative methods are flexible enough to accommodate and capitalize upon such turns of events in the course of a research project. This point about flexibility of research strategies has been seen as a great strength of qualitative research by other writers on social policy. Rist has argued that flexible research strategies are vital to capture events and persons which go their own way, not as predicted in advance; research strategies which cannot do this are 'doomed to reflect only that which stood still long enough to be measured' (Rist, 1984, p. 166). As with the example of playgroups, that may tell us little about what happens when policy aspirations are translated into social reality.

The capacity of qualitative methods to study social processes also means that they are well suited to studying the process of policy-making itself. As Edwards (1981) notes, there have been very few studies of the policy-making process in Britain which have utilized qualitative methods, although Flynn's (1979, 1981 and 1983) study shows that it is possible. Flynn studied the Planning Department of a local authority, which he conceptualized as a study of urban managers using direct observation of their work, unstructured and semi-structured interviews, and analysis of documents such as minutes of meetings and correspondence. Flynn claims that this was a limited and exploratory exercise, but he is surely correct when he argues that survey methods could not so successfully reveal, for example, the extent of officials' involvement in decision making (Flynn, 1979, p. 744). An equivalent study at central government level is Kogan and Henkel's study of the commissioning of research by the Department of Health and Social Security, although unfortunately in this case the researchers say rather little about the methods which they used. However, it is clear that they did attend meetings as observers, had access to committee papers, and interviews with staff members of research units and civil servants (Kogan and Henkel, 1983).

Both of these studies are relatively limited in terms of capitalizing upon the potential of qualitative research for understanding the process of policy making. Edwards (1981) argues that direct and close contact with those being studied is essential if one wants to understand 'the assumptive worlds or social contructions of reality' of those who make social policies. Young and Mills (1980) make a rather similar point, when they argue that studies of policy-making should be centrally concerned with developing interpretations of purposive behaviour, and that this should be founded on the assumption that reality is conceived differently by different people. Thus research methods should enable us to interpret events in the light of their meaning for actors, rather than postulating motives, interests or goals in advance; that is, classic fieldwork methods. In this discussion which is strongly supportive of fieldwork methods for studying policy-makers themselves, they do, however, acknowledge that there are practical difficulties in getting access to the closed world of government departments, and also of conducting qualitative interviews with people in elite positions where the researcher may well find it difficult to display familiarity and sympathy with the life experiences of the interviewee. They remain committed, however, to the potential value of research on the policy-making process which attempts to capture the subjective world of the actors. The process of educational policy-making offers a potentially rich but as yet almost untapped setting, for such studies, because of the various levels at which policies are made: the Department of Education and Science, the education departments of local authorities, school governing bodies, and senior staff in schools, to mention the most obvious.

Theoretically Grounded Qualitative Research

Earlier in this chapter, I indicated that one of the areas in which qualitative research could seek to improve upon much quantitative work is in providing clear theoretical frameworks for empirical work. This, of course, is also in line with the argument that we should be aiming essentially to provide policy-makers with reconceptualizations of the issues with which they deal, rather than with 'facts'. To argue that ethnographers and other qualitative researchers ought to be centrally concerned with theory is not therefore an *alternative* to an interest with policy — which is how it appeared in the context of the sociology of education in the 1970s (see chapter 1). Rather, I would endorse Pollard's view when he argues that developments in ethnography which would make it more policy relevant would also be conducive to theoretical developments (Pollard, 1984, pp. 179–83). In other words, rather than being alternatives, good ethnography which is theoretically grounded would have an *enhanced* capacity to make an impact upon policy.

Whether educational ethnography as it has developed in Britain is well placed to capitalize upon this potential would be a matter of debate amongst ethnographers themselves. Researchers who have sought to develop educational ethnography within a framework of Marxist theory have roundly dismissed other educational ethnographers for producing work which is purely descriptive and atheoretical. Willis (1980) puts forward a strong case on these grounds, arguing that ethnographic study conducted within the framework of Marxist theory is a quite different, and much more intellectually defensible, exercise. On the other hand his own study of working-class boys in and out of school can be criticized for offering a poor blend of ethnography and theory. Certainly it is the case that the two are presented quite separately as 'ethnography' and 'analysis', in discussions of roughly equal length. In the 'analysis', the ethnographic data are used to elaborate and refine Marxist theories about cultural and social reproduction, and the links between the two are a little tenuous at times (Willis, 1977; see Sharp and Green, 1975, for another study of Marxist ethnography which has conducted similar kinds of criticism).

The criticisms of Marxist ethnographers against those who use ethnographic methods from within a different tradition — principally symbolic interactionism — would be echoed by some writers from within that tradition itself. Woods argues that theory has been an underdeveloped area in educational ethnography, partly because the ethnographic task essentially is a descriptive one. Nonetheless, he takes the view that empirical description should never be an end in itself (Woods, 1985). If it is, ethnographic work is in danger of becoming as empiricist as the most atheoretical surveys. Hammersley, Scarth and Webb (1985) offer a similar analysis of the underdeveloped state of theory in educational ethnography, and suggest ways in which it can be tested and developed, especially through the selection of critical cases for study. These writers are agreed that the development of theory is a priority for educational ethnography, and that this also would make an important contribution more widely to the sociology of education in which, it can be argued, theorizing and empirical studies proceed all too often without reference to each other (Reynolds and Sullivan, 1979; Woods, 1985, pp. 63–4).

An interesting discussion of this issue in the context of social policy — and one which strikes a very positive note — is offered by David Hargreaves (1981) in his article on schooling and delinquency. Hargreaves identifies a clear gap between theory and research in this field, with theories being elaborated with little or no reference to evidence, and empirical research which is mostly atheoretical. He does not wish, however, to see a return to the positivist model of theory-testing, but puts forward the case that a blend of theory and data is entirely compatible with all good interpretivist work, from Max Weber onwards. He also takes the view that a blend of theory and research is precisely the kind of work which would be of use to policy-makers, and regrets that sociologists have singularly failed to address themselves to this.

This is not the place to discuss in detail whether these criticisms of the alleged atheoretical nature of ethnographic work are correct or misplaced. However, one is bound to challenge the claim that any piece of fieldwork can be 'purely descriptive', simply on the grounds that this implies a positivist concept of 'facts' which can straightforwardly be collected and presented without any interpretation; this is a view that would be rejected by many social scientists, on the grounds that 'facts' do not exist in this unproblematic way and that the researcher has made an active contribution to creating them in a particular form solely by selecting certain features of the social world as suitable for study (Hughes, 1980; Cain and Finch, 1981). The question, it seems to me, is not so much whether theory is totally absent from ethnographic studies, but to what extent underlying theoretical orientations are explicitly acknowledged by the researcher, and how they are used. In this respect, there may well be room for substantial improvement in much ethnographic — and other qualitative — research.

Further, these criticisms may be misplaced if they do not take into account the question of 'macro' and 'micro' analysis. Developments in 'theories' about education in recent years have been clearly pitched at the macro level of analyzing education as part of the structure of social control, or its function in serving the needs of the economy. Many writers would regard this work as excessively abstract and over-theorized (Reynolds and Sullivan, 1979), and it is certainly the case that the interests of ethnographic researchers have usually been very different and focussed on the minutiae of small-scale interaction — a gap which itself can be detrimental to developing an understanding of educational processes, as Hammersley (1984) has argued. My point here is that the gap between macro and micro analysis can be mistaken for a gap between theoretical and atheoretical work, if theory is always defined at the macro level. Theories about education and the needs of capitalism pitched at this level are not readily amenable to ethnographic — or perhaps to any empirical — study. One certainly can, however, address a more modest set of questions deriving from such theories at an empirical level, and through qualitative research: for example, how far do teachers in practice develop a capitalist work ethic in their pupils?

If 'theory' is defined in this broader, and also more modest, way, it becomes clear that qualitative research, including ethnographic research, can and should be theoretically informed. A possible model for this kind of work is that developed within the Chicago school (see chapter 5) — as Bulmer puts it, a central characteristic of their work was the development towards 'theoretically informed empirical research' (Bulmer, 1984, p. 108). Interestingly, it is British work closest to this model which Hammersley (a major critic of atheoretical educational ethnography) regards as an honourable exception to the general rule; namely the Manchester anthropological tradition of educational ethnography, where Hargreaves (1967), Lacey (1970) and subsequently Ball (1981) were explicitly testing out the theory of differentiation and polarization in schooling (Hammersley, 1984, p. 319). Further, and importantly, the Chicago and Manchester studies are precisely of the kind which, I have already argued, demonstrate the potential for policy-oriented, qualitative research (see chapter 1 and chapter 5), thus reinforcing the point that theoretical development and a policy orientation are congruent, not conflicting, aspirations for qualitative research.

In summary, I am suggesting that part of realizing the potential of qualitative methods in policy-oriented studies also entails what Bulmer calls 'theoretically informed empirical research'. I have argued first, that a concern with theory is quite compatible with qualitative research; second, that a blend of theory and data is the hallmark of good qualitative work; and third, that this particular blend produces precisely the kind of work which is likely to make an impact upon policy because it offers theoretical insights grounded in evidence.

Conclusion

The case for qualitative research in policy-related studies rests therefore on a number of grounds, and depends upon the capacity of reseachers to produce relevant work which adequately blends theory and data. If we consider qualitative research purely as a matter of methods, then the case for its utility rests principally on complementarity, that is, it can usefully supplement the kind of data provided by quantitative methods. If however the term 'qualitative research' is also taken to imply a particular epistemological orientation which emphasizes an understanding of the social world from the viewpoint of the participants, then its contribution to social policy is likely to be of a rather different order than the kind of quantitative research conventionally associated with social policy. By its very nature, it is likely to evaluate social policy from the perspective of those who are its targets rather than those who make the policy and, like the work which I placed in the 'alternative' tradition (chapter 3), it reflects the view from below, not the perspective of the administrator and the policy-maker. The relationship of the research to the policy issues studied is likely to be critical and questioning and at the very least this kind of research is bound to remind policy-makers of the complexity of the social situations which they seek to manage.

8   The Uses of Qualitative Research: Developing and Changing Policies

Like the previous chapter, my intention here is to make the case for the use of qualitative research in studies related to policy issues. I shall be focussing here upon the use of research in developing and changing policies.

Prospects for using research in policy development and change have to be considered in the light of the evidence which I discussed in chapter 6. This suggests that it is unrealistic to expect that social research will be used directly in most cases, but that its main effect is likely to be more diffuse: a policy-research relationship referred to in recent literature as 'enlightenment'. I suggested however, that reseachers might also be looking out for circumstances where they can promote the direct use of their work, even if only in a limited way. I shall be considering in this chapter some circumstances in which qualitative research might be used in that more direct way. I shall also be broadening out from an interest in influencing those who 'make' policy, to consider the potential usefulness of qualitative research to other groups who may be in a position to modify policy in a more limited way, especially in day-to-day practice, and to groups who are affected by decisions made elsewhere, and have an interest in pressing for change.

As in the last chapter, I shall concentrate my examples within two substantive fields and draw upon a third — pre-schooling — in a more limited way. The two areas which I shall introduce in this chapter both concern principally young people in the later years of secondary schooling. The first is policies towards preparation for work and/or unemployment and the transition out of schooling. Self-evidently this is an area which has been of substantial importance over the last decade, as it has been at other times in the past, and where educational policies (as narrowly defined) overlap considerably with other areas of social and economic policy (Reeder, 1979; Rees and Atkinson, 1982). My second example is perhaps less familiar and concerns 'education for parenthood' or 'family life'. Parenthood education can be seen as a field which encompasses not only schools, but is undertaken in a variety of settings such as ante-natal clinics, mother and toddler groups and so on (Pugh and De'Ath, 1984). I shall concentrate principally upon education for family life which goes on in secondary schools, where it can be seen as a contemporary version of the long-standing attempt in Britain to use schools to educate young women for motherhood (Lewis, 1980; Dyhouse, 1981; David, 1985). The particular form which this now takes has been shaped since the late 1960s, not only by a general concern about maternal deprivation, but also in the wake of Sir Keith Joseph's espousal of the 'cycle of deprivation' thesis, when preparation for parenthood came to be seen as 'one way of avoiding . . . a transference of inadequate parent behaviour from one generation to another' (Grafton *et al.*, 1983b, p. 153). Interpreted in this light, it represents the use of schools as a convenient site for intervention with young people to pursue social policies whose orientation is not concerned with schooling as such.

Qualitative Research Targeted on Policy-makers

I have already indicated (chapter 6) that there is limited scope for using *any* research to stimulate policy change on a large scale. Further, there are clearly additional difficulties when research has been based on qualitative methods, and when policy makers are operating within the dominant tradition, where research is expected to provide generalizable 'facts'. Qualitative researchers are therefore faced with making a case for the use of their work in a relatively inhospitable situation. However, a case can be made for the utility of qualitative research on the grounds that for certain purposes it is at least as good as — and in some ways better than — quantitative research. My discussion in this section draws and builds upon Rist's (1981a) arguments, where he identifies three grounds for the utility of ethnography in policy-making: restricting and shaping the definition of the problem; isolating the levers of change so that programmes can be targeted effectively; identifying the unintended consequences of policy decisions. In all of these areas, he argues, qualitative research is extremely valuable, provided that we do not expect research findings to have a major impact: the aim should be to inform rather than control the course of change.

Of these three areas which Rist discusses, the third — identifying the unintended consequences of policy decisions — is an extension of the task of evaluating the consequences of existing policies, which I discussed in the last chapter. Rist extends this by arguing that qualitative researchers can be involved at the stage of policy formulation, giving advice about the likely way in which the proposed changes will be received and implemented in practice, thus minimizing the chance that unintended and undesirable consequences will ensue. He argues that qualitative researchers can anticipate and guide policy-makers about how a policy is likely to be received because of their long-term familiarity with the group on whom the policy is targeted. In other words, he sees as a positive virtue the detailed knowledge of a specific setting which ethnographers acquire, which enhances their capacity to have an impact on policy-making. This does of course raise a range of ethical and political issues about the way in which research data are used and about whether researchers ought to be serving the interests of government in this way, which I shall return to in chapter 9. It seems to me that Rist is very close to the boundaries of what would be acceptable to many researchers when he suggests that qualitative researchers could assist by identifying those groups who are likely to be most receptive to the policy, and also the individuals who act as gatekeepers and could potentially deliver the support of others.

A weaker version of Rist's suggestion — and one which might be more congenial to researchers — is that qualitative researchers can use their detailed knowledge of social situations to advise policy-makers about what will *not* work. An illustration of this can be taken from studies of education for family life. As I have already indicated, this topic has achieved a prominence in social and educational policy during the 1970s and 1980s, and appears in the Department of Education and Science paper *The School Curriculum* (1981) in these terms:

> Preparation for parenthood and family life should help pupils to recognise the importance of those human relationships which sustain, and are sustained by family life, and the demands and duties that fall on parents. (Paragraph 25)

Even in the bland language of a government policy document, one can see that the exercise envisaged is a prescriptive one, designed to inculcate specific values; further, that there is an assumption that this can operate on the basis of a consensus about what constitutes 'the demands and duties' of parenthood and indeed, 'family life'.

When translated into practice in the classroom, what will happen? That question could clearly be tackled by devising an action-research project, in which a curriculum change is introduced and ethnographic research is associated with it (see below). However, even on the basis of existing evidence, there is a good case to be made for the view that the policy could not work as intended in this instance. For example, Prendegast and Prout's study of teenage girls' concepts of motherhood (1980), based on depth interviews, demonstrates just how subtle and complex are girls' images of future motherhood. Many seem to adopt at one and the same time a fairly negative view of motherhood in general, based upon their own experiences and observation of other women, and also positive expectations of their own satisfactions, based upon romantic ideologies. Any attempt to put across prescriptive messages about parenthood must clearly take into account the context into which those messages are received and, on the basis of this kind of evidence, one might predict that a curriculum programme which emphasizes the virtues and joys of motherhood could simply reinforce the gap between young women's assessment of the reality and their expectations for themselves. As Prendegast and Prout themselves note, if education in this area is to be anything more than an imposition of normative propositions, pupils' own knowledge — including that which they are inclined to suppress or overlook — needs to be opened up (p. 532).

Similarly, the assumption of a consensus view about what should be taught about parenthood can be questioned, not only from a moral standpoint, but also by looking at how teachers actually handle these issues. In a national study of existing schemes concerning education for parenthood, which was based principally on descriptive, quantitative data, the researchers did include some limited qualitative elements, including taped discussions with teachers (Grafton *et al.*, 1982 and 1983a). This material illustrates the hazards of translating policy directly into practice in these areas because, as the researchers argue 'such topics present teachers with difficulties which are not found elsewhere in the curriculum'. These difficulties arise because teachers have to make links between intimate aspects of their own lives and their professional practice and so they have to take decisions about whether to maintain a neutral or committed stance on different ways of living and bringing up children, and whether to make their own views and practices apparent. In fact, contrary to the aspirations of policy in this area, most teachers do not see themselves as authoritative figures, changing attitudes and encouraging a particular version of 'good practice', but rather as giving information, extending pupils' horizons and fostering pupils' capacity to make their own choices (Grafton *et al.*, 1982).

Presumably one way in which qualitative research could be used directly in such circumstances is that an ethnographer with a detailed knowledge of a particular school would be in a position to identify those teachers whose own professional practices are most consistent with the aspirations of policy-makers in this area, and therefore could advise on how the kind of programme which policy-makers want to encourage could be most effectively mounted. As I have already indicated, I see this raising serious ethical issues. It relates quite closely to another of Rist's (1981a) suggestions, which I find dubious on the same grounds: that qualitative researchers can help policy makers to isolate the levers for change, and thus ensure that programmes are targeted more effectively. Rist argues that quantitative research cannot provide this kind of guidance because it is a form of 'hit and run' social science, but that qualitative research, with its longitudinal perspective can reflect 'both developmental and comparative dimensions' in decisions about where to target resources. In the example which I am using, there is no doubt that an ethnographer with a detailed knowledge of a specific school could indeed provide that kind of guidance about where a concentration of resources would be most effective. Whether one would or should do that is partly a matter of confidentiality, trust and responsibility towards the people whom one has studied, and partly a matter of whether one endorses the aims of the policy (see chapter 9 for further discussion).

Rist's other category — restricting and shaping the definition of the problem — is much less ethically problematic and accords well with the 'enlightenment' model of the research-policy relationship. As Rist puts it, qualitative researchers are in 'an extremely advantageous position' to describe the dimensions of the problem because of their long-term familiarity with a particular group or setting, and can pay particular attention to competing definitions of the situation, including the way in which participants themselves define the issue (Rist, 1981a, p. 489). Again, he sees the positive virtue of qualitative research as lying in researchers' detailed familiarity with a particular setting, which may well mean that they are in a position to influence policy on the basis of existing knowledge, not only on the basis of specifically commissioned research.

The model being envisaged here is that researchers work alongside policy-makers in an advisory capacity, but the advice which they offer is not technical, but conceptual. This 'enlightenment' relationship, as I indicated in chapter 6, involves using research to reorient policy-makers' thinking, redraw the boundaries of problems and to formulate questions rather than provide answers. This is potentially an important and a radical role for research, and one to which qualitative research is well suited, although it may seldom be possible to capitalize upon the potential in this direct way. Such a role for research has, however, received the endorsement of two of the official reports on social research (see chapter 2). The Heyworth Committee (Report of the Committee on Social Studies, 1965) took the view that the research-policy relationship cannot be conceived as a direct one in the social sciences; nonetheless, social scientists should be working alongside policy-makers especially at the points where social problems emerge. The great value of the social sciences from the policy-makers' view, lies in their capacity to 'limit the scope of uncertainties within which policy decisions are taken' (paragraph 123). Some kinds of uncertainties can of course only be limited by quantification of the size of the population involved; but other uncertainties clearly require the kind of detailed knowledge of culture and social processes which qualitative research can provide. Similarly, Lord Rothschild's report on the SSRC makes the case for the use of social research in policy development, even if — as he puts it — the methodology may look uncertain to policy makers. Using the illustration of the mistakes made in policy decisions about slum clearance and public housing programmes through lack of attention to 'human needs and feelings', he argues that policy-makers need the 'check of organized enquiries of the kind that social scientists are trained to undertake'. The fact that 'clear results' cannot be guaranteed does not mean that such studies are a waste of time, because without them, policy decisions are governed only by 'commonsense and traditional wisdom' and 'uninstructed commonsense has proved . . . an unreliable guide' (paragraph 4.14).

Providing a check upon, and an antidote to, the commonsense notions upon which policy-makers rely is an area where qualitative research can potentially make a significant contribution through its capacity to reflect the detail of the situations in which policy-makers seek to intervene, and to reflect that from inside the situation: the view from below, to counteract the view from above. An example can be drawn from policies in the field of youth training schemes, using Williamson's (1982) study of trainees on the Youth Opportunities Programme (other studies dealing with similar issue are: Fiddy, 1983; Gleeson, 1983; Cohen, 1984). His study focussed upon a particular category of white male trainees, whose enthusiasm for the schemes on which they were working left something to be desired from the viewpoint of the schemes' supervisors, who saw these young men as lazy and lacking in motivation to work because they could be better off on the dole. Some of them had been in employment previously, and if they had been unable to hold down a job, their bad time-keeping, cheekiness or whatever was seen as a result of poor socialization into the discipline of work. The policy implications of defining the situation in this way are clearly that such young men need to be given a strong dose of the protestant ethic, backed up by removing the apparently attractive option of living on the dole — not too far removed from the kind of policies which were being pursued at the time this study was published. Williamson, however, on the basis of some observation and taped interviews with the young men concerned, shows that 'trainees have a different story to tell' (p. 106). He is able to show that they are operating already within a set of aspirations which strongly values work, but within which they aspire to an 'appropriate' job. In some ways entirely realistically, they see the YOP scheme as of no value in itself, but only as an alternative route to a conventional job: they judge the schemes as valuable only insofar as they improve their chances of getting the kind of job which previously they could have got on leaving school. The real problem which they faced was that they were 'holding out' for the right job in a labour market which was changing rapidly, and where the level of educational qualifications required for jobs was rising. The relationship between research findings of this kind and social policy is not straightforward of course: the implications which can be drawn range from the conclusion that training courses are a waste of time unless jobs available also expand, to the conclusion that the problem lies with the boys themselves, and their aspirations need to be reduced. In this instance, research does help to redefine the nature of the problem by challenging commonsense notions about the motivations of trainees, but in doing so it raises a range of further questions about the consequences of that redefinition. As I shall argue in chapter 9, there is a strong case for researchers not opting out at this point, but staying with the consequences of their findings as they are put to policy use.

Overcoming the Weaknesses Associated with Qualitative Data

My explicit aim in this book has been to make a positive case for the use of qualitative research. However, there are certain features of qualitative approaches which — if not handled very carefully — may undermine its potential. In particular, no such discussion can afford to ignore the weaknesses which are likely to be identified by anyone working within the dominant tradition of the research-policy relationship. Both the small-scale and case-study emphasis of the methods and the interpretivist epistemology are likely to contribute to a conclusion that the results of qualitative research are of dubious validity, not viable as the basis for generalization, quite possibly unrepresentative of the population in question and therefore, from the policy-makers' viewpoint, unusable (Reynolds, 1980–81; Finch, 1985). Not only is the problem one of small versus large-scale but it also arises from the fact that qualitative work is dominated by an approach to validity which emphasizes the meaning of events and situations to the participants (Magoon, 1977, p. 669); but in aiming for adequacy at the level of meaning, can fall far short of accounts which are causally adequate (see chapter 7 for further discussion).

How should qualitative researchers who want to have an impact on the policy-making process deal with these issues? One obvious possibility is to combine quantitative and qualitative methods so that one creates different types of data. The benefits here are that the inclusion of quantitative data increases the generalizability of findings, which will probably make them more convincing to policy-makers — and of course may also enhance their contribution to social science knowledge. Pollard (1984) suggests this as one solution in his discussion of ethnography and policy, on the grounds that ethnographic studies tend to focus on process whereas policy-makers tend to want measures of output. Pollard's position therefore complements the argument which I presented in chapter 2 in relation to a number of the research projects associated with official enquiries, where I argued that their weakness was that quantitative methods which they used allowed them to focus *only* on outcome and not on process. Pollard argues this in reverse, highlighting the relative weakness of ethnographic work in studying outcomes. Of course there are circumstances in which ethnographic work *can* address the outcomes of social processes. For example, Willis' well-known study *Learning to Labour* (1977), based on a combination of ethnography and Marxist theory, is sub-titled 'How working class kids get working class jobs' and is explicitly concerned with processes within the educational system which lead to this particular outcome. However, it is certainly true that any detailed case-study method will not be able to provide the predictive certainty about the social characteristics of young people who end up in manual jobs, which can be provided by a large-scale survey. So there is an obvious case for using appropriate methods for different kinds of study, which is rather similar to that which I discussed in chapter 7 about the complementarity of data.

One way, therefore, of overcoming the weaknesses likely to be associated with qualitative data in the eyes of policy-makers is to combine methods. The cynical case for this rests on pragmatic grounds: qualitative research can be smuggled in under cover of something more respectable. However, a case can also be made on the grounds that, since qualitative and quantitative approaches each have strengths and weaknesses, their combination provides the opportunity for research outcomes which are more authoritative and convincing. This is Pollard's (1984) position.

The question of how the weaknesses associated with qualitative data can be overcome can be answered in other ways, which do not necessarily entail a combination of methods. One such answer concerns the presentation of findings. Shipman (1985) in his discussion of educational ethnography and policy, argues that the perspective of the 'detached researcher' *is* valued by policy-makers, to set alongside reports of inspectors, advisers and teachers, but that enough information must be given to allow them to make an assessment of ethnographic findings. This means that the methods used must be spelled out in enough detail for others to be able to assess them. Further, control over methods must be sustained throughout the project and this must be clear when the findings are presented. This argument is rather similar to Becker's (1958), when he suggests that qualitative findings should be presented alongside a 'natural history' of the project; that is, an account which spells out the stages of the research, what data were used at each stage and how inferences were drawn from them, so that readers can make their own judgments about what confidence to place in the conclusions. These suggestions from Becker and Shipman involve making a positive virtue of the strengths of careful and rigorous study which good ethnography always pursues, and making one's methods open to the scrutiny of others in a sense is the only ultimate test of the validity of any piece of research, as I have argued elsewhere (Cain and Finch, 1981).

There are other ways in which the apparent weaknesses of qualitative data can be turned into strengths in the presentation of findings. One of these is highlighted by considering the debate about engineering versus enlightenment (see chapter 6). If one accepts that the most likely way in which one's research will find its way into policy-makers' thinking is through diffuse not direct means, and that this is most likely to happen where it provides a reconceptualization of issues and not just 'facts', then it is worth paying considerable attention to the terms in which accounts of research are formulated, so as to highlight clearly its major features in an understandable, even an eye-catching form. Once the eye is caught, so to speak, a more detailed appraisal may follow. This is not to suggest that qualitative researchers follow the lead of some of our quantitative colleagues and produce an arid list of 'policy recommendations' at the end of each study. Far from it. Formulating reconceptualizations of a 'social problem' requires far more imagination than that, and qualitative data offer the potential for just such imaginative presentation. For example, Martin Rein (1976) has suggested an interesting way in which research findings could be presented in his discussion of 'story telling'. This idea, in his view, is less rigorous than the effort of positivists to develop general laws, but at the same time, the logical structure developed is similar to a story which provides 'an interpretation of a complex pattern of events' (p. 266). The different elements in the story must of course be capable of being backed up with evidence, but the story puts the issues into a comprehensible form which at the same time includes normative implications for action. A central feature of such stories is the metaphor, which serves to offer analogies with events and actions familiar to the listeners, and which therefore helps to tease out patterns and draw lessons. Examples which he gives include 'the labour market queue' and 'fragmented social programmes' — in the case of the latter, for example, calling programmes 'fragmented' in itself implies a course of action, namely that they should be integrated (p. 77). The task of the social scientist as Rein defines it is one to which, it seems to me, ethnographic work is very much suited.

> To sum up, the task of the social scientist is to invent objectively grounded normative stories, to participate in designing programmes of intervention based upon them and to test the validity of stories that others commend. (p. 268)

So far I have suggested that qualitative researchers should meet the characteristic criticisms of their data by finding ways round those criticisms. However, I would also argue that they must be taken seriously, in the sense that the planning of qualitative research itself may need to be modified if it is to make a more sustained impact upon social policy. In particular, I want to argue that there are inherent weaknesses in the single, free-standing case study; but also that it is envisaged that these weaknesses could be overcome. My argument here is actually very much in line with another current debate which is concerned more with theoretical developments based on ethnographic work, and seeks to develop comparison between case studies.

There are two rather different ways in which one can envisage developing comparative cases in order to overcome the weakness of the single case study. The first entails setting up projects which are specifically designed as a series of parallel ethnographic studies in different settings, selected on criteria developed from existing theory to provide the most significant dimensions of comparison. The case for this type of 'team field research' has been made by Jack Douglas on the basis of his own experience in the United States. He argues that this approach combines the virtue of classic field research (ability to study in depth) with the classic aims of quantitative research (to get the extensive, representative, structured information) (Douglas, 1976, pp. 193–4). In the field of education, and again in the United States, Rist (1981b) has described a piece of team research which studied school demonstration projects concerned with youth employment and training. His discussion of the methods used (pp. 37–51) makes it clear that the field-workers based on each site were functioning as ethnographers, but their work was structured and coordinated by a central project team who provided them with 'analysis packets' which identified the main areas of interest, but did not specify how the data were to be collected. Data analysis was done by the central team, although fieldworkers were asked to provide their own interpretations. This procedure facilitates both comparison and generalization in ways which are not possible in a single case study. Team field research thus has many attractions, although it is undoubtedly an expensive undertaking. It may be possible, however, to build it into some research projects in a more modest way, with two or three parallel studies.

The second approach to developing comparative studies is eminently more attainable on grounds of cost. This is cumulative comparative studies: that is, designing individual studies in a way which builds explicitly on the previous work of other researchers, in such a way as to create significant comparisons, and to develop social knowledge in a cumulative way. By this, I do not mean to imply that there is likely to be a neat, linear unfolding of knowledge, as I indicated in chapter 6, but that the development of cumulative comparative case studies in an explicit way makes it more possible not only to extend evidence beyond a single setting, but also to redefine and advance understanding at a more conceptual level. Other recent writers have drawn attention to the importance of this approach as a way of advancing theoretical developments based on ethnography (Woods, 1985; Hammersley, Scarth and Webb, 1985). As these writers note, the only serious attempt to develop comparative qualitative case studies of educational settings in Britain has been the Manchester-based studies undertaken in the 1960s, of which Hargreaves' (1967) and Lacey's (1970) work are the best known, although Lambart's (1976) study was an integral part. Interestingly, as I argued in chapter 1, these studies also represent an approach to ethnographic study in education which do have a clear relevance to social policy.

The Chicago school also developed this kind of approach in the 1920s (see chapter 5), encouraging individual researchers to be guided in their selection of projects by considerations of how research in the department could be mutually reinforcing (Bulmer, 1984, pp. 136–43). The Chicago research serves to highlight another point about developing studies which build upon each other: comparisons can be made across narrowly-defined sub-disciplinary boundaries such as the 'sociology of education', and may indeed be more fruitful if this is done. Intellectual questions about what happens in schools, or how the educational system operates may well be developed by considering findings and concepts from studies in other analogous situations. Delamont (1981) has argued that educational ethnographers are very narrow in this respect and has suggested, for example, that studies of teachers would benefit substantially if they drew upon concepts and insights from another sub-disciplinary area, studies of the workplace.

It seems to me that the cumulative comparative development of qualitative research does offer substantial benefits in creating the kind of data which one can claim to have a real authority in the policy-making process — a view which has also been expressed by Pollard (1984). This argument can be made firmer by considering the philosophical underpinnings of the kind of comparisons which can be made by these procedures. This argument has been set out very clearly by Philip Abrams (1984), writing on the contribution of qualitative research to social policy but in relation to a rather different topic: the informal, neighbourhood care of elderly people. Abrams argues that the quality of care provided and the circumstances under which it is available are topics which have not proved amenable to quantitative study or experimental design, and he argues that the only possible way to proceed is 'from soft data to hard evaluations'. This must be based, in his view, on the comparative method; that is, by comparing cases through procedures of analytic induction. He offers a detailed example of how this can be done based, inter alia, on his

own empirical studies of neighbouring, and argues that the researcher's aim should be to work towards a classification of types of
relationship which can then be used as the basis of further research
and/or policy change.

The case which Abrams makes, which is equally applicable in the
field of education, underlines not only the importance of comparative
cases, but also the need for researchers to develop a heightened
theoretical awareness of the procedures which underlie the comparisons made. The logical procedures underlying analytic induction, as
an alternative to deductive logic, were initially set out by Znaniecki
(1934) and subsequently developed, among others by Glaser and
Strauss (1967) and are very much part of the symbolic interactionist
tradition within which many qualitative researchers work. The
underlying logic of the procedure entails developing a hypothetical
explanation of the phenomenon under study, and then studying a
few cases in depth to see whether the hypothesis fits the data. If it
does not fit, the explanation has to be reformulated; if it does fit,
further cases are examined to search for evidence which does not fit.
This search for negative evidence is the hallmark of analytic induction, and it means, as Bulmer has noted, that the empirical test of an
hypothesis 'is particularly rigorous, even a single negative case
requiring a reformulation of the hypothesis' (Bulmer, 1977, p. 280).
To proceed by analytic induction not only within a single ethnographic study, but also in making comparison between case studies,
offers the prospect of producing accounts which go some way
towards meeting a policy-maker's desire for reliable data, although
the presentation of such accounts must spell out these procedures and
make clear the alternative approach to 'validity' which is implied
there.

To summarize, I am arguing that qualitative researchers do have
a range of possible strategies which can be used to overcome the
features of qualitative work which make it look unusable to policy-
makers: combination of methods; appropriate presentation of
findings; building up comparative cases. These strategies partly entail
modifications in the way in which qualitative work is planned and
presented, but also imply the response to such criticism should
involve offensive as well as defensive strategies. That is, as well as
paying attention to those features of qualitative work which could
make it a more authoritative basis for policy, researchers need to be
able to explain clearly and convincingly that qualitative data have
been carefully collected and analyzed, and that the process of drawing
conclusions from such data is based on rigorous and logical proce-

dures. This case will always need to be made whilst the dominant tradition, with its very different notions of the nature of evidence in social research, holds sway.

Policy Change From Below

So far in this chapter I have been discussing the use of qualitative research in policy development and change as a matter between researchers and those who 'make' policy at a formal level, either nationally or locally. However, the operation of qualitative research at a small-scale level makes it especially suited to assisting change at grassroots level, where policies are put into practice. This may entail working alongside practitioners — teachers, counsellors, welfare officers and so on — as they interpret and operationalize 'policies' in the course of their daily work, or alongside groups composed of and representing those who are the recipients of services and assisting them to challenge and change policies whose directions are not in their interests. This view from below is very much part of that social research which I identified as the 'alternative' tradition (see chapter 3).

One version of what this grassroots style of policy-related research can mean has been suggested by W F Whyte, in his presidential address to the American Sociological Association (Whyte, 1982). He argued that there is a need to improve the practical relevance of sociology, and suggested that this should be done by reorienting sociological research towards the 'discovery, description and analysis of social interventions for solving human problems'. The concept of 'social interventions' being used here draws upon ideas developed in the 1920s and 1930s, but since fallen into disuse: it does not mean interventions imposed from above, but the mechanisms in which participants themselves have developed for solving problems as they define them. The kind of research appropriate to this task, he argues, means that the 'subjects' of the research have to be regarded as active participants in it, and it also means a research design which is flexible and which does not give the questionnaire survey pride of place. It seems to me that the methodological points which Whyte makes apply to the whole range of research situations where one is reflecting the view from below, not just those modelled on his concept of social interventions.

The reasons why researchers become involved in stimulating and implementing change at grassroots level are of course many and various but not least among them is a feeling that this is the only way in which any impact will be made. Higgins (1978), in her discussion of strategies for social change in the poverty demonstration projects in Britain and the USA argues that the consistent experience of researchers is that the presentation of facts to governments of itself has seldom brought about change. For this reason some researchers, notably those working on the British Community Development Projects, rejected the conventional 'up, along and down' model of disseminating research findings (that is, pass the recommendations upwards and eventually the changes will be passed downwards), in favour of the 'lateral ripple' approach, which involved working with and strengthening community groups who would press for and implement changes themselves.

The best known model of researchers taking an active part in stimulating change in the British educational context is the model of 'action research', a concept which can mean many different things but essentially denotes that a project includes both action to change a specific situation and also research designed to understand the situation better, or to monitor the change, or both (Town, 1973; Smith, 1975; Kelly, 1985). The most spectacular example of its use at the level of national policy-making was of course the EPA projects, which did themselves entail a 'lateral ripple' element, for example in the Liverpool and West Riding projects. A more recent, and more modest, example in the field of education is the GIST project in Manchester, which was designed to encourage more girls to choose scientific and technological subjects in secondary schooling. The research element of the programme (which was both quantitative and qualitative) aimed both to understand the underlying reasons for girls' subject choice and also to monitor the impact of changes introduced into certain schools, which included the introduction of some single sex teaching, the development of suitable curriculum materials, and visits to the schools by women scientists. This project was also attempting a 'lateral ripple' effect, and the researchers worked closely with teachers, feeding back information to them at each stage (Kelly, Whyte and Smail, 1984; Kelly, 1985).

The concept of action research on the surface appears to be a version of the natural science model of experimental design, where a controlled intervention is made and 'before' and 'after' measurement can be taken. This implies that quantitative techniques are an essential feature of action research. However the experience of both projects mentioned underlines the inappropriateness of this model for social science research. The GIST team rejected it from the outset (Kelly,

Whyte and Smail, 1984, p. 13). The EPA projects attempted it, but this experience clarified for those involved in them the impossibility of working within the natural science model of experimental design, because, as Karabel and Halsey put it, action research exposes in a sharp form the fact that 'social science which is to be significant must be value-based. It cannot be a value-free collection of facts' (Karabel and Halsey, 1977, p. 17). A similar conclusion is reached by Marris and Rein, in their discussion of their involvement as researchers alongside the 'action' in demonstration projects in the United States. Indeed they take this further by arguing that the experimental research design which they were trying to operate fitted the projects very badly, and methods which are more exploratory and rely less on quantification and measurement might have been much more appropriate (Marris and Rein, 1967).

More generally, I think it can be argued that qualitative methods are particularly appropriate to action research of a certain type: that is, action research on the 'lateral ripple' model, which seeks to work with practitioners at grassroots level and feed research findings back to them, rather than to pass findings 'up' to policy-makers at some other level. The experience of the research teams working on the EPA projects seems to bear out the conclusion that qualitative methods — whilst not necessarily offering the prospects of producing statistically valid and generalizable results — could nonetheless have been recognized as the most suited to many of the tasks which the teams were set. I noted in chapter 2 that the West Riding EPA team did in fact adopt a strategy which they found especially useful and which they saw as 'participant evaluation', but that they were nervous about whether other people would accept this as 'real research'. The London EPA team were also drawn away from the grand design of large-scale change to activities which seemed much more within their grasp and which entailed stimulating change at a small-scale level, working with local teachers and other professionals. Again, however, they seem to have been nervous about their methods. As Barnes, who directed this part of the programme, puts it in the official report:

> The work was pragmatic and eclectic rather than generated from any theory of managed social change. We might almost say it was parochial. Certainly a paramount concern was to get something done at a particular place and time, in particular circumstances, and the problems of generalising from this were only dealt with as a secondary issue. (Department of Education and Science, 1975a, p. 17)

The central focus of the coordinated EPA action research projects was intervention at the pre school level, planned carefully in an experimental design and its outcomes monitored statistically (see chapter 2). A quite different approach to working with nursery teachers to monitor their practice was adopted in the Oxford pre-school project and this — although it does not represent a full-scale ethnography — does rest much more heavily on detailed qualitative work which, it seems to me, is clearly more appropriate to the task in hand. One element of the study entailed exploring how nursery teachers and play leaders go about their educational goals with a view to helping them to come closer to achieve those goals (Bruner, 1980). This was done by getting the teacher to record about 15 or 20 minutes of her own interaction with children, at a time selected by herself; this was then transcribed and the research team coded and analyzed it. A member of the research team who was also herself experienced at working with young children then discussed the transcript and the analysis with the teacher, focussing in this project on the gaps between the teacher's intentions and what happened in practice. Teachers then had the opportunity of repeating the procedure as many times as they wished.

The techniques used here are by no means unique to this project, but they illustrate the potential of using qualitative methods in the context of an action-research project whose orientation is comparable to the EPA projects. The case for the utility of such methods in bringing about policy change at the 'micro' level, especially working with teachers, has been put strongly by Pollard (1984). He argues that ethnography can now capitalize upon the theoretical developments which have occurred at a macro level in the sociology of education, where it has increasingly been acknowledged that teachers cannot be regarded as simply agents of the state, or of capitalism, but do in fact have opportunities to act independently within their classrooms. In terms of my argument, one must see the practice of teaching on a day-to-day basis as part of the 'policy' making process, as well as the site where much policy is implemented. In Pollard's view, this means that the ethnography of schools and classrooms can make an important contribution to social policy at this level; and the apparent weaknesses of ethnographic methods from the perspective of government policy-makers looks much more like strengths to 'practitioner policy-makers such as teachers'. Not only do ethnographic methods offer the opportunity for detailed study on a small scale, but the humanistic — in contrast with the scientific — paradigm can more easily address issues like the quality of learning experience (p. 185).

From the perspective of this concept of policy change, one of the most interesting developments in the British educational scene in recent years has been the work associated principally with Stenhouse and his colleagues, who have pursued a version of action research based on qualitative, case-study methods as a means of professional and curriculum development, which entails teachers researching their own practice. This work has it origins in Lawrence Stenhouse's direction of the Humanities Curriculum Project, and the continuing of its focus is curriculum research and development. Stenhouse (1975, pp. 142–65) outlines the underlying philosophy as one where 'curriculum research and development ought to belong to the teacher' (p. 142), which means that teachers need to be actively involved in the critical testing of ideas, not just in accepting and applying them. In that sense, this is a type of action research (Nixon, 1981). In a recent discussion of one project in this genre, Elliott (1985), defines action-research as 'the institutionalization of collaborative reflection about the practice of teaching'. Putting this into operation entailed a complex project in nine schools; and within each one, full-time researchers, external consultants, school-based coordinators and teams of teachers. Individual self-evaluation by teachers, supported by external consultants and researchers, was followed by a variety of strategies for collective reflection on the 'private' knowledge thus gained, as a way of stimulating change in practice.

Qualitative research does seem to have considerable potential in relation to action research of this type and offers the opportunity for researchers to be directly involved in changing policy and practice at this small-scale level. Its potential is not confined to curriculum development (although this is where it has been most extensively used to date) but also is clearly relevant to modifying the nature of teacher-pupil interactions (as in the Oxford pre-school project which I discussed above), and in altering the range of educational experiences which are provided for children, and the way in which such experiences are organized and delivered.

Three features of this type of qualitatively-based action research are particularly important in relation to its further development. First, the focus and the aims are very modest, and are acknowledged to be so from the outset. There is clearly therefore the possibility that — even if such changes are successfully introduced in a handful of schools — the impact will extend no further, making this a very low-level version of 'policy change'. In response to that criticism, I would argue that all the evidence (reviewed in the earlier chapters of this book) suggests that more ambitious attempts to use research to change policy on a wider scale have met with remarkably little success, and this small-scale approach represents the possibility of at least changing what is offered to *some* people. Further, such small-scale experiments can provide key examples of 'good practice' which can be used subsequently as part of the political pressure to accomplish change on a larger scale. Therefore researchers who have worked on such projects bear some responsibility to stay with the results of their research and to use and publicize it in appropriate settings, if their potential as examples of good practice is to be realized.

Second, projects of this kind clearly embody what Higgins (1978) calls the 'lateral ripple' model of research used (see above) rather than the 'up along and down' model which has been characteristic of the dominant research-policy relationship, most clearly articulated in its Fabian version (see chapter 5). The 'lateral ripple' approach attempts to place the knowledge created in the process of research into the hands of those whom it directly concerns, and who are either in a position to implement it themselves, or who can make use of it when engaging in the political processes through which policy change may be accomplished. The case for handing over the knowledge to the participants rather than handing it upwards to policy-makers rests partly on the pragmatic grounds that they are more likely to do something with it, but also on principled grounds concerning the democratization of knowledge — a principle most clearly articulated in the work of Mass-Observation (see chapter 3). Action-research raises very sharply the question of who owns the data which are created in the course of social research, and the lateral ripple principle puts into effect the principle that the research subjects do have rights over them by seeking, as part of the research, to strengthen their capacity to continue making use of such knowledge once the project is completed.

Third, the whole emphasis of this approach to action research implies a collaboration between the researchers and the researched, to which qualitative methods are uniquely suited. In a sense, this represents not only the democratization of knowledge but also the democratization of skills — that is, the skills of research — and in some ways is reminiscent of Mass-Observation's use of volunteers as 'amateur' researchers and of panellists, who reported what was happening in their own lives (see chapter 3). Qualitative case-studies such as that discussed by Elliott (see above) involve teachers in evaluating their own practice, and this collaborative principle can also be extended to children, as Pollard (1985) has interestingly shown.

This is very far removed from the model of the objective researcher and clearly makes a project vulnerable to criticisms of subjectivity and 'bias', an issue which I take up in chapter 9. Leaving that aside for the moment, if one accepts collaborative research in principle then one can argue that qualitative methods have great potential for involving research subjects in a collaborative way and thereby of putting the means of change into participants' own hands. The research process itself in a sense becomes a means of empowering the powerless, by sharing with them the ability to reflect upon one's own position, to see one's circumstances as a product of social forces, to modify one's self image, or to identify points at which the means of social change lie within one's own grasp.

9 Values, Ethics and Politics

Issues concerning values, ethics and politics have been implicit (and sometimes explicit) throughout much of the discussion in the preceding chapters. The purpose of this chapter is to draw these together and to consider them explicitly. Many of the issues which I shall consider can arise in all kinds of social research, but my intention here is to look at them specifically in relation to policy-oriented research of a qualitative kind, drawing upon the models of this type of work which I have developed in previous chapters. I shall group the issues under three main sections: questions of objectivity and values in research; research ethics; and finally, a discussion of the political position of the researcher and its implications.

Objectivity, Values and the Policy-oriented Researcher

The dominant tradition of the research-policy relationship in Britain sees research as providing objective, factual information which is handed over to policy-makers for their use, as I demonstrated in chapter 5. This approach therefore embodies a clear distinction between facts and values, and sees 'fact-finding' and 'making value-judgments' as two separate activities which are pursued sequentially. This is so even in those versions of the dominant tradition — ameliorism in the nineteenth century and Fabianism in the twentieth — which anticipated that the end point of research will be a set of moral prescriptions for change which arise out of the data, and which any rational administrator is therefore bound to accept. This classic approach in British social administration is, as Bulmer puts it, 'a peculiar blend of empirical data and philosophy' which pays little attention to theory, with the result that 'too much is prescribed and too little is explained; values intrude too forcefully' (Bulmer, 1982a, p. 165). In Bulmer's view, the problem lies in the lack of attention paid to theoretical accounts of the phenomena studied. This approach also clearly overlooks the extent to which 'facts' are themselves imbued with values, for example, by the kinds of questions which are asked.

However, insofar as the dominant position still is influential, any researcher who aspires to undertake the kind of research which is aimed at policy-makers is likely to meet the expectation that the research ought to be providing objective facts, and consequently will be assigned the role of technician in policy-making, providing 'facts' but no more. Qualitative researchers are likely to find themselves in difficulties on both counts. The methods by which qualitative data are collected are less likely to make claims to value-free objectivity credible, even if researchers should wish to make such claims. This is substantially compounded where research is being conducted in the on-going collaborative ways which I discussed in chapter 8, where the researcher is working alongside the researched, not standing apart from them.

A well-documented British example of difficulties of this kind is Cohen and Taylor's (1977) discussion of their attempts to get permission to continue their research on the experience of long-term imprisonment, which developed initially from education classes which they took in Durham prison. Their decision to continue and develop this was sparked off by the prisoners' hostility to Home Office researchers, who had arrived to study the experience of long-term imprisonment by standard quantitative methods, including psychological tests. Their own attempts to continue their very different style of investigations into the same issue — which involved long-term familiarity with a small group of prisoners based on conversation and group discussions, with the researchers feeding back their analysis to the prisoners for further discussion — were ultimately unsuccessful. A major source of criticism from the Home Office centred on their methods, which were said to concentrate on a 'small minority' and therefore not to give a representative picture, and to amount to a project which was not 'proper research', falling 'somewhere between research and journalism' (p. 72). Their departure from the conventional model of the objective researcher was in this case made the reason for denying them access — or at least, for laying down conditions associated with access which would have made it into a quite different project. There is, of course, a sense in which one could argue that research methods were made the public issue, but that the real reason for excluding them was the potentially subversive content of their findings. However, the position which Cohen and Taylor adopt is somewhat more subtle than that. They argue that the Home Office had developed over the years a highly circumscribed definition of 'research' which is quite consonant with its legitimate correctional aims in respect of the prison population. However, in doing so, they had effectively developed a mechanism for excluding outsiders from undertaking research on its territory, by defining all research which does not fall within that definition as 'not proper research' (p. 77). It seems to me that the point which they make about the Home Office links more generally in an important way with the argument that one of the reasons why quantitative research has always been the dominant mode in a policy context is its utility for enabling administrators to categorize the population as a basis for developing more efficient bureaucratic methods of control (see chapter 5). So qualitative researchers are not simply in the position of having to persuade policy-makers that their concept of 'objective' research is a naive one, but also have to cope with the reality that the quantitative methods which provide 'objective research' are exceedingly useful in relation to the daily task of maintaining the status quo — whether it be in prisons, schools, or whatever. Qualitative research, in contrast, is much more likely to offer up findings and insights which will disturb the status quo, while at the same time the methods employed make it impossible to claim credibility on grounds of objectivity.

The difficulties which qualitative researchers face with respect to questions of objectivity therefore will not easily go away. They do, of course, lead straight back to classic debates about whether social science can ever be 'value-free', associated principally with Weber (1949) and Myrdal (1958). More recently, the discussions of Becker (1967) and Gouldner (1970 and 1973) on similar issues have also been influential. Questions of objectivity and values as set out in these debates may be regarded as having been settled some time ago by many social scientists, but they remain live issues in policy-related research. Partly this is a consequence of the dominant tradition itself which remains strong within the discipline of social administration, and partly it is a result of undertaking research where there is a clear and direct engagement with the social world, which highlights questions of values that remain dormant in other kinds of research. As Barnes (1979) has put it:

In advocating change, values have to be made explicit,

> whereas values can more easily be taken for granted, or never made explicit, when studying the reproduction of the present state of affairs. (p. 175)

Undertaking policy-oriented work therefore necessarily implies that the researcher needs to address these questions of fact and value, especially in the presentation of findings. This presents the qualitative researcher with a rather difficult tightrope to walk: on the one hand, being unable and probably disinclined to claim that the research provides objective, value-free facts, but on the other hand, wanting to assert that ethnographic and other qualitative data do offer authoritative descriptions of the social world. In relation to education, much of the work which I discussed in chapter 7 especially would make such a claim. To accomplish this one needs to be able to demonstrate convincingly that facts and values cannot be separated, but that research is not thereby invalidated. Rein (1976) has provided a strong statement of that position in relation to social policy, arguing that claims of value-neutrality in policy-related research mean that 'we take the risk of winning objectivity at the cost of usefulness' (p. 42). He argues that the only way to develop social science capable of taking a position on policy issues is to integrate descriptive analysis with normative questions — a position rather like Myrdal's, who argues that the important issue is to introduce value premises openly into research, to face questions of value rather than evade them (Myrdal, 1958, p. 54). Some support for the position that facts and values are inevitably intertwined can be found in the official report on the SSRC produced by Lord Rothschild (1982), in which he argues that some parts of social science (for example, population studies) can more genuinely claim to be value-free than others, but that:

> Other parts of social science cannot be value-free without distorting their aim, for example, the sociological study of the effects of housing on a given population. Value judgments will be implicit in noting some of the effects, good and bad. (Paragraph 4.12)

All of this has considerable implications for the role which the qualitative researcher can adopt in relation to policy-makers, and in particular, for the model of the researcher as technician, which is so prominent in the dominant tradition (see chapter 5). Allocating the social scientist a technician role is a characteristic position where research is being conducted to feed into policy at the top, that is, for example, to officials at the Department of Education and Science, or to Members of Parliament or ministers. This is a 'top-down' model of social reform, where research is allocated a subordinate role as the 'handmaiden of policy' (Greer, 1977, p. 57). Within this model, although research as presented may include analysis as well as description, the fact/value distinction is sharply maintained and the role allocated to the researcher means that 'the description of *what* happened is more likely to be accepted than the explanation of *why* it happened' (Shils, 1949, p. 225). A vivid example of this can be found in chapter 4, where the British government's use of Mass-Observation during wartime was predicated on the assumption that the facts would be useful, but they could probably discard Tom Harrisson's opinions. In this example, and for a brief period, data generated by qualitative methods were regarded as useful to government, but the technician model was being nonetheless imposed upon a style of social research where it could not easily fit.

It is, in other words, rather difficult for qualitative researchers to adopt the role of the technicians of policy because the data which they generate do not lend themselves so readily to separating 'the facts' and handing them over. However, there is still often a temptation to define a research project of any kind as providing useful technical information, because either access or funding or both seem easier to secure on that basis. As Barnes puts it, government agencies themselves are under pressure to show that they are using tax-payers' money to fund research projects that are 'purported to be useful', and researchers for their part are likely to '(describe) over-optimistically the likely practical significance of their proposed research' (Barnes, 1979, p. 82). Casting oneself into a technician role may be tempting even for qualitative researchers, but the dangers of so doing are all too obviously displayed in the experience of Mass-Observation (see chapter 4) — a point which I shall take up below in relation to research ethics. Further, being cast in the technician role by definition gives the researcher a relatively limited amount of control over the kind of data which are to be generated and the kind of issues which are to be studied and therefore clearly carries the potential for being involved in research where one has grave doubts about the value of the exercise on intellectual grounds. Indeed, as I have already noted, it is possible for research to be used quite cynically by policy-makers, not genuinely to assist them in their deliberations, but to deflect criticism, or as a public relations exercise. The research conducted for the Plowden Committee is a well-documented case of research being used as 'stage management' (Acland, 1980; see also chapter 2).

It is very likely therefore that if one were to ask the simple question, 'Should you be prepared to act in the role of the technician of policy?' most qualitative researchers would answer an unambiguous 'no'. However, to pose the question in that way is too crude, and does not really reflect the kind of choice which most researchers are likely to be faced with: one's role may be ambiguous at the start of a project, for example, or it may seem that an initial agreement to provide 'useful facts' is a small price to pay for obtaining access or funding. Further, the structural position of a researcher in relation to policy-makers varies in a rather more complex way than the crude distinction 'technician or not?' implies. For example, the structural position in which the researcher is perhaps most vulnerable to being relegated to the technician role is where research has been directly commissioned by policy-makers, including where the task is defined as policy 'evaluation' in its narrow sense (see chapter 7). Evaluation using qualitative methods is as vulnerable here as is any other kind. Wolcott, for example, in his discussion of the development of ethnographic evaluation in American educational institutions, argues that there is inevitably an 'evaluation compromise', whereby ethnographers accept that they cannot engage in 'full-blown ethnographic studies' because the material required by their sponsors needs to be more focussed (Wolcott, 1984).

Another group of researchers who are equally if not more likely to be cast in the role of technicians are those who work as in-house researchers for central government or local authority departments. However, even in these two closely circumscribed structural positions, researchers are not necessarily and invariably in a position to adopt an over-rational view of the policy-making process itself, and to overlook the evidence that policy-makers actually look to research to offer reconceptualizations of the issues, and not just to provide facts (see chapter 6). So even where the researcher's structural position makes him or her look very much like a technician, there may be scope for a more independent input.

For other researchers whose structural position does not tie them so closely into government, it is clearly somewhat easier to avoid being defined as a technician, although pragmatic considerations may encourage a slide into that role, as I have already indicated. So, for the researcher who does want to pursue policy-oriented research, what are the alternatives? And among those alternatives, is it possible to define a researcher into a role which does not maintain the over-simple distinction between fact and values which, inter alia, is hospitable to qualitative research? These are crucial questions; but before answering them, I want to consider a related set of issues about the position of the researcher, not only in relation to policy-makers, but also in relation to those who have been researched. The ethical questions which I shall raise in the next section need to be considered alongside the questions of objectivity and values which I have discussed in this section, in developing alternative models of the political position of the researcher which better fit the kind of policy-related qualitative research which I have been advocating.

Ethical Issues in Policy-oriented Qualitative Research

Enthusiasm for promoting qualitative research as being of direct usefulness to policy-makers must be tempered by a recognition that this is a situation in which ethical issues are raised in a sharp form. An illustration of some dangers of over-enthusiasm can be drawn from Rist's (1981a) work, which is highly supportive of policy-oriented qualitative research in the field of education. Rist sees the qualitative researcher as a 'precious commodity' for policy-makers, because he or she has built up the trust and confidence of a particular social group, and can therefore give access to them, advise on how to target the programme and so on (see chapter 8 for further discussion). This of course builds on a key feature of qualitative research and especially ethnography, namely long-term familiarity with a particular setting and a particular group of people. The kind of role which Rist envisages for research could be totally unacceptable on ethical grounds to many researchers, depending somewhat upon issues like how the research was set up, the content of the policy, who pays the researcher, and how much control the researcher retains over the data. There are also parallels with the position of anthropological researchers whose work was made use of by colonial administrators (Asad, 1973).

An example and a warning of the particular ethical difficulties which are attendant upon policy-oriented qualitative research is provided by the experience of Mass-Observation's use by government during the Second World War. As I indicated in chapter 4, there was a clear recognition within the Ministry of Information that Mass-Observation's methods made it ideally suited quite literally to spying on the population. Despite the exclusion of qualitative methods within the dominant tradition, they have a clear superiority over quantitative methods in this regard. Much as the leaders of Mass-Observation were aware of this possibility and stated at the outset that they would not be used for 'espionage', they had no access to any means of control over their data which could prevent that in practice, other than the normal methods of formally concealing the identity of individuals; but that does not deal with the possibility of 'betraying' the practices of vulnerable social groups, as I shall argue in the next section. Being cast into the role of technician despite the fact that qualitative research fits this model rather badly, they were drawn into highly dubious situations such as concealing their links with government in order to maintain their credibility with the public including concealment from the observers, who did not know that the data which they collected were being fed into the Ministry of Information. This concealment was a direct result of their desire to preserve a commitment to the democratization of knowledge and the collaboration of large numbers of volunteers who researched their own social situation, whilst at the same time being useful to government. The lesson which can be derived from this experience is one which no researcher can afford to ignore if she wishes to pursue policy-oriented qualitative research, including that which entails collaboration with the researched.

In more general terms: what are the main ethical issues which arise in policy-oriented qualitative research specifically, and can they be overcome? First, there is the question of openness or concealment on the part of the researcher, as illustrated graphically by the Mass-Observation experience. Issues concerning covert research strategies have been widely debated amongst social researchers, and these debates are well summarized in the collection edited by Bulmer (1982b). In his introduction to his collection, Bulmer acknowledges that there are clear parallels to be drawn in particular between covert participant observation and espionage (p. 4), and notes that a minority of social researchers — perhaps Douglas (1976) being the best known — defend its positive virtues in this regard, arguing that since the whole of social life is characterized by suspicion and deceit there is no particular reason for social research to stand aside from this. The majority, however, would reject that view, arguing, as for example, Warwick does in the same collection, that the ends do not justify the means in social research, even if one can demonstrate that research conducted covertly has in some way benefited the group studied (Warwick, 1982).

So far as policy-related research is concerned, there may be some temptation to indulge in an ends-justify-the-means argument in relation to covert observation, particularly in research which is oriented to policy change. A particular danger arises here in policy-related research which is commissioned or sponsored by policy-makers as part of a top-down exercise in policy evaluation and change. In these circumstances, there can be serious ethical questions about what one 'takes' from the people being studied, as MacDonald and Norris note in their discussion of educational evaluation based on fieldwork (MacDonald and Norris, 1981, pp. 284–7). Where the research is sponsored by those who have the power to make and change policy, there may well be the opportunity for a researcher to engage covertly in research, in the guise of an official, for example, or indeed a client. Such research is, it seems to me, a particularly dangerous example of covert social research, because the findings are not being used merely to illuminate our knowledge of the social world, but potentially to change it. As with the whole debate about covert research, the argument is in the end about moral and political issues, points which I take up later in this chapter. However, policy-related research which is concerned with the view from below, and which attempts to engage collaboratively with the recipients and the 'makers' of policy at the grassroots, is far less likely to raise these kinds of ethical questions. The very essence of such activities precludes concealment almost by definition. However, there may be some danger — as there always is within qualitative research — that the nature of the research enterprise is not clearly understood by the researched just because participant observation as a research strategy is much less understood than a questionnaire (Barnes, 1979, pp. 77–8). People being researched by observational methods are also far less able to control the flow of information than interview subjects, and there often are ambiguities built into such situations about when the researcher is supposed to be 'off duty'. Nonetheless, it seems to me that the severe ethical difficulties associated with concealment of the research purpose are far less likely to arise in 'bottom-upwards' policy research, than in the 'top down' versions.

Another important set of ethical issues, which arises in policy-oriented qualitative research of both kinds, are questions of confidentiality of the data and the protection of the respondents. In quantitative research, these are frequently dealt with as technical issues, requiring simply the rigorous application of procedures to detach the names of respondents from the interview schedules; but, as I have argued elsewhere, questions about confidentiality are magnified in qualitative research because of the position of trust which the researcher aims to develop, and because research on a small scale makes individuals much more easily identifiable (Finch, 1985).

Qualitative, policy-oriented research raises issues of confidentiality at two levels: the individual and the collective. At the individual level, there are questions of quite literally, who gets their hands on the data. It is the 'raw' data which are of particular significance here, especially fieldnotes and interview transcripts, because these are almost bound to contain material which will embarrass or incriminate named individuals, either the person who gives the information, or others whom they name. It is, of course, recognized practice for researchers to give assurances that such data will be seen in its raw state by themselves alone. A further procedure described by Stenhouse and used by himself and his collaborators in case-study research in schools, involves sending interviewees a copy of the interview transcript, inviting them to check it and — if they feel it necessary — to erase any material which is too sensitive to be used. After that, they are asked to sign a cover sheet which gives permission for the material to be used in an anonymized form (Stenhouse, 1985). In policy-oriented research it may not always be possible either to give or to honour conventional promises of confidentiality. Again, this is a problem which is especially likely to arise with 'top-down' commissioned or sponsored research; but researchers wishing to engage in small-scale, grassroots research in a policy context can find themselves in similar difficulties if they need the cooperation of policy-makers and administrators to secure access to their research setting.

An account of precisely this situation is given by Cohen and Taylor in relation to their prison research. At one point during their negotiations with the Home Office (which were ultimately unsuccessful), they requested that they should be allowed to tape-record some of their conversations with prisoners. This was agreed, but in a form which they found unacceptable. They were told that they should tape *all* interviews, and that these should be transcribed on Home Office premises; after transcription and any 'necessary editing' of objectionable material, the Home Office would hold onto the tapes until the researchers needed them (Cohen and Taylor, 1977, p. 84). A suggestion of this kind which puts raw data into 'official' hands would be potentially extremely damaging to the people interviewed — a point which is especially obvious in relation to prison research. Faced with a stark choice of this kind, probably most researchers would abandon the project, as Cohen and Taylor ultimately did. But often the situation may be less clear-cut: the potential damage to the researched may be less obvious, for example, and the whole project seem more inocuous; or researchers may be given access and only realize later that the data are to be treated as the property of the sponsors. This situation has been explored in the

American context by Trend (1980), using the example in which fieldworkers had been collecting data on low-income households and had given written guarantees of confidentiality; subsequently, there was a request for the material to be handed over to the General Accounting Office for audit. Trend argues that ethnographers working on government contracts are uniquely vulnerable to disagreements over the use of data, because of its personalized nature. He suggests some rules of advice which fieldworkers in such situations might follow: read your contract carefully before you sign, looking especially for whether you are expected to hand over the data when the project is finished; decide how much confidentiality you can promise in the light of this; do not collect unnecessary data which could be used adversely later; and do not imagine that you can avoid the law ultimately by planning wild schemes such as shipping the data off to a foreign country (pp. 347–8). Trend's basic approach is to make sure that any such research is embarked upon with one's eyes open, and with a realistic appraisal of what can be accomplished within the law — advice which seems eminently sensible, and pertinent in the British context also, especially since the effects of the Police and Criminal Evidence Act 1984 on official access to social research data could be substantial, although have yet to be tested (*Network*, 1984).

Questions about confidentiality and protection of individuals do not stop, however, at the matter of who controls access to the data. Even where this is firmly in the researcher's hands, there are questions about how the findings get fed back into the situation studied. Ethnographic studies in schools offer plenty of examples of information generated in the course of research which could be damaging to individuals if it were made public. Researchers routinely have to face such issues whilst the research is actually being conducted: what, for example, do you do when you find a pupil smoking or otherwise breaking the school rules (Corrigan, 1979)? Perhaps in that situation, many researchers would find it relatively easy to turn a blind eye, but there are other circumstances where events occur which are vital to the research issues being studied, and yet also damaging to individuals. If these are then fed back into the research setting, the implications for the individuals concerned could be damaging. An example of such a situation can be taken from Ball's (1984) discussion of what happened at the school which he studied when he was presenting some of his findings to teachers. In the course of this, he described one lesson in detail, as illustrative of what went on in the classrooms. The lesson described happened to be

French, and the response of the French staff was very hostile, accusing Ball of 'picking' on them. Ball says that he concluded from this experience that in future he would build in features to any such account which would actively mislead anyone trying to identify the subjects. A parallel, and very interesting, discussion can be found in Richardson's (1973) work on leadership and staff relationships in a secondary school. Richardson worked in a collaborative way with staff and, by her own account, built up good and trusting relationships with them. However, she shows that she still had to face two occasions when the whole basis of her activities was called into question, both of which concerned the circulation of research material beyond the school as well as within it. In her view, these problems arose essentially from a conflict of views about who should control the 'boundary' around the school, that is, who should be able to decide upon the nature of material presented to the outside world (pp. 45–59).

These ethical issues which arise when feeding back material into a situation, although on one level they apply to the publication of any qualitative research, arise most sharply in the kind of collaborative, 'bottom-upwards' research which seeks to introduce change at grassroots level. Where any information is fed back directly into the small-scale situation, there is much greater potential for identifying individuals than usually is possible in the publication of a book, where simple concealment of the setting means that the individuals remain anonymous to the great majority of readers — although total anonymity can probably never be guaranteed. An additional dimension of concern about feeding back research into small-scale educational settings in the mid-1980s concerns their potential use in evaluation of individual teachers. If teacher appraisal becomes a reality, educational researchers working in a collaborative way with teachers will have to address the ethical issues which I am raising here in a particularly sharp form.

Finally, so far as individual protection is concerned, there is the question of whether all research subjects have equal rights to expect this. As I have already indicated, much policy-related research concerns the recipients of policy, but there is also considerable potential for qualitative research to be used to study the policy-making process itself, if access were granted (see chapter 7). Discussions of research ethics often distinguish between the relative power of different research subjects, arguing that questions of privacy and protection are paramount where research concerns powerless groups, but such considerations can be at least partially suspended in research on the powerful, who already have the means whereby they can protect themselves, and in a real sense are 'fair game'; where research concerns people who hold public office, there is an additional argument that it is entirely legitimate to openly scrutinize their actions (Barnes, 1979). In the educational context, this would mean perhaps that civil servants in the DES, politicians at central and local government level, education officers of the LEA and perhaps head-teachers would be 'fair game' for research strategies which have less protection for subjects built into them. Clearly such issues are matters to be considered, decided and justified in relation to the circumstances of a particular case by researchers who do get access to policy-makers. However, in many cases studying the policy-making process is likely to mean, for example, as in Flynn's (1979) study of a town planning department, that one spends most of one's time with officials who themselves are relatively powerless in the setting being studied. Hence, the ethical issues may not be so clearly different from policy-oriented research on client groups.

As well as the question of the protection of individuals, policy-oriented research raises questions of protection at a collective level. These issues become especially acute when one is studying relatively powerless groups. The problem here is not so much that individuals might be damaged, but that a whole social group may be stigmatized by the research findings, or popular prejudices about them may be confirmed. I have described elsewhere the difficulties which I faced in deciding whether to write up findings of a research project on working-class playgroups, some of which I felt could be interpreted in such a way as to reinforce popular prejudices about the inade-quacies of a particular powerless group of women — working class mothers in inner city areas (Finch, 1984d and 1985). I described this as a sense that I could potentially betray my informants as a group, not as individuals, and the potential for betrayal is even more obviously present in situations where research findings reveal, for example, strategies which informants use (possibly including illegal strategies) to avoid the worst aspects of the effects of current policies upon their own lives, or where informants as a group are engaged in pursuits whose organization could be damaging if publicly revealed. A well-known rather dramatic example of this is Humphreys' study of homosexual behaviour in public lavatories, where he was able to describe in detail how this is organized and controlled. This research also raises questions about the use of covert research strategies in such circumstances (Humphreys, 1970: see Warwick, 1982, for discussion of the ethical issues raised by this study).

The possibility for all such betrayals is far greater in qualitative than in quantitative research, because of its emphasis upon the reality and the details of how people organize their lives. Where qualitative research is designed not merely to add to the stock of knowledge about social life but also to influence change in policies, an additional layer of difficulty may arise, because there is conflict between the researcher's desire to protect informants (whether individually or collectively) and the need to maintain credibility with policy-makers. To put it crudely, one cannot argue that the situation in which the recipients of policies are placed is intolerable without producing the evidence which supports that conclusion; but such evidence may seem weak without the inclusion of material which shows the lengths that people go to cope with their present difficulties. In grassroots as well as 'top-down' research, such difficulties may also arise, if the researcher is seeking to identify areas for potential change without identifying individuals whose present practice is particularly in need of such change. A good illustration of these kind of problems can be found in Burgess' (1985b) discussion of some ethical aspects of his study of a comprehensive school. This study was not specifically policy-oriented, but the issues raised in this instance are very similar. Burgess was concerned in particular to study pupils who were receiving a Newsom curriculum designed for the 'less able'. He admits that he found it difficult to decide how to write up some of this research on Newsom classes, 'where pupils smoked, swore at, and with, the teachers and where little school work was done' (p. 156). Eventually, after all the teachers concerned had left the school, Burgess did show some draft chapters describing these classes to the headteacher who was furious that he had not been told sooner what was going on. In this instance, it was clear that there would have been direct and negative consequences for the individuals involved if the data had been fed immediately into the policy process (at the level of the headteacher). Holding it back until the individuals left the school partly resolved that problem, although Burgess was well aware that his data could nonetheless rebound on subsequent generations of Newsom pupils who, whilst perhaps being offered better 'educational experiences' might also find that there is 'some curtailment of the strategies that pupils adopt to come to terms with their schooling' (p. 157).

Having raised some of the ethical issues which relate to policy-oriented, qualitative research especially, I make no pretence that I can give recipes for resolving them. Like Burgess, it seems to me inevitable that there are no certain answers and that ethical compromises have to be reached on the basis of what seems to be the most feasible agreement which offers maximum protection to all parties, including the researcher. There is, of course, always the possibility that — like Cohen and Taylor — one will decide that the only compromises which are feasible are not actually acceptable and there seems little honest choice other than to abandon that piece of research. Whatever decisions are ultimately taken, it seems to me that there can never be neatly applicable rules, and therefore that codes of ethics may produce useful guidelines, but are not the ultimate answer. Indeed, as I have argued elsewhere (Finch, 1984d), insofar as codes of ethics may imply that such considerations are merely technical issues, they could be positively dangerous, since in practice, research questions described as 'ethical' are ultimately moral and political matters, in which the researcher has to engage as a member of the society, and not simply as a technician of policy. I return, therefore, to questions concerning the political position of the researcher in the next section.

The Political Position of the Researcher

Earlier in this chapter, I argued that the qualitative researcher in particular cannot realistically adopt the stance of being 'objective', even if one can do this in the case of quantitative research — an issue which itself is debatable. In this final section, I shall consider alternative positions which a researcher might adopt in the policy-research process, bearing in mind also the kind of ethical and moral questions which I outlined in the previous section.

The arguments which I have been developing in previous chapters suggest that policy-oriented research of a qualitative kind can realistically be carried out only on the understanding that the knowledge created cannot be 'objective' in the sense of being neutral in relation to the political processes of policy-making. The idea that all social science knowledge is ultimately political and not neutral is a well-established position in sociology (Bell and Newby, 1977; Cain and Finch, 1981), and this of course is especially pertinent to any research which aims to be policy-oriented. As Karabel and Halsey (1977) put it, in the context of their discussion of action-research in the educational field:

Explicit recognition of the political character of social science research — as well as a clear awareness of the interest of state policy-makers in its findings — is, we suggest, a necessary development if social science is to retain its commitment to the quest for knowledge while at the same time continuing to negotiate public support. (p. 28)

In one sense, this position does have resonance within the dominant tradition of the research-policy relationship, and especially within Fabianism, where the political character of research findings *was* recognized, albeit in a specific form: that is, it was assumed that the facts would speak for themselves, but that they would inevitably proclaim reformist, socialist measures (see chapter 5). In official reports on research, the Rothschild report on the SSRC is notable for its clear recognition of the essentially contested and political nature of social science research. Indeed, Rothschild sees one major role for empirical research as submitting government policies to empirical trial — an activity which he sees as very much in the public interest (Rothschild, 1982, paragraph 3.12).

To argue in this way seems to point to a position for the researcher which is openly partisan, rather than objective and politically neutral; or, at the very least, it implies that the researcher cannot stay out of the political arena within her or his research may be used to shape policies. This is the position which Rein (1976) adopts in his influential work, when he argues against the idea of a 'policy science' which can be above ideological disagreements, since good research can never be conducted without being grounded in a specific paradigm. It is especially clear in policy-related research that different paradigms are not simply an intellectual matter of different schools of thought, but are issues relating to power and the representation of sets of interests. As a consequence:

> Academic debate is therefore much nastier than it might be if only intellectual disagreements were involved. (Rein, 1979, p. 257)

In the case of qualitative research, as I have already suggested, there is a strong likelihood that the political stance adopted will be oppositional, perhaps subversive, in respect of the status quo, since the methods used get close up to the people studied, and are very likely to challenge the 'official version' of their situation (see chapter 3). Moreover, qualitative researchers are likely to make themselves 'visible' in the research process and its outcome. Further, where a study is a commissioned evaluation, designed to feed into policy-making directly, there is a sense in which the researcher can scarcely avoid a partisan stance, whether that is made explicit or not. As MacDonald has argued in respect of educational evaluation, the evaluator has to make decisions about what information will be of most use and how to obtain it, and taking those decisions commits him or her to a political stance on issues of educational change (MacDonald, 1977).

To adopt an openly partisan approach may seem attractive for its simplicity and its apparent honesty, but there is clearly a danger that this will undermine claims to any authority which derives from the knowledge created through research, potentially relegating it to the status of just one version of issue in question, which is to the taste of some people but not others. Bulmer sees this kind of danger in the whole debate about objectivity in social science which derives from Weber and Myrdal, arguing that its consequence is often to exaggerate the value-laden character of social science 'to the point where all differences of view are seen as a matter of taste and no standards are admitted for judging the rightness and wrongness of particular analyses, (Bulmer, 1982a, p. 165). It seems to me that this is a real danger especially in relation to qualitative research, which already has to overcome accusations of subjectivity because of the methods used. If one then also adopts a political stance that can be seen simply as one's own taste, the potential for qualitative research to make an impact on policy has been lost. Even where the policy-makers' political taste accords with one's own, the research may be seen as adding little if it simply demonstrates what both are in agreement about in any case. Rather, a much stronger position to adopt is that an acceptance that all social science knowledge is intrinsically political does not necessarily entail a slide into total relativism. On the contrary, it remains an important task of social scientists to evaluate one account of a particular set of circumstances against another by weighing the quality of the evidence and the argument which supports each (Cain and Finch, 1981).

Following on from this recognition of the political nature of research, but without losing sight of the independent input which research potentially can make to social policy, I want to suggest that there are four possible positions which a researcher can adopt in relation to the policy-making process, all of which are alternatives to the model of the objective scientist who provides technical knowledge.

The first of these alternatives is the role as provider of enlightenment. In chapter 6, I outlined in some detail the case for this approach, which has the considerable merits of aligning with the way in which policy-makers appear actually to use research in most cases. The emphasis is upon the indirect effects of research findings, not so much for their factual context, as for the reorientation of the issues and the reconceptualizations which researchers can provide. As I noted, qualitative research seems particularly well suited to this, and there is no doubt that the enlightenment model provides a very attractive role for researchers, and one which many will feel it appropriate to adopt. It fits well not only with the evidence about how research is actually used, but can accommodate the 'political' view of social science knowledge, since its emphasis is upon ways of thinking about social issues, not on the provision of facts. It is rather similar to what Rein has called the 'value-critical' approach to the place of moral values in policy research, which emphasizes the inherently controversial nature of policy issues, and envisages a role for research which is rather modest: to generate a 'plausible understanding of social processes', and to see values themselves as part of those processes. The value-critical approach always generates conclusions which are provisional, which do not attempt to discover causal relationships that are stable over time, and which represent 'a best guess in the circumstances' (Rein, 1976, p. 74).

Given the appropriateness of the enlightenment model for qualitative research and its other attractions, it may well be the model of policy-oriented research to which most qualitative researchers are drawn. Whilst broadly I would welcome that, it also seems important to point out some of the dangers associated with the enlightenment model. Essentially these stem from the fact that the role of the researcher in this model is somewhat removed from the action, in that it implies that the researchers themselves are not actively engaged in problem-solving. This means that it fits rather less well the model of grassroots policy-oriented research which entails a collaborative work with the researched. Here, the researcher is by definition amongst the action, and if he or she then attempts to adopt the purely passive role implied by the enlightenment model, offering insights but declining to discuss how they should be acted upon, this runs counter to the concept of collaboration, especially if the project has been conceptualized as 'action-research'.

Where the research aims to feed into policy-making at a higher level, there are also potential dangers in adopting a passive approach. By definition, one is dependent on someone else taking up one's research and using it, and the scope for one's insights to be misinterpreted and modified are as great in the case of 'factual' data. Thus, as I have argued elsewhere, to act *only* as the provider of knowledge and insights can be to abdicate responsibility for how that knowledge is used (Finch, 1985). A graphic illustration of this is offered by Julienne Ford, in a discussion of her study of *Social Class and the Comprehensive School* (Ford, 1969). She describes how she heard a radio broadcast in which Professor Cox (an educationalist associated with the Black Papers whose position was very different from her own) was using her findings to support the view that educational selection should be retained. Her work was, as she puts it, 'being used to fuel his very different fire' (Ford, 1976, p. 58).

A somewhat more active stance on the part of the researcher is therefore implied, although one may then have to confront paradox of the kind which Merton identified in his discussion of the intellectual in a public bureaucracy. Distinguishing between 'bureaucratic' and 'unattached' intellectuals (the former work directly within public bureaucracies, the latter do not), he argued that unattached intellectuals who are interested in policy can retain their independence of thought but may have difficulty in getting access to those who hold power; bureaucratic intellectuals have access to power, but at the price of having limits placed upon the research which they can undertake. To act as an unattached intellectual, in Merton's view means that at best one can produce critiques of public policy which have an effect on the climate within which decisions are made (Merton, 1957). Whilst I accept Merton's general point about the limitations placed upon both kinds of intellectuals, I find the distinction which he poses between the two rather too sharp. There are various ways in which a researcher can adopt an active stance towards the use of research without necessarily being drawn into the structures of government itself. Indeed, the other models which I shall consider are all of this type.

The second position which I see for a policy-oriented researcher is the role of adviser. This is one example of a role which is something in between the completely 'unattached' and the 'bureaucratic' intellectual, in that an adviser is someone who is not necessarily structurally incorporated into government bureaucracies, but nonetheless is invited to make a direct input to policy. This is very much the role sought by the Webbs and later Fabians, and the most successful examples of it in relation to the use of social science were, as I argued in chapter 6, those academics who made an input to Labour party policy-making in opposition and in government in the 1950s and 1960s. Educational policies were centrally involved in this, especially comprehensive reorganization in secondary education, and the EPA experiments. Payne and his colleagues argue that it is only when social scientists are used as consultants or advisers, rather than as research technicians, that the full potential of the contribution of social science to policy can be realized (Payne, Dingwall, Payne and Carter, 1981, pp. 157–9). The importance of the role of the adviser was also outlined by Znaniecki in his (1940) discussion of the social role of the 'man of knowledge', where he argues that those in power seek advisers as a response to changes in economic or social conditions which disturb the established patterns. The advisers sought are people who have 'superior knowledge' in the sense that they are familiar with a range of ways of coping with the problem in hand, and can therefore both diagnose it and suggest alternative solutions (pp. 34–6).

The role which an adviser can hope to play is therefore something of a mixture of partisanship and distance from the political arena. On the one hand, it is difficult to envisage that those who hold power will seek as advisers any social scientists whose own political position is known to be out of sympathy with their own. As I argued in chapter 5, the Webbs ultimately failed in their attempts to promote their 'good ideas' with policy-makers on a non-partisan basis; but their successors in the 1960s were much more successful when they were specifically working with politicians whose views they shared. On the other hand, the adviser is sought precisely because she or he has a different kind of (in Znaniecki's terms) 'superior knowledge' to offer, which makes it possible to envisage alternative policies and to assess their viability. In that sense, the adviser is distanced from the policy-making process.

This kind of advisory role is, it seems to me, quite accessible to qualitative researchers provided, as I argued in chapter 8, their expertise goes beyond single case-studies, and enables comparisons between relevant situations to be made. However, the advisory role is very much a matter of opportunity, and opportunities to act as an adviser in government policy-making at various levels are likely to arise only when the political complexion of the government aligns with the political orientation (in its broadest sense) of the researcher. Such opportunities are easier to cultivate at grassroots level precisely because there is variation in the ways in which policies are interpreted and applied in different local authorities or different schools, and the opportunities for qualitative researchers to be 'advisers' at this level of policy are correspondingly greater.

The third role which I shall consider for the researcher is the role of advocate on behalf of the research subjects. This is a model that appears to fit naturally with qualitative research, where the aim is to achieve an understanding of the world from the perspective of those studied who, in the case of policy-oriented research, are often the recipients of social policy and therefore relatively powerless groups in society, as I have already argued. The qualitative researcher is therefore in a position where she is, quite literally 'giving a voice' to the relatively powerless, simply by conducting this kind of research. The potential of that is well expressed by Cohen and Taylor, in their discussion of the difficulties which they encountered in doing research with an education class in a prison, where they argue that the right to control 'talk' is the prerogative of the powerful in our society, and enabling the powerless to 'talk' can be a highly political activity: 'talk can be deviant . . . and controlling the right to talk is a tool for protecting the powerful' (Cohen and Taylor, 1977, p. 76). It is a short step from conducting a piece of research which allows the powerless to 'talk', to using that research as an advocate on their behalf. A possible analogy for this, which is used by Pollard (1984), is between an ethnographic researcher and a trade union official:

Because of its fundamentally appreciative attributes (ethnography) can articulate the perspectives of particular groups and present them forcefully in much the same way as a good union might do. (p. 185)

In a sense, the advocacy role is one which a qualitative researcher doing work of this kind almost cannot avoid. Simply by writing up the research findings in this 'appreciative' way, the researcher is presenting 'their story'. It is precisely because of this position, that some of the ethical issues which I discussed in the preceding section are especially pertinent to qualitative research: there is great potential for telling that story in a way which actually ultimately damages the collective position of the researched. It is possible to turn that around and to argue — as some writers would — that the only justification for undertaking qualitative research on powerless groups is to be able to act as an advocate on their behalf (James, 1977, p. 198). This is to envisage a type of advocacy which moves beyond the writing of a research report, and takes the demands of the researched group more clearly into the political arena. As Abrams (1985) puts it in a discussion critical of this approach, it involves:

acting as a 'mouthpiece' for a client group or as a 'community lawyer' accepting briefs only of the deserving downtrodden. (p. 203)

This kind of advocacy seems a dangerous position to adopt, for a variety of reasons. As I have argued elsewhere, a researcher acting as an advocate for a powerless group may simply have the effect of reinforcing popular prejudices about the incapacity of that group to act on its own behalf. Further, one's claim to be an advocate may not be directly endorsed by the group themselves — and in a sense often cannot be, since the researcher will be in contact with only a limited number of delinquent pupils, mothers of pre-school children, or whatever. Effectively, the researcher is a self-appointed advocate, articulating demands on the basis of her own interpretation of a group's needs as they have emerged in a research project, not necessarily demands which the group themselves have articulated. To do this in a real sense is paternalistic (Finch, 1985).

My own doubts about the advocacy role, have been echoed by other writers, from a variety of perspectives. Platt (1972) writing about survey research and social policy, argues against the position that the research should act as an advocate, even though she recognizes that the idea of reflecting the views of the researched seems 'uniquely democratic'. It is, however, in her view naive, because it assumes inter alia that the views of that group are relatively permanent, and that overlooks the fact that, unless there is unanimity, the view of the majority will be advocated at the expense of the minority. Frances Piven, discussing the development in the United States of 'advocacy planning' (not necessarily associated with research) produces a strong argument against professionals acting as advocates on behalf of the poor, on the grounds that this seldom produces any real change which would not have happened anyway, and meanwhile serves to blunt the more disruptive kind of protests through which the poor and powerless sometimes *have* been able to achieve their own demands (Piven, 1972, pp. 43–8). Thus, although simply by writing a report of qualitative research one is putting oneself in an advocacy role, there are a variety of moral reasons for questioning whether a researcher should go beyond that, and act on behalf of the group researched.

The fourth role which is in principle open to the researcher is that of direct engagement with policy — the most active role of all. I see this as differing from advocacy in the sense that one is acting on no-one's behalf other than one's own, but nonetheless one is directly engaged at some level with the process of making and changing policy.

There are a variety of ways in which this can happen. The most accessible of these — and the way in which all researchers can engage with policy, I would argue   is to enter the arena of public debate. This means not simply presenting findings in an accessible form, but also spelling out their practical consequences and offering interpretations of one's own findings which do engage with questions of policy. It may also entail writing in non-academic publications if those are more likely to make an impact; indeed the evidence which I discussed in chapter 6 suggested that government policy-makers get much of their information about research from sources like newspapers, as do other citizens. My argument about entering the arena of public debate rather echoes Bryant's position in his discussion of 'sociology in action'. He suggests that sociologists do not have to get directly involved in practical change but that:

> they should show much more research interest in strategies for deliberate social change, social intervention and the realisation of ideas than has been the case to date. Those who believe in the social and political significance of their work might at least ask themselves in all seriousness how its potential can be given practical effect. (Bryant, 1976, p. 347)

Abrams (1985) has endorsed a rather similar position, for which he uses the term 'advocacy'. He uses that term in a different way from its usage in my earlier discussion, where the researcher acts as a 'mouthpiece' for the research subjects. Abrams argues for a different sort of 'advocacy', which he sees as a relatively weak version of the enlightenment model of the research-policy relationship (see chapter 6). In this version of advocacy, the social scientist does directly engage with public debate about policy but acting as a social scientist (rather than as a representative of some other group) who can draw upon 'a social wisdom which has been slowly acquired in a 150 years of sociological work' (pp. 203–4). The advocacy in a sense is advocacy of social science itself, where social science knowledge is recognized to be 'argumentative knowledge', which can be used in a critical yet constructive way to comment upon policy by raising questions about possible unintended consequences, about the uncertainty of planning, or about the diversity of interests involved in any set of decisions. Abrams regards the work of Floud and of Halsey in the field of education as exemplary of social scientists who have operated on this model (p. 197).

Beyond engaging in public debate, there may be times when there are opportunities to make direct interventions in policy and practice. Some opportunities do exist to press findings on government ministers or civil servants (Thomas, 1983). This is not to suggest that social science knowledge will be so compelling and authoritative that it will automatically be accepted, as it suggested by the linear model of the research-policy relationship, but that this is one kind of knowledge which can and ought to be available in the policy-making process and may occasionally be decisive; more frequently its impact will be diffuse (see chapter 6 for discussion of linear and diffuse models).

A rare example of a social researcher making a significant and direct input to policy can be found in David Hargreaves' work for the Inner London Education Authority. Following the publication in 1982 of his proposals for the fuller implementation of the comprehensive principle in secondary schools (pp. 166–91) Hargreaves left his academic post and went to work full-time for the ILEA and wrote a concrete set of proposals for the authority (Hargreaves, 1984). Subsequently, about thirty schools became involved in implementing these innovations, which include greater autonomy for pupils in matters of school organization such as uniform, involvement of pupils in decision-making structures including decisions about the curriculum, and new forms of assessment (*Times Educational Supplement*, 24 June 1985).

On other occasions, research findings can be and are used as political ammunition by one or more parties in the political process. For example, Husen (1984, pp. 16–17) has discussed how his own work on differentiation by academic ability in Swedish schools was used in a significant way as political ammunition to support the case against early differentiation. In this instance, Husen indicates that he was not directly involved with the Social Democratic Party who used his findings; but clearly one option for researchers is to work with relevant parties and pressure groups, and to engage directly with policy debate and political change in that way.

These are all possible forms of direct engagement with policy at governmental level (whether local or national), and all assume the 'up, along and down' model of change (see chapter 8). However, if one adopts the 'lateral ripple' model there are rather different possibilities for direct engagement with policy. In the grassroots, collaborative kind of research which I discussed in chapter 8, the researcher is engaged directly in policy change almost by definition, but on a small scale. For the policy-oriented researcher who is dissatisfied simply with the hope that her research may eventually provide policy-makers with enlightenment, direct engagement with small-scale change is likely to prove the most satisfying complementary activity, although it does, of course, entail accepting that one's research activities are not going to change the world. It is important not to undervalue the importance of small-scale change, however, which can ultimately amount to a movement of some significance, if, for example, it is repeated in several local authorities (Finch, 1985). Collaborative, small-scale research oriented to policy change is also likely to prove intellectually challenging for a researcher, since it provides a direct opportunity to test and refine ideas, in contrast to small-scale 'evaluation' research, which entails studying and analyzing a programme of change which the researcher has had no part in shaping. Halsey makes this point forcibly in his discussion of different models of action research based on the experience of the Educational Priority Areas programmes. He argues that the 'planning approach' to action research assigns the researcher the role of answering technical questions about what worked; whereas in the 'research approach' (which he regards as superior if far less common) the researcher helps to define the objectives and the methods for reaching them (Department of Education and Science, 1972, pp. 169–77).

All of these 'active' researcher roles (and to an extent the more 'passive' one of enlightenment) derive from an acknowledgement of the political nature of the knowledge created by research and contrast sharply with the model of the objective scientist. They also contrast with the dominant tradition of the research-policy relationship, insofar as that relationship involves a very small number of people: the researchers and the policy-makers. By contrast, the roles which I have outlined very much involve the researched as part of the policy-making process, and implicitly reject the top-down models of social reform, in favour of something much more like the bottom-upwards version represented in the 'alternative' tradition, and most vividly in Mass-Observation's concept of the democratization of knowledge, where in an 'us-and-them' model of social relationships, the researcher is very much on the side of 'us' (see chapters 3 and 4). I have argued that policy-oriented qualitative research is particularly suited to this model (see chapter 8). It can also be argued that an honest resolution of the ethical dilemmas involved in social research point in this direction. As Barnes puts it, 'any worthwhile, practical attempt to resolve ethical issues in social inquiry has to take into account the distribution of power between scientist, citizens, sponsors, and gatekeepers (Barnes, 1979, p. 24). Ultimately, therefore, questions of 'ethics' are not technical issues, but can only be considered with reference to the structures of power within which research operates: in that sense, they are political questions.

Any researcher who engages in policy-oriented or indeed any research capable of being used in a political context, cannot stand aside from power structures and therefore meets the classic dilemma outlined by Becker in his well-known article entitled 'Whose side are we on?' which, it is interesting to note, was first given as his presidential address to the Society for the Study of Social Problems (Becker, 1967). As Becker expresses it, the dilemma is that we cannot avoid taking sides, since 'we must always look at the matter from someone's point of view'. But the decision about whose side we are on is itself a political act. If — as is frequently the case in qualitative research — we reflect the viewpoint of a relatively powerless group, we ourselves become automatically entangled in power relations, since in general our society operates on a 'hierarchy of credibility' that accords more credence to the views of those in top positions. Thus, by giving credence to another view, sociologists fail to respect this hierarchy of credibility and 'express disrespect for the entire establishment order' (p. 242). Gouldner (1973, pp. 27–68) has challenged this view arguing, inter alia, that Becker presents his rejection of the non-partisan position as self-evident and never justifies it. This is not the place to engage in detail with the Becker-Gouldner debate, but I would agree at least with Gouldner's view that the value-free position should not be rejected too glibly (p. 27); indeed, I argued earlier in this chapter that this could be damaging to the potential of qualitative research in policy-oriented studies. However, Becker is right to emphasize that all social research takes place in a political context and researchers have to work out how they relate to that.

Finally, a further implication of this discussion of positions which is viable for the researcher to adopt in relation to policy is that the researcher needs to stay with the results of the research well beyond the official end of the project. The enlightenment model implies that the time-scale over which any research is likely to have an impact is much longer than the time-scale of a single project, and the more active roles outlined here clearly require some kind of sustained commitment on the part of the researcher. Indeed, as soon as one abandons a 'fact-finding' model of policy research in favour of a model which stresses interpretation within an overall recognition of the intrinsically political nature of such knowledge, researchers themselves become crucial in the continued use of their products. The potential for reinterpretation and misinterpretation is one important reason for that. More positively there is potentially a promotional role of the researcher, where the likely impact of a project which involved change in a single school or single local authority is greatly enhanced if it becomes widely known as a model of 'good practice' — or even simply, as an illustration that things can be done differently (see chapter 8). Participants may themselves be able to do this kind of promotional work, but the researcher is in a special position because of the skills which he or she initially brought to the project, and because of the unique position of the researcher of having an overall, analytical view of it.

In conclusion, it will be apparent that the whole area of values, ethics and politics raises some very complex issues in policy-oriented qualitative research. In my view, there are no easy ways of resolving these — certainly there are no neat and easily applicable formulae. But ultimately the problems are a particular combination of difficulties common to all kinds of social science research, and do not present problems of so special and severe a kind as to preclude this kind of research altogether. Once one abandons the model of the objective scientists acting as the technicians of social policy, all social research becomes messy and complex, and at least qualitative researchers have the great advantage of long-term familiarity with precisely the kinds of ethical and political questions which do have to be considered in policy-related research.

Conclusion: Developing Policy-oriented Qualitative Research

This concluding chapter is brief, and simply draws together the threads of the arguments developed in diverse ways in the preceding chapters, to highlight the prospects and possibilities for developing policy-oriented qualitative research to a point where it has a greater prominence than hitherto. I shall do this first, by summarizing what I see as the major limitations on the development of policy-oriented, qualitative research in the past, and how far these apply in the present. Second, I shall draw together and summarize my arguments about what a more highly developed version of policy-oriented qualitative research would be like.

In the past, the limitations on the greater development of qualitative research in a policy context have derived substantially from dominant conceptions of what constitutes policy-oriented research. Such definitions have set criteria for 'useful' research which qualitative studies have usually been unable to meet. Most importantly, these are: the concept of the direct use of research for policy purposes, which favours both an unproblematic notion of objective 'facts' and a model of the researcher as a technician who produces such facts but has no part in decisions about their interpretation and use. This concept of the direct use of research runs through the dominant tradition of the research-policy relationship since the mid-nineteenth century in Britain (chapter 1) and also forms the major theme of government reports on social research since the Second World War. Its most vivid version is the consumer-contractor principle (chapter 2). From this perspective qualitative research almost inevitably looks unconvincing, because the kind of data produced by qualitative techniques do not lend themselves to separating 'facts' from the researcher's 'opinions'; and where the underlying epistemology is interpretivist, the data themselves are unlikely to appear politically neutral (chapter 5). This indeed was precisely one of the difficulties encountered when the British government did try to make use of the qualitative data collected by Mass-Observation during the Second World War (chapter 4).

A further, and linked, problem concerns not so much definitions of what constitutes 'policy research' as the actual utility for governments of the kind of research data produced by quantitative techniques. In particular, the statistical documentation and classification of a population is an important prerequisite for developing mechanisms of administrative control in the management of an industrial society: a utility which was very apparent in the nineteenth century development of social research, including research in the field of education (chapter 1), but which also continued to form an important theme in official reports on the use of social research by governments well into the twentieth century (chapter 2). It is certainly possible for quantitative research to challenge the status quo, and this was apparent, for example, in the 'political arithmetic' tradition of research in education, which was oriented towards social reform (chapter 1). However, this approach still takes the perspective of the administrator in the sense that social change is seen as coming 'from above', and the role of research is to feed administrative intelligence to those enlightened policy-makers who will be able to use it to develop reformist measures. The most explicit version of this developed within the Fabian tradition, and is well illustrated by the Webbs' involvement in reforming education in London. This has remained the dominant model. It is a concept of policy-oriented research which leaves little space for qualitative work (chapter 5). Although there was some space for qualitative techniques in the work of the Webbs themselves (and indeed in the studies of Charles Booth and the early statistical societies), these were always accorded a secondary importance because of the underlying positivist epistemology, with its unproblematic concept of fact-gathering.

This all points to the strong likelihood that those who wanted to use social research would not find qualitative work convincing. For their part, researchers have not been notably eager to provide policy-oriented qualitative work, despite the expansion of qualitative research in education and other policy-related fields, especially since the late 1960s. I have suggested that this is a result of the particular orientation of social science disciplines in Britain, and of the boundaries which have been drawn between them (chapter 5). However, when one looks at the situation in the mid-1980s, on this level at least there seems to be more space for qualitative, policy-oriented work to develop than was apparent a decade earlier. The dominant mood within sociology is less hostile to both empirical research and to a policy orientation; whilst the discipline of social administration has become much more diverse and open, much less clearly wedded to the Fabian model as the only way of operating and engaging in some of the critical questioning about the use of social science by governments which characterized sociology two decades earlier. I have suggested that the orientation within each discipline is likely to be reflected in studies of education undertaken from the standpoint of either sociology or social administration. There are therefore far more opportunities for cross-fertilization between these two disciplines — and to a lesser extent with anthropology — in policy-related research. Within the substantive area of education in particular, there now seem to be signs that some qualitative researchers are increasingly recognizing the importance of a policy orientation (chapter 5).

So from the side of social scientists — the 'supply' side as it were — the prospects for the development of policy-oriented qualitative research look much more favourable than previously. On the demand side, one cannot point so directly to an increased desire on the part of policy-makers to utilize qualitative research, but a more explicit endorsement of the relative merits of qualitative research could help to open up some space for it. This can be done, first, by clearly highlighting the limitations and weaknesses of an over-concentration on quantitative research. In this book I have considered that most explicitly in my discussion of the use of research in official reports on education, where the over-concentration on quantitative techniques and positivist epistemology can be demonstrated to have led to research which was only partially adequate for its purpose and — in the case of HMI reports — downright misleading (chapter 2). Without necessarily dismissing the value of quantitative research for circumstances where it *is* appropriate, it is not the only possible type of policy-oriented research. Second, and following from this, qualitative research has clear strengths in respect of policy-oriented studies. Chapters 7 and 8 were concerned with discussion of how those strengths could be built upon. These include: a concern for process as well as outcome; a capacity to study processes over time, including the policy-making process itself; the capacity to provide descriptive detail which makes situations 'comprehensible'; the study of social processes in their natural contexts; a capacity to reflect the subjective reality of people being studied, including most importantly those who are the target groups for social policy action.

At the level of techniques, a case can be made for the utility of qualitative research in a policy context. However, a case made solely on grounds of technique may not be very convincing. Whether a convincing case for the utility of qualitative research can ultimately be made depends very much on the extent to which one can assume that those who use research have a more sophisticated awareness of the nature of social science knowledge than that which supported the dominant tradition. Certainly there is a more sophisticated awareness among social scientists themselves that knowledge cannot be straight-forwardly 'objective' and 'value-free', and that most social science knowledge does not come in a form where it can be directly used. But what of politicians and administrators? There are some optimistic signs there also. First, two of the official reports on research — Heyworth and the Rothschild Report on the SSRC — did themselves incorporate this more sophisticated understanding of the intrinsically political nature of social science knowledge, and indeed have sup-ported the view that in a democratic society, governments ought to support social science research which is critical of their own policies (chapter 2). The Rothschild Report in particular, envisages social science research being fed into political *debate* at various levels, not necessarily directly used by those in power. Second, the evidence about how social research does actually get used by policy-makers suggests that it is unrealistic to expect it to be used directly in most cases. Its use is actually far more diffuse, and operates most impor-tantly at the level of offering alternative conceptualizations of issues, rather than providing useful facts (chapter 6). Evidence of this kind points to a contemporary situation in which the relationship between research and policy is understood in a more complex and sophisti-cated way, and one which does not define out qualitative work in the same way as the historically dominant tradition.

There may be grounds therefore for some limited optimism that qualitative research can have more impact on policy-makers than it has to date. Whether or not this optimism is justified, that does not exhaust the potential uses of research in relation to social policy. The idea that policy-related research *means* knowledge passed to those in power is characteristic of the dominant tradition, but is only one of a range of possibilities. The examples of policy-oriented research which I have placed in the 'alternative' tradition are of a different order, not only because they make much more extensive use of qualitative techniques, but also because they reflect the perspective of the relatively powerless, see research as giving a voice to ordinary people and its potential for the democratization of knowledge, and reflect a view of social change and social reform from below rather than from above (chapter 3). Although this 'tradition' is far more fragmented than the dominant one, and the elements which I have identified are not always fully articulated, it does represent a different conception of what 'policy-oriented research' can mean. This is a conception in which those who 'make' policy are not the central focus, and where the potential is acknowledged for research to serve different interests.

I therefore see the prospects for the further development of qualitative policy-oriented work in two rather different ways: some possibility of expansion in the conventional sense (that is, to be targeted on policy-makers); but more importantly, the development of different kinds of research with a policy focus or orientation, to be used by a wide range of social groups in consolidating and changing their own situations.

So what would a more highly developed version of policy-oriented qualitative research be like? The discussion in the preceding chapters has suggested that it would be characterized by a series of linked and overlapping features, which collectively outline a programme for policy-oriented research which is especially suited to the use of qualitative techniques and to non-positivist epistemologies. Those features are as follows:

(a) *It is research which is technically competent, rigorously and professionally analyzed and interpreted*
Perhaps it almost goes without saying that any research should meet these criteria. But I put them at the top of this list to emphasize that policy-oriented research must be at least as rigorous as any other kind. Because the audience for policy-oriented work is composed less of one's academic peers and more of groups and individuals who may not be well informed about social science research, there may be some temptation to cut corners, especially where research is commissioned. But the prospect that the results of research may be used in the 'real' social and political world place a special obligation on the technical and professional conduct of researchers (chapter 9).

(b) *The research produced will be theoretically informed*
The relationship of theory to research has been more extensively discussed than the relationship of research to policy in recent writings on qualitative research, a point which is well illustrated in relation to educational ethnography (chapter 7). A relative lack of theoretical input is one of the characteristics of the dominant tradition of social policy

research, but in principle there is no necessary contradiction between research being policy-oriented and being strong theoretically. Indeed, as I argued in chapters 7 and 8, it is necessary for qualitative policy-oriented research also to be theoretically grounded if it is to achieve its full potential; conversely, undertheorized research is likely to be less useful in a policy context as well as less intellectually challenging. Policy and theory are therefore complementary, not alternative, orientations for qualitative research, and current developments of theory ought to support and sustain the development of more policy-oriented work.

(c) *Some developments of methods is necessary, especially in the use of comparative cases*
The lack of generalizability from the single, free-standing case study is perhaps the most obvious weakness of qualitative methods from a policy perspective. On one level, one needs to defend case study as a method, and to highlight its considerable alternative strengths. However, I argued in chapter 8 that the development of comparative cases, probably on a cumulative basis, would substantially enhance the potential of policy-oriented, qualitative research, especially if the underlying logic of analytic induction is well understood, carefully applied and explained clearly. Partial models are offered by the Manchester school of educational ethnographies, and by some of the curriculum studies inspired by Stenhouse (chapter 8), but there is much need for development of these approaches in relation to policy-oriented studies.

(d) *It will not necessarily serve the agenda of those in power and those who 'make' policy*
Research which is conducted from the perspective of a government in power is not precluded by my argument, but the point is that 'policy-oriented' research need not be of this type. In the 1960s policy-oriented researchers, including those working in the field of education, were heavily criticized for 'taking' the administrative problems of government rather than 'making' their own research problems, and as a result there was a widespread rejection of policy research, especially in sociology. The sociology of education was affected as much as, if not more than, other areas of the discipline (chapter 5). That rejection to some

extent threw the baby out with the bath water, in that it closed off the possibilities for developing research which is still concerned with areas of social life which are the targets for social policy, but looking at those issues from a non-governmental perspective.

(e) *It will tend to develop 'policy-oriented research' which is critical, challenging and oppositional, but not necessarily allied to a party-political position*

This point is very much linked with the previous one. The use of qualitative techniques is very likely to produce an account of social life which challenges the 'official view', as is apparent in the research in the 'alternative' tradition (chapter 3). The adoption of non-positivist epistemologies is likely to reinforce this. So the kind of 'policy-oriented research' implied by these approaches is one where social scientists are providing alternative accounts of social reality — a position which one can argue is the proper role for social science in a democratic society (chapter 6). Two well-known 'schools' of social research can serve as pointers to what this means. First, in the United States, the Chicago school specifically rejected the kind of reformist social science which developed in Britain, and also the concept of straightforward links between knowledge creation and social change. Nonetheless, the Chicago department of sociology has a long and distinguished tradition of qualitative research concerned with public issues of the day, and with areas of social life defined politically as 'social problems'. This research challenged dominant conceptions of why individual actions and social processes occur as they do (chapter 5). Second, recent feminist research in Britain has been significant in modifying the concerns of both sociology and social administration, including studies related to education. It is characteristically concerned not only with understanding the social world, but with questions about how it could be changed, and it reflects the interests of women, a relatively powerless group. Feminists have also actively promoted the use of qualitative research as being most appropriate to the task in hand (chapter 5).

(f) *It will have relatively modest aspirations for the impact of research, especially for its direct use*

A realistic appraisal of the likely impact of any piece of

research suggests that it is rare for 'findings' to be directly translated into 'policy', and indeed very little social science research is produced in a form which makes that possible. In relation to the findings of qualitative research, that is especially apparent (chapter 6). Simply on pragmatic grounds therefore, there are good reasons for having very limited aspirations about the direct use of research. In the case of qualitative research, these are reinforced by the fact that there are potential dangers associated with its direct use. These are well illustrated by the experience of Mass-Observation's use by the British government in wartime: its tendency to challenge the official view made its work vulnerable to being overlooked or dismissed; the researchers were unable to maintain the critical independence which they thought vital once incorporated into the structures of government; and the potential for spying on the population was well recognized (chapter 4). This last issue — the fact that qualitative techniques can quite literally be used as a form of espionage — ought to make any qualitative researcher wary about having their work directly used by governments, should that ever be an option. The prospects of the use of such research in relation to teacher appraisal raises those issues in a sharp form (chapter 9).

(g) *It will emphasize the indirect use and the 'enlightenment' role of research*
The point here is closely linked to the previous one. The evidence of how social research actually gets used by the powerful suggests a pattern of diffuse and indirect use, and indicates that those in power are most likely to use research as 'enlightment' — that is, the conceptualizations of an issue offered as a result of research are more important than concrete 'findings' (chapter 6). Qualitative research is well suited to providing such conceptualizations, and therefore on pragmatic grounds it makes sense to target policy-oriented research in that way. It also means that the potential impact of research is seen not just in relation to a few powerful individuals who 'make' policy, but as possible at different times and with different groups. This emphasis acknowledges the political nature of the situation into which research is being fed, and envisages research being used 'from below' as well as 'from above', by those

who are the targets of policy and who are pressing for change in their own situation.

(h) *It may well contain a specific commitment to the democra-*
tization of knowledge and the skills through which it is
created
The techniques of quantitative research necessarily abstract data from the individual to the aggregate level, whilst qualitative techniques give individuals far more prominence, and get close up to research subjects rather than keeping them at arms' length. These features make it likely that policy-oriented qualitative research will decisively reject the model of the detached researcher, collecting data to hand over to the powerful, in favour of a model of the research process which accords the researched a more active role. Such a model was most clearly articulated in Mass-Observation's desire to use ordinary people (not just professional researchers) to research their own situation, as an exercise in the democratization of knowledge and therefore of power (chapter 3). More generally, democratic and collaborative styles of research are possible when qualitative techniques are used, and are encouraged by interpretivist epistemology. Thus, one important implication of policy-oriented qualitative research is that it has the potential for engaging the researched as well as the researcher in evaluating the status quo and bringing about change. That particular insight has been developed in relation to some teacher-based curriculum research and development (chapter 8), but it could be used much more widely.

(i) *It will be concerned with policy at all levels, including grass-*
roots policy change
Following on from the previous point, it is clear that if a researcher is to actively engage the researched in studying their own situation and possibly bringing about change in it, this will almost always be change of a small-scale kind. The model of using research, not to pass information upwards to remote 'policy-makers', but to be used by the people researched fits well with both qualitative techniques and with a commitment to the democratization of knowledge. It involves acknowledging that policy is not only implemented, but often 'made' and re-made at a very small-scale level. I argued in chapter 8 that this kind of grassroots

policy change is a potential use for policy-oriented, qualitative research.

(j) *It implies researcher-involvement with policy as well as research*

It is evident from the features outlined that engaging in policy-oriented research must mean a relatively active role for the researcher in respect of policy itself. I say 'relatively active', in that it certainly means rejecting the passive role of technician which is characteristic of the dominant tradition of policy-oriented research. The technician role is not actually possible for a qualitative researcher, because there are self-evidently no straightforward 'facts' which can simply be handed over for someone else to use; it can also be argued that the role of technician cannot be justified on ethical grounds (chapter 9). There are, however, a range of possible 'relatively active' roles for the researcher which I discussed in chapter 9; adviser, advocate, or direct engagement in the political process.

In the introductory chapter of this book, I suggested that qualitative researchers may need to be convinced of the value of undertaking policy-oriented research. I hope that the subsequent discussion in this book has served not only to strengthen the major reason which I gave there for undertaking such research — that all social research is unavoidably a political activity — but also to make the prospect of policy-oriented research more congenial than it is if one simply adopts the dominant model of the research-policy relationship. At the same time, I take the view that undertaking policy-oriented research ought properly to be conceived as a rather limited exercise. This book has not been about the politics of social change in general (or even about a sociological understanding of how such change comes about) but about the use of research as such to bring about change, or to consolidate the status quo, or to provide a vision of what alternative social arrangements could be like. As a citizen, the researcher may be engaged directly in various ways in struggles to bring about social change, but that is a different matter from what it is possible to accomplish specifically as a social researcher. The use of qualitative research in a policy context is, in my view, likely to amount to a much more modest exercise than that to which the dominant tradition has aspired during the last 150 years; but it is also more viable, more intellectually challenging and more ethically justifiable.

References

ABRAMS, M. (1951) *Social Surveys and Social Action*, London, Heinemann.

ABRAMS, P. (1968) *The Origins of British Sociology 1834–1914*, Chicago, University of Chicago Press.

ABRAMS, P. (1981) 'The collapse of British sociology?' in ABRAMS, P., DEEM, R., FINCH, J. and ROCK, P. (Eds) *Practice and Progress: British Sociology 1950–1980*, London, Allen and Unwin.

ABRAMS, P. (1984) 'Evaluating soft findings: Some problems of measuring informal care', *Research, Policy and Planning*, 2, 2, pp. 1–8.

ABRAMS, P. (1985) 'The uses of British sociology 1831–1981', in BULMER, M. (Ed.) *Essays on the History of British Sociological Research*, Cambridge, Cambridge University Press.

ACLAND, H. (1980) 'Research as stage management: The case of the Plowden committee', in BULMER, M. (Ed.) *Social Research and Royal Commissions*, London, Allen and Unwin.

ANDERSON, D. (Ed.) (1980) *The Ignorance of Social Intervention*, London, Croom Helm.

ASAD, T. (Ed.) (1973) *Anthropology and the Colonial Encounter*, London, Ithaca.

ASHTON, T.S. (1934) *Economic and Social Investigations in Manchester 1833–1933*, London, King.

BALL, S. (1981) *Beachside Comprehensive: A Case Study of Secondary Schooling*, Cambridge, Cambridge University Press.

BALL, S. (1984) 'Beachside reconsidered: Reflections on a methodological apprenticeship', in BURGESS, R. (Ed.) *The Research Process in Educational Settings: Ten Case Studies*, Lewes, Falmer Press.

BANTING, K. (1979) *Poverty, Politics and Poverty: Britain in the 1960s*, London, Macmillan.

BARNES, J.A. (1979) *Who Should Know What? Social Science, Privacy and Ethics*, Harmondsworth, Penguin.

BECKER, H. (1958) 'Problems of inference and proof in participant observations', *American Sociological Review*, 23, pp. 652–60.

BECKER, H. (1967) 'Whose side are we on?', *Social Problems*, 14, pp. 239–47.

BELL, C. and NEWBY, H. (Eds) (1977) *Doing Sociological Research*, London, Allen and Unwin.

BENNETT, N. (1976) *Teaching Styles and Pupil Progress*, London, Open Books.

BENNETT, N. and McNAMARA, D (1979) 'Introduction', in BENNETT, N. and McNAMARA, D. (Eds) *Focus on Teaching*, London, Longmans.

BERNBAUM, G. (1977) *Knowledge and Ideology in the Sociology of Education*, London, Macmillan.

BLOOMFIELD, B.C. (Ed.) (1964) *The Autobiography of Sir James Kay Shuttleworth*, Education Libraries Bulletin, London, Institute of Education.

BLUME, S. (1977) 'Policy as theory', *Acta Sociologica*, 20, 3, pp. 247–62.

BLUME, S. (1979) 'Policy studies and social policy in Britain', *Journal of Social Policy*, 8, 3, pp. 311–34.

BOOTH, C. (1902) *Life and Labour of the People of London*, London, Macmillan.

BRENNAN, E.J.T. (Ed.) (1975) *Education For National Efficiency: The Contribution of Sidney and Beatrice Webb*, London, Athlone Press.

BROWN, J. (1978) "Social control" and the modernisation of social policy 1890–1929', in THANE, P. (Ed.) *The Origins of British Social Policy*, London, Croom Helm.

BRUCE, M. (1968) *The Coming of the Welfare State*, London, Batsford.

BRUNER, J. (1980) *Under Five in Britain*, London, Grant McIntyre.

BRYANT, C.G.A. (1976) *Sociology in Action: A Critique of Selected Conceptions of the Social Role of the Sociologist*, London, Allen and Unwin.

BRYMAN, A. (1984) 'The debate about quantitative and qualitative research', *British Journal of Sociology*, XXXV, 1, pp. 75–92.

BULMER, M. (Ed.) (1977) *Sociological Research Methods*, 2nd edn 1984, London, Macmillan.

BULMER, M. (1978a) 'The prospects for applied sociology', *British Journal of Sociology*, 29, pp. 128–35.

BULMER, M. (1978b) 'Social science research and policy-making', in BULMER, M. (Ed.) *Social Policy Research*, London, Macmillan.

BULMER, M. (1980) 'Introduction', in BULMER, M. (Ed.) *Social Research and Royal Commissions*, London, Allen and Unwin.

BULMER, M. (1981) 'Quantification and Chicago social science: A neglected tradition', *Journal of the History of Behavioural Sciences*, 17, 3, pp. 312–31.

BULMER, M. (1982a) *The Uses of Social Research*, London, Allen and Unwin.

BULMER, M. (Ed.) (1982b) *Social Research Ethics*, London, Macmillan.

BULMER, M. (1984) *The Chicago School of Sociology*, Chicago, University of Chicago Press.

BULMER, M (1985) 'The development of sociology and empirical social research in Britain', in BULMER, M. (Ed.) *Essays on the History of British Sociological Research*, Cambridge, Cambridge University Press.

BURGESS, R.G. (1983) *Experiencing Comprehensive Education: A Study of Bishop McGregor School*, London, Methuen.

BURGESS, R.G. (1984a) 'Exploring frontiers and settling territory: Shaping the sociology of education', *British Journal of Sociology*, 35, 1, pp. 122–37.

BURGESS, R.G. (1984b) *In The Field: An Introduction to Field Research*, London, Allen and Unwin.

BURGESS, R.G. (Ed.) (1985a) *Strategies of Educational Research: Qualitative Methods*, Lewes, Falmer Press.

BURGESS, R.G. (1985b) 'The whole truth? Some ethical problems of research in a comprehensive school', in BURGESS, R.G. (Ed.) *Field Methods in the Study of Education*, Lewes, Falmer Press.

CAIN, M. and FINCH, J. (1981) 'Towards a rehabilitation of data', in ABRAMS, P., DEEM, R., FINCH, J. and ROCK, P. (Eds) *Practice and Progress: British Sociology 1950–1980*, London, Allen and Unwin.

CALDER, A. and SHERIDAN, D. (Eds) (1984) *Speak For Yourself: A Mass-Observation Anthology 1937–49*, London, Jonathan Cape.

CAPLAN, N. (1976) 'Social research and national policy: Who gets used, by whom, for what purpose, and with what effects?' *International Social Science Journal*, 28, pp. 187–94.

CAPLAN, N., MORRISON, A. and STAMBAUGH, R. (1975) *The Use of Social Science Knowledge in Policy Decisions at National Level*, Ann Arbor, MI, University of Michigan.

CARLEY, M. (1980) *Rational Techniques in Policy Analysis*, London, Policy Studies Institute/Heinemann.

CARSON, W.G. and WILES, P. (Eds) (1971) *The Sociology of Crime and Delinquency in Britain, Vol. 1: The British Tradition*, Oxford, Martin Robertson.

CENTRE FOR CONTEMPORARY CULTURAL STUDIES (1981) *Unpopular Education: Education and Social Democracy in England Since 1944*, London, Hutchinson.

CHERNS, A. (1972) 'Social sciences and policy', in CHERNS, A., SINCLAIR, R. and JENKINS, W.I. (Eds) *Social Science and Government*, London, Tavistock.

CHERNS, A. (1979) *Using the Social Sciences*, London, Routledge and Kegan Paul.

CICOUREL, A.V. (1964) *Method and Measurement in Sociology*, New York, Free Press.

COBBETT, W. (1830) *Rural Rides*, reprinted 1975, London, Macdonald Facsimile Edition.

COHEN, A.K. (1955) *Delinquent Boys: The Culture of the Gang*, New York, Free Press.

COHEN, D. and WEISS, J. (1977) 'Social science and social policy: Schools and race', in RIST, R. and ANSON, R. (Eds) *Education, Social Science and the Judicial Process*, New York, Teachers' College Press.

COHEN, P. (1984) 'Against the new vocationalism', in BATES, I., CLARKE, J., COHEN, P., FINN, D., MOORE, R. and WILLIS, P. *Schooling For The Dole: The New Vocationalism*, London, Macmillan.

COHEN, S. and TAYLOR, L. (1977) 'Talking about prison blues', in BELL, C. and NEWBY, H. (Eds) *Doing Sociological Research*, London, Allen and Unwin.

COLE, M. (1974) 'Labour research', in COLE, M. (Ed.) *The Webbs and Their Work*, first published 1949, Brighton, Harvester.

COLEMAN, J.S. (1966) *Equality of Educational Opportunity*, Washington D.C., U.S. Government Printing Office.

COLEMAN, J.S. (1984) 'Issues in the institutionalisation of social policy', in HUSEN, T. and KOGAN, M. (Eds) *Educational Research and Policy: How Do They Relate?*, Oxford, Pergamon.

COMMITTEE OF ENQUIRY INTO THE EDUCATION OF HANDICAPPED CHILDREN AND YOUNG PEOPLE (1978) *Special Educational Needs*, The Warnock Report, Cmnd. 7212, London, HMSO.

COMMITTEE OF INQUIRY INTO THE EDUCATION OF CHILDREN FROM ETHNIC MINORITY GROUPS (1981) *West Indian Children in Our Schools*, The Rampton Report, Cmnd. 8273, London, HMSO.

COMMITTEE OF INQUIRY INTO THE EDUCATION OF CHILDREN FROM ETHNIC MINORITY GROUPS (1985) *Education For All*, The Swann Report, Cmnd. 9453, London, HMSO.

COMMITTEE ON HIGHER EDUCATION (1963) *Higher Education*, The Robbins Report, Cmnd. 2154, London, HMSO.

CORRIGAN, P. (1979) *Schooling the Smash Street Kids*, London, Macmillan.

CORRIGAN, P. (Ed.) (1980) *Capitalism, State Formation and Marxist Theory: Historical Investigations*, London, Quartet Books.

CORRIGAN, P. and CORRIGAN, V. (1978) 'State formation and social policy until 1871', in PARRY, N., RUSTIN, M. and SATYAMURTI, C. (Eds) *Social Work, Welfare and the State*, London, Edward Arnold.

DAVID, M. (1985) 'Motherhood and social policy — a matter of education?' *Critical Social Policy*, 12, pp. 28–43.

DAVIES, L. (1979) 'Deadlier than the male? Girls' conformity and deviance in school', in BARTON, L. and MEIGHAN, R. (Eds) *Schools, Pupils and Deviance*, Driffield, Nafferton Books.

DAVIES, L. (1984) *Pupil Power: Deviance and Gender in School*, Lewes, Falmer Press.

DAVIES, L. (1985) 'Ethnography and status: Focusing on gender in educational research', in BURGESS, R.G. (Ed.) *Field Methods in the Study of Education*, Lewes, Falmer Press.

DELAMONT, S. (1981) 'All too familar? A decade of classroom research', *Educational Analysis*, 3, 1, pp. 69–83.

DELAMONT, S. and ATKINSON, P. (1980) 'The two traditions in educational ethnography: Sociology and anthropology compared', *British Journal of the Sociology of Education*, 1, 2, pp. 139–52.

DENZIN, N. (1970) *The Research Act in Sociology*, Chicago, Aldine.

DEPARTMENT OF EDUCATION AND SCIENCE (1967) *Children and Their Primary Schools*, Report of the Central Advisory Council for Education, The Plowden Report, London, HMSO.

DEPARTMENT OF EDUCATION AND SCIENCE (1972) *Educational Priority: Vol. 1: EPA Problems and Policies*, London, HMSO.

DEPARTMENT OF EDUCATION AND SCIENCE (1974) *Educational Priority, Vol. 2: EPA Surveys and Statistics*, London, HMSO.

DEPARTMENT OF EDUCATION AND SCIENCE (1975a) *Educational Priority, Vol. 3: Curriculum Innovation in London's EPAs*, London, HMSO.

DEPARTMENT OF EDUCATION AND SCIENCE (1975b) *Educational Priority, Vol. 4: The West Riding Project*, London, HMSO.

DEPARTMENT OF EDUCATION AND SCIENCE (1977) *Ten Good Schools: A Secondary School Enquiry*, HMI Matters for Discussion No. 1, London, HMSO.

DEPARTMENT OF EDUCATION AND SCIENCE (1978) *Primary Education in England: A Survey by H.M. Inspectors of Schools*, London, HMSO.

DEPARTMENT OF EDUCATION AND SCIENCE (1981) *The School Curriculum*, London, HMSO.

DEPARTMENT OF EDUCATION AND SCIENCE (1984) *The Education Welfare Service: An HMI Enquiry in Eight LEAs*, London, HMSO.

DIBBLE, V. (1975) *The Legacy of Albion Small*, Chicago, University of Chicago Press.

DONNISON, D. (1978) 'Research for policy', in BULMER, M. (Ed.) *Social Policy Research*, London, Macmillan.

DOUGLAS, J.B. (1964) *The Home and the School*, London, MacGibbon and Kee.

DOUGLAS, J. (1976) *Investigative Social Research: Individual and Team Field Research*, London, Sage.

DYHOUSE, C. (1981) *Girls Growing Up in Late Victorian and Edwardian England*, London, Routledge and Kegan Paul.

DYOS, H.J. (1967–8) 'The slums of Victorian London', *Victorian Studies*, 11, 1, pp. 5–40.

EDWARDS, J. (1975) 'Social indicators, urban deprivation and positive discrimination'. *Journal of Social Policy*, 4, 3, pp. 275–87.

EDWARDS, J. (1981) 'Subjectivist approaches to the study of social policy making', *Journal of Social Policy*, 10, 3, pp. 289–310.

ELLIOT, J. (1981) 'Foreword', in NIXON, J. (Ed.) *A Teacher's Guide to Action Research*, London, Grant McIntyre.

ELLIOT, J. (1985) 'Facilitating action-research in schools: Some dilemmas', in BURGESS, R.G. (Ed.) *Field Methods in the Study of Education*, Lewes, Falmer Press.

ENGELS, F. (1892) *The Conditions of the Working Classes in England from Personal Observations and Authentic Sources*, reprinted 1969, London, Panther.

FARIS, R.E.L. (1970) *Chicago Sociology 1920–32*, Chicago, University of Chicago Press.

FETTERMAN, D.M. (Ed.) (1984) *Ethnography in Educational Evaluation*, Beverly Hills, Sage.

FIDDY, R. (Ed.) (1983) *In Place of Work: Policy and Provision for the Young Unemployed*, Lewes, Falmer Press.

FINCH, J. (1983) 'Dividing the rough and the respectable: working-class women and pre-school playgroups', in GAMARNIKOW, E., MORGAN, D., PURVIS, J. and TAYLORSON, D. (Eds) *The Public and the Private*, London, Heinemann.

FINCH, J. (1984a) *Education as Social Policy*, London, Longman.

FINCH, J. (1984b) 'The deceit of self help: Preschool playgroups and working class mothers', *Journal of Social Policy*, 13, 1, pp. 1–20.

FINCH, J. (1984c) 'A first class environment? Working class playgroups as pre-school experience', *British Educational Research Journal*, 10, 1, pp. 3–17.

FINCH, J. (1984d) '"It's great to have someone to talk to": The ethics and politics of interviewing women', in BELL, C. and ROBERTS, H. (Eds) *Social Researching: Politics, Problems, Practice*, London, Routledge and Kegan Paul.

FINCH, J. (1985) 'Social policy and education: Problems and possibilities of using qualitative research', in BURGESS, R.G. (Ed.) *Issues in Educational Research: Qualitative Methods*, Lewes, Falmer Press.

FLOUD, J. (1957) Report of discussion at the British Sociological Association Annual Conference, *British Journal of Sociology*, 8, p. 172.

FLOUD, J. and HALSEY, A.H. (1958) 'The sociology of education', *Current Sociology* VII, 3, pp. 165–93.

FLYNN, R. (1979) 'Urban managers in local government planning', *Sociological Review*, 27, 4, pp. 743–53.

FLYNN, R. (1981) 'Managing consensus: Strategies and rationales in policy-making', in HARLOE, M. (Ed.) *New Perspectives in Urban Change and Conflict*, London, Heinemann.

FLYNN, R. (1983) 'Co-optation and strategic planning in the local state', in KING, R. (Ed.) *Capital and Politics*, London, Routledge and Kegan Paul.

FORD, J. (1969) *Social Class and the Comprehensive School*, London, Routledge and Kegan Paul.

FORD, J. (1976) 'Facts, evidence and rumour: A rational reconstruction of "Social Class and the Comprehensive School"', in SHIPMAN, M. (Ed.) *The Organisation and Impact of Social Research*, London, Routledge and Kegan Paul.

A Framework for Government Research and Development (1971) Cmnd. 4814, London, HMSO.

FRANKENBERG, R. (Ed.) (1982) *Custom and Conflict in British Society*, Manchester, Manchester University Press.

FULLER, M. (1984) 'Dimensions of gender in a school: Reinventing the wheel?' in BURGESS, R.G. (Ed.) *The Research Process in Educational Settings: Ten Case Studies*, Lewes, Falmer Press.

GALTON, F.W. (1974) 'Investigating with the Webbs', in COLE, M. (Ed.) *The Webbs and Their Work*, first published 1949, Brighton, Harvester.

GALTON, M. and DELAMONT, S. (1985) 'Speaking with forked tongue? Two styles of observation in the ORACLE project', in BURGESS, R.G. (Ed.) *Field Methods in the Study of Education*, Lewes, Falmer Press.

GEORGE, V. and WILDING, P. (1976) *Ideology and Social Welfare*, London, Routledge and Kegan Paul.

GLASER, B. and STRAUSS, A. (1967) *The Discovery of Grounded Theory*, Chicago, Aldine.

GLASS, D.V. (Ed.) (1954) *Social Mobility in Britain*, London, Routledge and Kegan Paul.

GLEESON, D. (Ed.) (1983) *Youth Training and the Search for Work*, London, Routledge and Kegan Paul.

GOLDING, P. (1980) 'From Charles Booth to Peter Townsend: Poverty research in the U.K.', *Social Policy and Administration*, 14, 2, pp. 169–72.

GOLDING, P. and MIDDLETON, S. (1982) *Images of Welfare*, Oxford, Martin Robertson.

GOULDNER, A.W. (1970) *The Coming Crisis of Western Sociology*, London, Heinemann.

GOULDNER, A. (1973) 'The sociologist as partisan: Sociology and the welfare state', in *For Sociology: Renewal and Critique in Sociology Today*, London, Allen Lane.

Government Statistical Services (1981) Cmnd. 8236, London, HMSO.

GRAFTON, T., MILLER, H., SMITH, L., VEGODA, M. and WHITFIELD, R. (1983) 'Gender and curriculum choice in relation to education for parenthood', in HAMMERSLEY, M. and HARGREAVES, A. (Eds) *Curriculum Practice: Sociological Case Studies*, Lewes, Falmer Press.

GRAFTON, T., SMITH, L., VEGODA, M. and WHITFIELD, R. (1983) *Preparation for Parenthood in the Secondary School Curriculum*, A Research Report, University of Aston.

GRAFTON, T., VEGODA, M., SMITH, L. and WHITFIELD, R. (1982) ' "Getting personal": The teachers' dilemma', *International Journal of Sociology and Social Policy*, 2, 3, pp. 85–94.

GRAHAM, H. (1983) 'Do her answers fit his questions? Women and the survey method', in GAMARNIKOW, E., MORGAN, D., PURVIS, J. and TAYLORSON, D. (Eds) *The Public and the Private*, London, Heinemann.

GREER, S. (1977) 'On the selection of problems', in BULMER, M. (Ed.) *Sociological Research Methods*, London, Macmillan.

GRIFFIN, C. (1985) 'Qualitative methods and cultural analysis: Young women and the transition from school to un/employment', in BURGESS, R.G. (Ed.) *Field Methods in the Study of Education*, Lewes, Falmer Press.

GRIMSHAW, R., HOBSON, D. and WILLIS, P. (1980) 'Introduction to ethnography at the centre', in HALL, S., HOBSON, D., LOWE, A. and WILLIS, P. (Eds) *Culture, Media, Language*, London, Hutchinson.

HALDANE COMMITTEE (1917) *Machinery of Government*, Cmnd. 9230, London, HMSO.

HALFPENNY, P. (1979) 'The analysis of qualitative data', *Sociological Review*, 27, 4, pp. 799–825.

HALSEY, A. (1972) *Educational Priority*, Vol. 1, London, HMSO.

HALSEY, A. (1982) 'Provincials and professionals', *Times Higher Education Supplement*, 25 June, pp. 10–11.

HALSEY, A.H. (1985) 'Provincials and professionals: The British post-war sociologists', in BULMER, M. (Ed.) *Essays on the History of British Sociological Research*, Cambridge, Cambridge University Press.

HALSEY, A.H., FLOUD, J. and ANDERSON, C.A. (Eds) (1961) *Education, Economy and Society*, New York, Free Press.

HALSEY, A.H., HEATH, A.F. and RIDGE, J.M. (1980) *Origins and Destinations: Family, Class and Education in Modern Britain*, Oxford, Clarendon.

HAMMERSLEY, M. (1984) 'Some reflections upon the macro-micro problem in the sociology of education', *Sociological Review*, 32,2, pp. 316–24.

HAMMERSLEY, M. (1985) 'From ethnography to theory: A programme and paradigm in the sociology of education', *Sociology*, 19, 2, pp. 244–59.

HAMMERSLEY, M., SCARTH, J. and WEBB, S. (1985) 'Developing and testing theory: The case of research on student learning and examinations', in BURGESS, R.G. (Ed.) *Issues in Educational Research: Qualitative Methods*, Lewes, Falmer Press.

HARGREAVES, D.H. (1967) *Social Relations in a Secondary School*, London, Routledge and Kegan Paul.

HARGREAVES, D. (1981) 'Schooling and delinquency', in BARTON, L. and WALKER, S. (Eds.) *Schools, Teachers and Teaching*, Lewes, Falmer Press.

HARGREAVES, D. (1982) *The Challenge for the Comprehensive School*, London, Routledge and Kegan Paul.

HARGREAVES, D. (1984) *Improving Secondary Schools*, London, Inner London Education Authority.

HARGREAVES, D., HESTOR, S. and MELLOR, F. (1975) *Deviance in Classrooms*, London, Routledge and Kegan Paul.

HIGGINS, J. (1978) *The Poverty Business: Britain and America*, Oxford, Blackwell/Martin Robertson.

HOBSBAWM, E. (1964) 'The Fabians reconsidered', in HOBSBAWM, E., *Labouring Men: Studies in the History of Labour*, London, Weidenfeld and Nicolson.

HOGBEN, L. (Ed.) (1938) *Political Arithmetic*, London, Allen and Unwin.

HUGHES, E. (1960) 'Introduction: The place of fieldwork in social science', in JUNKER, B. (Ed.) *Fieldwork*, Chicago, University of Chicago Press.

HUGHES, J.A. (1980) *The Philosophy of Social Research*, London, Longman.

HUMPHREYS, L. (1970) *The Tea-Room Trade*, London, Duckworth.

HUSBANDS, C.T. (1981) 'The anti-quantitative bias in postwar British sociology', in ABRAMS, P., DEEM, R., FINCH, J. and ROCK, P. (Eds) *Practice and Progress: British Sociology 1950–1980*, London, Allen and Unwin.

HUSEN, T. (1984) 'Issues and their background', in HUSEN, T. and KOGAN, M. (Eds) *Educational Research and Policy: How Do They Relate?*, Oxford, Pergamon.

JACKSON, B. and MARSDEN, D. (1962) *Education and the Working Class*, London, Routledge and Kegan Paul.

JAMES, J. (1977) 'Ethnography and social problems', in WEPPNER, R.S. (Ed.) *Street Ethnography*, Beverly Hills, Sage.

JAMES, P. (1980) *The Reorganisation of Secondary Education*, Slough, National Foundation for Educational Research.

JANOWITZ, M. (1972) *Sociological Models and Social Policy*, Morristown, NJ, General Learning Systems.

JENNINGS, H. and MADGE, C. (Eds) (1937) *May 12th: an Account of Coronation Day*, London, Faber and Faber.

JOHNSON, R. (1970) 'Educational policy and social control in early Victorian England' *Past and Present*, 49, pp. 96–119.

KALLÓS, D. (1981) 'The study of schooling: What is studied? Why? And how?' in POPKEWITZ, T.S. and TABACHNICK, B.R. (Eds) *The Study of Schooling: Field Based Methodologies in Educational Research and Evaluation*, New York, Praeger, pp. 31–68.

KARABEL, J. and HALSEY, A.H. (1977) 'Educational research: A review and an interpretation', in KARABEL, J. and HALSEY, A.H. (Eds) *Power and Ideology in Education*, New York, Oxford University Press.

KAY, J.P. (1832) 'The moral and physical conditions of the working classes of Manchester in 1832', reprinted in KAY-SHUTTLEWORTH, J. (1973) *Four Periods of Public Education*, Brighton, Harvester.

KAY, J.P. (1839) 'Recent measures for the promotion of education in England', reprinted in KAY-SHUTTLEWORTH, J. (1973) *Four Periods of Public Education*, Brighton, Harvester.

KEAT, R. (1979) 'Positivism and statistics in social science', in IRVINE, J., MILES, I. and EVANS, J. (Eds) *Demystifying Social Statistics*, London, Pluto.

KEATING, P. (Ed.) (1976) *Into Unknown England, 1866–1913: Selections from the Social Explorers*, London, Fontana.

KELLY, A. (1985) 'Action research: Some definitions and descriptions', in BURGESS, R.G. (Ed.) *Issues in Educational Research: Qualitative Methods*, Lewes, Falmer Press.

KELLY, A., WHYTE, J. and SMAIL, B. (1984) *Girls into Science and Technology: Final Report*, Manchester, University of Manchester, Department of Sociology.

KOGAN, M. and HENKEL, M. (1983) *Government and Research: The Rothschild Experiment in a Government Department*, London, Heinemann.

KOGAN, M., KORMAN, N. and HENKEL, M. (1980) *Government's Commissioning of Research: A Case Study*, Brunel University, Department of Government.

KOGAN, M. and PACKWOOD, T. (1974) *Advisory Councils and Committees in Education*, London, Routledge and Kegan Paul.

KUPER, A. (1983) *Anthropology and Anthropologists: The Modern British School*, 2nd edn, London, Routledge and Kegan Paul.

KURTZ, L.R. (1984) *Evaluating Chicago Sociology: A Guide to the Literature with Annotated Bibliography*, Chicago, University of Chicago Press.

LACEY, C. (1970) *Hightown Grammar: The School as a Social System*, Manchester, Manchester University Press.

LACEY, C. (1976) 'Problems of sociological fieldwork: A review of the methodolodgy of "Hightown Grammar"', in SHIPMAN, M. (Ed.) *The Organisation and Impact of Social Research*, London, Routledge and Kegan Paul.

LACEY, C. (1982) 'Freedom and constraint in British education', in FRANKENBERG, R. (Ed.) *Custom and Conflict in British Society*, Manchester, Manchester University Press.

LAMBART, A. (1976) 'The sisterhood', in HAMMERSLEY, M. and WOODS, P. (Eds) *The Process of Schooling: A Sociological Reader*, London, Routledge and Kegan Paul/Open University Press.

LAYARD, R. and KING, J. (1973) 'The impact of Robbins', in FOWLES, G., MORRIS, V. and OZGA, J. (Eds) *Decision Making in British Education*, London, Heinemann/Open University Press.

LEWIS, J. (1980) *The Politics of Motherhood 1919–39*, London, Croom Helm.

LINDBLOM, C. (1968) *The Policy-Making Process*, Englewood Cliffs, NJ, Prentice-Hall.

LINDBLOM, C. and COHEN, D. (1979) *Usable Knowledge: Social Science and Social Problem Solving*, New Haven, Conn., Yale University Press.

LUBENOW, W.C. (1971) *The Politics of Government Growth: Early Victorian Attitudes Toward State Intervention, 1833–1848*, Newton Abbot, David and Charles.

McCARTNEY, J.L. (1984) 'Setting priorities for research: New politics for the social sciences', *The Sociological Quarterly*, 24, 4, pp. 437–55.

MACDONAGH, O. (1977) *Early Victorian Government, 1830–1870*, London, Weidenfeld and Nicolson.

MacDONALD, B. (1977) 'A political classification of evaluation studies', in

HAMILTON, D., JENKINS, D., KING, C., MacDONALD, B. and PARLETT, M. (Eds) *Beyond the Numbers Game: A Reader in Educational Evaluation*, London, Macmillan.

MacDONALD, B. and NORRIS, N. (1981) 'Twin political horizons in evaluation fieldwork', in POPKEWITZ, T.S. and TABACHNICK, B.R. (Eds) *The Study of Schooling: Field Based Methodologies in Educational Research and Evaluation*, New York, Praeger.

McGREGOR, O.R. (1957) 'Social research and social policy in the nineteenth century', *British Journal of Sociology*, 8, pp. 146–57.

MACKENZIE, N. and MACKENZIE, J. (1977) *The First Fabians*, London, Quartet Books.

MADGE, C. and HARRISSON, T. (Eds) (1938) *First Year's Work 1937–38 by Mass-Observation*, London, Lindsay Drummond.

MADGE, C. and HARRISSON, T. (1939) *Britain by Mass-Observation*, Harmondsworth, Penguin.

MAGOON, J. (1977) 'Constructivist approaches in educational research', *Review of Educational Research*, 47, 4, pp. 651–93.

MALINOWSKI, B. (1939) 'A nation-wide intelligence service', in MADGE, C. and HARRISSON, T. (Eds) *The First Year's Work 1937–38 by Mass-Observation*, London, Lindsay Drummond.

MARRIS, P. and REIN, M. (1967) *Dilemmas of Social Reform: Poverty and Community Action in the United States*, London, Routledge and Kegan Paul.

MARSH, C. (1982) *The Survey Method*, London, Allen and Unwin.

MARSH, C. (1985) 'Informants, respondents and citizens', in BULMER, M. (Ed.) *Essays on the History of British Sociological Research*, Cambridge, Cambridge University Press.

MARSHALL, T.H. (1965) *Social Policy*, London, Hutchinson.

MARWICK, A. (1967) 'The Labour Party and the welfare state in Britain 1900–1948', *American Historical Review*, 73, 2, pp. 380–403.

Mary Adams Papers (1939–41) Tom Harrisson Mass Observation Archive, University of Sussex.

Mass Observation File Reports (1937–51) Tom Harrisson Mass Observation Archive, University of Sussex.

MAYHEW, H. (1851) *London Labour and the London Poor, Vol. 1 The London Street-Folk*, reprinted 1967, London, Frank Cass and Co. Ltd.

MERTON, R.K. (1957) 'The role of the intellectual in public bureaucracy', in MERTON, R.K. *Social Theory and Social Structure*, first published 1949, New York, Free Press.

MERTON, R.K. (1973) 'Technical and moral dimensions of policy research', in MERTON, R.K. *The Sociology of Science: Theoretical and Empirical Investigations*, first published 1949, Chicago, University of Chicago Press.

MESS, H.A. (1928) *Industrial Tyneside: A Social Survey*, London, Ernest Benn.

MILLER, S.M. (1974) 'Policy and science', *Journal of Social Policy*, 3, 1, pp. 53–8.

MILLS, C. WRIGHT (1959) *The Sociological Imagination*, reprinted 1970, Harmondsworth, Penguin.

MINISTRY OF EDUCATION (1959) *Fifteen to Eighteen*, Report of the Central Advisory Council for Education, The Crowther Report, London, HMSO.

MINISTRY OF EDUCATION (1963) *Half Our Future*, Report of the Central Advisory Council for Education, The Newsom Report, London, HMSO.

MISHRA, R. (1977) *Society and Social Policy*, London, Macmillan.

MORRIS, N. (1973) 'Introduction', in KAY-SHUTTLEWORTH, Sir J. *Four Periods of Public Education*, Brighton, Harvester.

MORGAN, D.H.J. (1981)'Men, masculinity and the process of sociological research', in ROBERTS, H. (Ed.) *Doing Feminist Research*, London, Routledge and Kegan Paul.

MOSS, L. (1953) 'Sample surveys and the administrative process', *International Social Science Bulletin*, 5, pp. 482–94.

MYRDAL, G. (1958) 'The relation between social theory and social policy', in MYRDAL, G. *Value in Social Theory: A Selection of Essays on Methodology*, first published 1953, London, Routledge and Kegan Paul.

Network (1984) Newsletter of the British Sociological Association, 30 October, London, British Sociological Association.

NISBET, J. and BROADFOOT, P. (1980) *The Impact of Research on Policy and Practice in Education*, Aberdeen, Aberdeen University Press.

NIXON, J. (1981) 'Introduction', in NIXON, J. (Ed.) *A Teacher's Guide to Action Research*, London, Grant McIntyre.

NORMAN-BUTLER, B. (1972) *Victorian Aspirations: The Life and Labour of Charles and Mary Booth*, London, Allen and Unwin.

OAKLEY, A. (1981) 'Interviewing women: A contradiction in terms', in ROBERTS, H. (Ed.) *Doing Feminist Research*, London, Routledge and Kegan Paul.

PARKER, J. (1974) 'The Fabian Society and the New Fabian Research Bureau' in COLE, M. (Ed.) *The Webbs and Their Work*, first published 1949, Brighton, Harvester.

PARKINSON, M. (1982) 'Politics and policy-making in education', in HARTNETT, A. (Ed.) *The Social Sciences in Educational Studies: A Selective Guide to the Literature*, London, Heinemann.

PATRICK, J. (1973) *A Glasgow Gang Observed*, London, Eyre-Methuen.

PATTON, M.Q. (1980) *Qualitative Evaluation Methods*, Beverly Hills, CA, Sage.

PAYNE, G., DINGWALL, R., PAYNE, J. and CARTER, M. (1981) *Sociology and Social Research*, London, Routledge and Kegan Paul.

PEMBER REEVES, M. (1913) *Round About A Pound A Week*, London, Bell.

PINKER, R. (1971)*Social Theory and Social Policy*, London, Heinemann.

PIVEN, F.F. (1972) 'Whom does the advocate planner serve?, in CLOWARD, R. and PIVEN, F.F. (Eds) *The Politics of Turmoil: Essays in Poverty, Race and the Urban Crisis*, New York, Pantheon Books.

PLATT, J. (1972) 'Survey data and social policy', *British Journal of Sociology*, 23, 1, pp. 77–92.

PLATT, J. (1981a) 'The social construction of "positivism" and its significance in British sociology', in ABRAMS, P., DEEM, R., FINCH, J. and ROCK, P. (Eds) *Practice and Progress: British Sociology 1950–1980*, London, Allen and Unwin.

PLATT, J. (1981b) 'Evidence and proof in documentary research', *Sociological Review*, 29, 1, pp. 31–52 and 53–66.

POLLARD, A. (1984) 'Ethnography and social policy for classroom practice', in BARTON, L. and WALKER, S. (Eds) *Social Crisis and Educational Research*, London, Croom Helm.

POLLARD, A. (1985) 'Opportunities and difficulties of a teacher-ethnographer', in BURGESS, R.G. (Ed.) *Field Methods in the Study of Education*, Lewes, Falmer Press.

POPKEWITZ, T.S. (1981a) 'The study of schooling: paradigms and field-based methodologies in educational research and evaluation', in POPKEWITZ, T.S. and TABACHNICK, B.R. (Eds) *The Study of Schooling: Field Based Methodologies in Educational Research and Evaluation*, New York, Praeger.

POPKEWITZ, T.S. (1981b) 'Qualitative research: Some thoughts about the relation of methodology and social history', in POPKEWITZ, T.S. and TABACHNICK, B.R. (Eds) *The Study of Schooling: Field Based Methodologies in Educational Research and Evaluation*, New York, Praeger.

POPPER, K. (1963) *The Poverty of Historicism*, London, Routledge and Kegan Paul.

PORTER, M. (1984) 'The modification of method in researching postgraduate education', in BURGESS, R.G. (Ed.) *The Research Process in Educational Settings: Ten Case Studies*, Lewes, Falmer Press.

POULTON, G.A. and JAMES, T. (1975) *Pre-school Learning in the Community: Strategies for Change*, London, Routledge and Kegan Paul.

PREMFORS, R. (1984) 'Research and policy-making in Swedish higher education', in HUSEN, T. and KOGAN, M. (Eds) *Educational Research and Policy: How Do They Relate?*, Oxford, Pergamon.

PRENDEGAST, S. and PROUT, A. (1980) 'What will I do...? Teenage girls and the construction of motherhood', *Sociological Review*, 28, 3, pp. 517–35.

PUGH, G. and De'ATH, E. (1984) *The Needs of Parents: Practice and Policy in Parent Education*, London, Macmillan.

REEDER, D. (1979) 'A recurring debate: Education and industry', in BERNBAUM, G. (Ed.) *Schooling in Decline*, London, Macmillan.

REES, T.L. and ATKINSON, P. (Eds) (1982) *Youth Unemployment and State Intervention*, London, Routledge and Kegan Paul.

REIN, M. (1976) *Social Science and Public Policy*, Harmondsworth, Penguin.

REIN, M. (1980) 'Methodology for the study of the interplay between social science and social policy', *International Social Science Journal*, 32, 2, pp. 361–8.

REIN, M. (1983) *From Policy to Practice*, London, Macmillan.

Report of the Committee on the Provision for Social and Economic Research (1946) The Clapham Report, Cmnd. 6868, London, HMSO.

Report of the Committee on Social Studies (1965) The Heyworth Report, Cmnd. 2660, London, HMSO.

REPORT OF THE COMMITTEE OF INQUIRY INTO THE EDUCATION OF CHILDREN FROM ETHNIC MINORITY GROUPS (1985) *Education for All*, The Swann Report, Cmnd. 9453, London, HMSO.

REYNOLDS, D. (1976a) 'The delinquent school', in HAMMERSLEY, M. and WOODS, P. (Eds) *The Process of Schooling*, London, Routledge and Kegan Paul.

REYNOLDS, D. (1976b) 'When pupils and teachers refuse a truce: The secondary school and the process of delinquency', in MUNGHAM, G. and PEARSON, G. (Eds) *Working Class Youth Culture*, London, Routledge and Kegan Paul.

REYNOLDS, D. (1980–81) 'The naturalistic model of educational and social research: A Marxist critique', *Interchange*, 11, 4, pp. 77–89.

REYNOLDS, D. and JONES, D. (1978) 'Education and the prevention of juvenile delinquency', in TUTT, N. (Ed.) *Alternative Strategies for Coping with Crime* Oxford, Blackwell.

REYNOLDS, D. and SULLIVAN, M. (1979) 'Bringing schools back in', in BARTON, L. and MEIGHAN, R. (Eds) *Schools, Pupils and Deviance*, Driffield, Nafferton.

RICHARDSON, E. (1973) *The Teacher, the School and the Task of Management*, London, Heinemann.

RIST, R. (1981a) 'On the utility of ethnographic research for the policy process', *Urban Education*, 15, 4, pp. 485–9.

RIST, R. (1981b) *Earning and Learning: Youth Employment Policies and Programmes*, Beverly Hills, CA, Sage.

RIST, R. (1984) 'On the application of qualitative research to the policy process: An emergent linkage', in BARTON, L. and WALKER, S. (Eds) *Social Crisis and Educational Research*, London, Croom Helm.

ROCK, P. (1979) *The Making of Symbolic Interactionism*, London, Macmillan.

ROSSI, P. (1980) 'The challenge and opportunities of applied social research', *American Sociological Review*, 45, pp. 889–904.

ROTHSCHILD, Lord (1982) *An Enquiry into the Social Science Research Council*, Cmnd. 8554, London, HMSO.

ROWNTREE, S. (1902) *Poverty: A Study of Town Life*, London, Macmillan.

SCOTT, S. (1984) 'The personable and the powerful: Gender and status in sociological research', in BELL, C. and ROBERTS, H. (Eds) *Social*

Researching· Politics, Problems, Practice, London, Routledge and Kegan Paul.

SCOTT, S. (1985) 'Working through the contradictions in researching postgraduate education', in BURGESS, R.G. (Ed.) *Field Methods in the Study of Education*, Lewes, Falmer Press.

SHARP, R. and GREEN, T. (1975) *Education and Social Control*, London, Routledge and Kegan Paul.

SHARPE, L. (1978) 'The social scientist and policy-making in Britain and America: A comparison', in BULMER, M. (Ed.) *Social Policy Research*, London, Macmillan.

SHARROCK, W.W. (1980) 'The possibility of social change', in ANDERSON, D.C. (Ed.) *The Ignorance of Social Intervention*, London, Croom Helm.

SHAW, C.R. (1930) *The Jack-Roller: A Delinquent Boy's Own Story*, Chicago, University of Chicago Press.

SHAW, G.B. (1974) 'Early days', in COLE, M. (Ed.) *The Webbs and Their Work*, first published 1949, Brighton, Harvester.

SHAW, M. (1975) *Marxism and Social Science*, London, Pluto.

SHAW, M. and MILES, I. (1979) 'The social roots of statistical knowledge', in IRVINE, J., MILES, I. and EVANS, J. (Eds) *Demystifying Social Statistics*, London, Pluto.

SHILS, E. (1949) 'Social science and social policy', *Philosophy of Science*, 16, pp. 219–42.

SHIPMAN, M. (1985) 'Ethnography and educational policy', in BURGESS, R.G. (Ed.) *Field Methods in the Study of Education*, Lewes, Falmer Press.

SILVER, H. (Ed.) (1973) *Equal Opportunity in Education*, London, Methuen.

SILVER, H. (1980) *Education and the Social Condition*, London, Methuen.

SIMEY, T.S. (1957) 'Social investigation: Past achievements and present difficulties', *British Journal of Sociology*, 8, pp. 121–30.

SMITH, F. (1974) *The Life and Work of Sir James Kay-Shuttleworth*, first published 1923, Bath, Cedric Chivers Ltd.

SMITH, G. (1975) 'Action-research: experimental social administration?' in LEES, R. and SMITH, G. (Eds) *Action-Research in Community Development*, London, Routledge and Kegan Paul.

SMITH, G. and JAMES, T. (1977) 'The effects of pre-school education: Some American and British evidence', *Oxford Review of Education*, 1, 2, pp. 223–40.

SMITH, T. (1980) *Parents and Preschool*, London, Grant McIntyre.

SOCIAL SCIENCE RESEARCH COUNCIL (1981) *A Change in Structure for Changing Circumstance*, London, Social Science Research Council.

SPRING RICE, M. (1939) *Working-class Wives: Their Health and Conditions*, Harmondsworth, Penguin.

STANLEY, L. and WISE, S. (1983) *Breaking Out: Feminist Consciousness and Feminist Research*, London, Routledge and Kegan Paul.

STANLEY, N.S. (1981) *"The Extra Dimension": A Study and Assessment of the Methods Employed by Mass-Observaton in its First Period, 1937–1940*, PhD thesis, CNAA.

STENHOUSE, L. (1975) *An Introduction to Curriculum Research and Development*, London, Heinemann.

STENHOUSE, L. (1980) *Curriculum Research and Development in Action*, London, Heinemann.

STENHOUSE, L. (1985) 'Library access, library use and user education in academic sixth forms: An autobiographical account', in BURGESS, R.G. (Ed.) *The Research Process in Educational Settings: Ten Case Studies*, Lewes, Falmer Press.

SUMMERFIELD, P. (1985) 'Mass-Observation: Social research or social movement?' *Journal of Contemporary History*, July.

SUTHERLAND, G. (1984) *Ability, Merit and Measurement: Mental Testing and English Education, 1880–1940*, Oxford, Clarendon.

SWANN, Lord (1985) *Education For All: A Brief Guide to the Main Issues of the Report*, Annex to the Swann Report, Cmnd. 9453, London, HMSO.

SYLVA, K., ROY, C. and PAINTER, M. (1980) *Childwatching at Playgroup and Nursery School*, London, Grant McIntyre.

SZRETER, R. (1984) 'Some forerunners of sociology of education in Britain: An account of the literature and influences c.1900–1950', *Westminster Studies in Education*, 7, p. 13–43.

TAYLOR-GOOBY, P. (1981) 'The empiricist tradition in social administration', *Critical Social Policy*, 1, 2, pp. 6–21.

TAYLOR-GOOBY, P. and DALE, J. (1981) *Social Theory and Social Welfare*, London, Edward Arnold.

THOMAS, P. (1983) 'Social research and government policy: Heyworth, Rothschild and after', in LONEY, M., BOSWELL, D. and CLARKE, J. (Eds) *Social Policy and Social Welfare*, Milton Keynes, Open University Press.

THOMAS, W.I. and ZNANIECKI, F. (1918–20) *The Polish Peasant in Europe and America*, Chicago, University of Chicago Press.

THOMPSON, E.P. (1967–68) 'The political education of Henry Mayhew', *Victorian Studies*, 11, 1, pp. 41–62.

THOMPSON, E.P. and YEO, E. (Eds) (1973) *The Unknown Mayhew*, Harmondsworth, Penguin.

Tom Harrisson Mass Observation Archive (1983) Microfiche text, Brighton, Harvester.

THORPE, D., SMITH, D., PALEY, J. and GREEN, C. (1980) *Out of Care*, London, Allen and Unwin.

TOWN, S. (1973) 'Action research and social policy', *Sociological Review*, 12, 4, pp. 573–98.

TOWNSEND, P. (1981) 'Guerillas, subordinates and passers-by: The relationship between sociologists and social policy', *Critical Social Policy*, 1, 2, pp. 22–34.

TREND, M. (1980) 'Applied social research and government: Notes on the limits of confidentiality', *Social Problems*, 27, 3, pp. 342–9.

TROW, M. (1984) 'Researchers, policy analysis and policy intellectuals', in HUSEN, T. and KOGAN, M. (Eds) *Educational Research and Policy: How Do They Relate?*, Oxford, Pergamon.

WAGENAAR, H. (1982) 'A cloud of unknowing: Social science research in a political context', in KALLEN, D., KOSSE, G., WAGENAAR, H., KLOP-KOGGE, J. and VORBECK, M. (Eds) *Social Science Research and Public Policy-Making: A Reappraisal*, Windsor, NFER-Nelson.

WALKER, A. (1981) *Unqualified and Underemployed: Handicapped Young People and the Labour Market*, London, Macmillan.

WARWICK, D (1982) '"Tearoom Trade": Means and ends in social research', in BULMER, M. (Ed.) *Social Research Ethics*, first published 1973, London, Macmillan.

WASS, Sir D. (1983) 'Participation — the sole bond', Reith Lecture VI, *The Listener*, 15 December, pp. 15–17.

WEBB, B. (1926) *My Apprenticeship*, London, Longmans, Green & Co.

WEBB, B. (1948) *Our Partnership*, London, Longmans, Green & Co.

WEBB, S. (1901) *The Education Muddle and the Way Out*, Fabian Tract No. 106, reprinted in BRENNAN, E.J.T. (Ed.) *Education For National Efficiency: The Contribution of Sidney and Beatrice Webb*, London, Athlone Press.

WEBB, S. (1904) *London Education*, London, Longmans, Green & Co.

WEBB, S. and WEBB, B. (1932) *Methods of Social Study*, Cambridge, Cambridge University Press.

WEBER, M. (1949) *On the Methodology of the Social Sciences*, Glencoe, Ill., Free Press.

WEISS, C. (1979) 'The many meanings of research utilization', *Public Administration Review*, 39, 5, pp. 426–31.

WEISS, C. (1982) 'Policy research in the context of diffuse decision making', in KALLEN, D., KOSSE, G., WAGENAAR, H., KLOPKOGGE, J. and VORBECK, M. (Eds) *Social Science Research and Public Policy-Making: A Reappraisal*, Windsor, NFER-Nelson.

WEISS, C. with BUCUVALAS, M. (1980) *Social Science Research and Decision Making*, New York, Columbia University Press.

WELLS, A.F. (1935) *The Local Social Survey in Great Britain*, London, Allen and Unwin.

WEST, D.J. and FARRINGTON, D.P. (1973) *Who Becomes Delinquent?*, London, Heinemann.

WEST, E.G. (1975) *Education and the Industrial Revolution*, London, Batsford.

WHITEHEAD, F. (1985) 'The Government Social Survey', in BULMER, M. (Ed.) *Essays on the History of British Sociological Research*, Cambridge, Cambridge University Press.

WHYTE, W.F. (1982) 'Social inventions for solving human problems', *American Sociological Review*, 47, 1, pp. 1–13.

WILCOX, K. (1982) 'Ethnography as a methodology and its applications to the study of schooling: A review', in SPINDLER, G. (Ed.) *Doing the Ethnography of Schooling: Educational Anthropology in Action*, New York, Holt, Rinehart and Winston.

WILES, P. (1977) *The Sociology of Crime and Deviance in Britain, Vol. 2: The New Criminologies*, London, Martin Robertson.

WILLCOCK, H.D. (1949) *Mass-Observation Report on Juvenile Delinquency*, London, The Falcon Press.

WILLIAMS, R. (1980) 'Social research and sociology: Problems in the funding of knowledge', in ANDERSON, D.C. (Ed.) *The Ignorance of Social Intervention*, London, Croom Helm.

WILLIAMSON, H. (1982) 'Client response to the Youth Opportunities Programme', in REES, T.L. and ATKINSON, P. (Eds) *Youth Unemployment and State Intervention*, London, Routledge and Kegan Paul.

WILLIAMSON, W. (1974) 'Continuities and discontinuities in the sociology of education', in FLUDE, M. and AHIER, J. (Eds) *Educability, Schools and Ideology*, London, Croom Helm.

WILLIS, P. (1977) *Learning To Labour: How Working Class Kids Get Working Class Jobs*, London, Saxon House.

WILLIS, P. (1980) 'Notes on method', in HALL, S., HOBSON, D., LOWE, A. and WILLIS, P. (Eds) *Culture, Media, Language*, London, Hutchinson.

WILLMOTT, P. (1985) 'The Institute of Community Studies', in BULMER, M. (Ed.) *Essays on the History of British Sociological Research*, Cambridge, Cambridge University Press.

WOLCOTT, H.F. (1984) 'Ethnographers sans ethnography: The evaluation compromise', in FETTERMAN, D.M. (Ed.) *Ethnography in Educational Evaluation*, Beverly Hills, Sage.

WOODS, P. (1983) *Sociology and the School: An Interactionist Viewpoint* London, Routledge and Kegan Paul.

WOODS, P. (1984) 'Ethnography and theory construction in educational research, in BURGESS, R.G. (Ed.) *Field Methods in the Study of Education*, Lewes, Falmer Press.

WOODS, P. and HAMMERSLEY, M. (1977) *School Experience: Explorations in the Sociology of Education*, New York, St. Martin's Press.

YEO, E. (1973) 'Mayhew as a social investigator, in THOMPSON, E. and YEO, E. (Eds.) *The Unknown Mayhew*, Harmondsworth, Penguin.

YOUNG, K. and MILLS, L. (1980) *Public Policy Research: A Review of Qualitative Methods*, London, Social Sciences Research Council.

YOUNG, M.F.D. (1971) *Knowledge and Control*, London, Collier-Macmillan.

YOUNG, M.F.D. (1973) 'Curricula and the social organisation of knowledge', in BROWN, R. (Ed.) *Knowledge, Education and Cultural Change*, London, Tavistock.

ZNANIECKI, F. (1934) *The Method of Sociology*, New York, Farrer and Rinehart.

ZNANIECKI, F. (1940) *The Social Role of the Man of Knowledge*, New York, Columbia University Press.

Suggestions for Further Reading

ABRAMS, P. (1968) *The Origins of British Sociology 1834–1914*, Chicago, University of Chicago Press.

The first half of this book consists of an excellent evaluative review of the early development of British sociology, in which issues concerning the relationship of social research and social policy are central. The second half of the book consists of readings from authors of the period, which illustrate key developments.

ABRAMS, P., DEEM, R., FINCH, J. and ROCK, P. (Eds) (1981) *Practice and Progress: British Sociology, 1950–1980*, London, Allen and Unwin.

A collection of papers given originally at the British Sociological Association conference in 1980, reviewing the development of sociology over the previous three decades. Articles especially pertinent to social research are those by Abrams, Cain and Finch, Husbands, Platt and Stacey.

BARNES, J.A. (1979) *Who Should Know What? Social Science, Privacy and Ethics*, Harmondsworth, Penguin.

An accessible discussion of research ethics in anthropological and sociological research, focusing on ethical dilemmas and different strategies for resolving them, and highlighting the rights of citizens to protection against negative consequences of social science research.

BARTON, L. and WALKER, S. (Eds) (1984) *Social Crisis and Educational Research*, London, Croom Helm.

Contains important articles by Ray Rist and Andrew Pollard on qualitative research and social policy.

BRYMAN, A. (1984) 'The debate about quantitative and qualitative research', *British Journal of Sociology*, XXXV, 1, pp. 75–92.

An important article, although it assumes some knowledge of the debate about the relative merits of quantitative and qualitative research. Bryman argues that in these debates there is an inherent confusion between matters of technique and matters of epistemology. If the two are separated, he argues, there is not a neat correspondence between epistemological positions and particular techniques.

BULMER, M. (Ed.) (1980) *Social Research and Royal Commissions*, London, Allen and Unwin.

A useful collection of articles contributed by social scientists who have been involved with various Royal Commissions. Acland contributes an important, and highly critical, article on the research undertaken for the Plowden Committee. Bulmer's introduction sets out clearly the ways in which British Royal Commissions have utilized social research.

BULMER, M. (1982) *The Uses of Social Research*, London, Allen and Unwin.

An important book, which reviews the development of applied social research in Britain and evaluates its potential. Case studies are used to illustrate key themes, including a case study of research on deprivation and disadvantage. There is a good discussion of the institutional context of social research and its implications; also of the engineering and enlightenment models of research. However, the book reflects the dominant tradition of policy-oriented research, and the contribution of qualitative methods is not specifically discussed.

BULMER, M. (Ed.) (1985) *Essays on the History of British Sociological Research*, Cambridge, Cambridge University Press.

A collection of essays in honour of Philip Abrams, who died in 1981. Essays cover the development of research methods, especially but not exclusively survey methods, used by sociologists in the nineteenth and twentieth centuries. Useful contributions on the more recent history of social research include essays on: Mass-Observation; the Government Social Survey; the Institute of Community Studies. The section on uses of research includes an essay by Abrams, published posthumously, in which a central theme concerns the social scientist as advocate.

BURGESS, R.G. (Ed.) (1984a) *The Research Process in Educational Settings: Ten Case Studies*, Lewes, Falmer Press.

A collection of autobiographical articles about undertaking qualitative research in educational settings. The authors reflect on a range of issues: methodological, ethical, political and personal. They offer valuable insights into the 'natural history' of some well-known research projects, as well as some which were undertaken as postgraduate work.

BURGESS, R.G. (1984b) *In The Field: An Introduction to Field Research*, London, Allen and Unwin.

An introductory textbook on field research methods, which uses throughout examples drawn from Burgess' own ethnographic work in a secondary school, as well as a wide range of other examples from published studies.

BURGESS, R.G. (Ed.) (1985) *Field Methods in the Study of Education*, Lewes, Falmer Press.

A collection of articles about the research process, by authors who have conducted qualitative research in educational settings, covering the full range from primary schools to postgraduate education. An article by Shipman on ethnography and educational policy-making is of direct relevance to the themes which I have developed. Other valuable contributions are: Woods on theory and ethnography; two articles on gender by Davies and by Griffin; Burgess' discussion of ethical dilemmas; and articles by Stenhouse, Elliot and Pollard, each of which address certain issues concerning a collaborative approach to research.

CALDER, A. and SHERIDAN, D. (Eds) (1984) *Speak For Yourself: A Mass-Observation Anthology 1937–49,* London Jonathan Cape.

An anthology, with commentary, of the work of Mass-Observation. This provides a useful introduction for readers not familiar with the organization's work.

CHERNS, A. (1979) *Using the Social Sciences*, London, Routledge and Kegan Paul.

A collection of articles by Cherns (many of them previously published elsewhere) which cover both public policies towards the development of the social sciences themselves, and also the ways in which social science has been used in British public policy-making.

FINCH, J. (1984) *Education as Social Policy*, London, Longman.

A textbook aimed at students and professional workers in social policy and education, which sees the education service as part of the welfare state in Britain since 1944. Consequences of locating educational developments as part of a broader social policy strategy are discussed, and conceptual frameworks used in the study of social policy are applied to education, thus highlighting certain features of the educational system which are often invisible in other studies.

GOULDNER, A. (1973) 'The sociologist as partisan: Sociology and the welfare state', in *For Sociology: Renewal and Critique in Sociology Today*, London, Allen Lane.

An influential discussion which engages critically with Becker's question 'Whose side are we on?' in social research. Ethical and political questions about how far a sociologist can or should be partisan are considered, with policy questions much to the fore.

HUGHES, J.A. (1980) *The Philosophy of Social Research*, London, Longman.

A good introductory textbook, which presents complex philosophical issues in an accessible way. Hughes considers both orthodox positivist approaches to social research, and 'humanist' alternatives.

HUSEN, T. and KOGAN, M. (Eds) (1984) *Educational Research and Policy: How Do They Relate?*, Oxford, Pergamon.

A collection of papers from a conference in honour of Torsten Husen, the distinguished Swedish educational researcher whose work has been closely related to the development of educational policies in Sweden and elsewhere. International contributors from western Europe, the United States and Scandinavia address the question of the relationship between social science research and policy in the field of education.

KELLY, A., WHYTE, J. and SMAIL, B. (1984) *Girls into Science and Technology: Final Report*, Manchester, University of Manchester, Department of Sociology.

A well-written report which summarizes the approach and the outcome of the GIST project. This is a good example of a piece of policy-oriented action research in education, which was conducted in collaboration with teachers and used both quantitative and qualitative methods.

KURTZ, L.R. (1984) *Evaluating Chicago Sociology: A Guide to the Literature with Annotated Bibliography*, Chicago, University of Chicago Press.

Useful as an introductory guide to the research conducted by the 'Chicago school'.

LINDBLOM, C. (1968) *The Policy-Making Process*, Englewood Cliffs, NJ, Prentice-Hall.

The classic source for discussion of decision-making as 'incrementalism', not a single, defined event.

MARSH, C. (1982) *The Survey Method*, London, Allen and Unwin.

An excellent discussion of the survey research model and its potential, although it does assume a basic working knowledge of survey methods. Marsh considers the history of the use of social surveys and also their contemporary political application. Key chapters which discuss the philosophical basis of survey research make an important contribution to the debate about the utility of these methods.

NIXON, J. (Ed.) (1981) *A Teacher's Guide to Action Research*, London, Grant McIntyre.

A collection of articles, by researchers and by practising teachers, on teachers' involvement in researching their own classroom practice. A useful collection which displays a range of work undertaken by teacher-researchers, reflecting the concern of the movement principally with matters of curriculum and professional practice.

PAYNE, G., DINGWALL, R., PAYNE, J. and CARTER, M. (1981) *Sociology and Social Research*, London, Routledge and Kegan Paul.

A critical review of developments in British sociology which argues a need (at that time at least) to reorient the discipline more centrally to undertaking research, and to develop institutional contexts which encourage that. The book is openly supportive of both ethnographic work and of a policy orientation.

POLLARD, A. (1984) 'Ethnography and social policy for classroom practice', in BARTON, L. and WALKER, S. (Eds) *Social Crisis and Educational Research*, London, Croom Helm.

An important and rare example of a mainstream British educational ethnographer considering social policy implications of his work. Pollard's particular focus is 'policy' at the level of classroom practice.

POPKEWITZ, T.S. and TABACHNICK, B.R. (Eds) (1981) *The Study of Schooling: Field Based Methodologies in Educational Research and Evaluation*, New York, Praeger.

A collection of articles by British and American authors on the uses of qualitative research in applied educational settings. Two articles by Popkewitz, and one by MacDonald and Norris, and another by Kallós, are particularly pertinent to policy issues.

REIN, M. (1976) *Social Science and Public Policy*, Harmondsworth, Penguin.

A classic discussion by a well-known American writer. Rein's discussion on the fact-value dilemma is particularly important, and he extends this in relation to value issues in the contribution of social science to social policy.

RIST, R. (1981) *Earning and Learning: Youth Employment Policies and Programmes*, Beverly Hills, Sage.

Report of a study of youth employment 'demonstration projects' in schools in the United States. This study is an example of qualitative research being used in commissioned evaluation of an experimental project in education. It is also an example of team research based on fieldwork techniques.

SHIPMAN, M. (Ed.) (1976) *The Organisation and Impact of Social Research*, London, Routledge and Kegan Paul.

A useful and interesting collection of articles written by the people who have conducted well-known pieces of research in the field of education: Douglas, the Newsoms, Ford, Lacey, Barker Lunn and Dale. The authors discuss the methodology of their studies and the impact which each had. The studies discussed include examples of both qualitative and quantitative techniques.

WEBB, S. and WEBB, B. (1932) *Methods of Social Study*, Cambridge, Cambridge University Press.

The Webb's methods textbook, which still contains some very valuable insights into research methods appropriate to policy-oriented studies. Both quantitative and qualitative methods are covered (although those terms are not used), and some of the discussion of qualitative methods is excellent, including interviewing, observation and note-taking.

WOODS, P. (1983) *Sociology and the School: An Interactionist Viewpoint*, London, Routledge and Kegan Paul.

A book which sets out to demonstrate how the perspective of interactionism can illuminate sociological understanding of school life, drawing on a range of empirical studies. For readers unfamiliar with interactionism, it provides a useful introduction to its application in educational settings.

Author Index

Abrams, M., 100, 233
Abrams, P., 13, 19, 24, 26, 41, 111,
  116, 117, 118, 122, 123–4, 125,
  153, 186–7, 215, 217, 233, 251
Abrams, P. *et al.*, 251
Acland, H., 59–60, 140, 199, 233
Adams, M., 96–106
  see also Mary Adams Papers
  [Subject Index]
Anderson, D., 154, 233
Asad, T., 201, 233
Ashton, T.S., 17, 233
Atkinson, P.
  see Delamont and Atkinson; Rees
  and Atkinson

Ball, S., 34, 173, 205–6, 233
Banting, K., 115, 151, 233
Barnes, J.A., 3, 190, 197–8, 199, 203,
  207, 219, 233, 251
Barton, L. and Walker, S., 251
Becker, H., 26, 82–3, 183, 197, 220,
  233–4
Bell, Lady, 84
Bell, C. and Newby, H., 3, 209, 234
Bennett, N., 6, 234
Bennett, N. and McNamara, D., 6,
  234
Bernbaum, G., 32, 36, 234
Bloomfield, B.C., 16, 17, 18, 234
Blume, S., 47, 112, 114, 140, 149,

156, 234
Booth, C., 19–22, 25, 27, 31, 58, 74,
  78, 79, 82–3, 109, 122, 124, 160,
  162, 224, 234
Bowley, A.L., 27
Brennan, E.J.T., 23, 119, 120, 234
Broadfoot, P.
  see Nisbet and Broadfoot
Brown, J., 24, 234
Bruce, M., 92, 234
Bruner, J., 167, 191, 234
Bryant, C.G.A., 217, 234
Bryman, A., 5, 7, 9, 10, 234, 251–2
Bucuvalas, M.
  see Weiss and Bucuvalas
Bulmer, M., 13, 14, 15, 19–20, 27,
  29, 41, 54, 56, 78, 80, 84, 110, 111,
  118, 120, 130, 131, 132, 153, 173,
  174, 186, 187, 195–6, 202, 211,
  234–5, 252
Burgess, E.W., 84
Burgess, R.G., 5, 6, 34, 67, 132, 161,
  163, 208, 235, 252–3

Cain, M. and Finch, J., 163, 172,
  183, 209, 211, 235
Calder, A. and Sheridan, D., 87, 88,
  89, 235, 253
Caplan, N., 235
Caplan, N. *et al.*, 141, 146, 147, 148,
  235

Subject Index